KEEP Your Cash, SAVE Your Social Security, and LIVE Worry-Free!

The Smart Senior's FINANCIAL ANSWER BOOK

Publisher's Note

This book is intended for general information only. It does not constitute medical, legal, or financial advice or practice. The editors of FC&A have taken careful measures to ensure the accuracy and usefulness of the information in this book. While every attempt has been made to ensure accuracy, errors may occur. Some websites, addresses, and telephone numbers may have changed since printing. We cannot guarantee the safety or effectiveness of any advice or treatments mentioned. Readers are urged to consult with their professional financial advisers, lawyers, and health care professionals before making any changes.

Any health information in this book is for information only and is not intended to be a medical guide for self-treatment. It does not constitute medical advice and should not be construed as such or used in place of your doctor's medical advice. Readers are urged to consult with their health care professionals before undertaking therapies suggested by the information in this book, keeping in mind that errors in the text may occur as in all publications and that new findings may supersede older information.

The publisher and editors disclaim all liability (including any injuries, damages, or losses) resulting from the use of the information in this book.

The plans of the diligent lead to profit as surely as haste leads to poverty.
Proverbs 21:5 (NIV)

FC&A Publishing®
103 Clover Green
Peachtree City, GA 30269
www.fca.com

Produced by the staff of FC&A
ISBN 978-1935574897

TABLE OF CONTENTS

A BRIGHTER FUTURE
Chart your path to financial freedom

STEADY CASH FLOW
How to make your wealth last a lifetime

END THE MONEY DRAIN
Smart strategies keep more dollars in your pocket

SAFE & SOUND
Protect what matters most

HEALTHY LIVING
Get the right care at the right price

LOW-COST LODGING
Open the door to
powerhouse savings

UTILITIES & SERVICES
Stay up and running
without breaking the bank

EAT ON THE CHEAP
Bite-sized wisdom to pad
your piggy bank

WHEEL & DEAL

Drive down the price of getting there

AT YOUR LEISURE

Cut-rate ways to live it up

A BRIGHTER FUTURE

Chart your path to financial freedom

1 | Your financial checkup

> "Every financial worry you want to banish and financial dream you want to achieve comes from taking tiny steps today that put you on a path toward your goals."
>
> Suze Orman

Your ultimate retirement roadmap begins here

You check in with your doctor every year, zip by the dentist for a cleaning, get your eyes tested, and probably show your hair some TLC on a regular basis. But do you give your finances the same attention to make sure they're just as healthy?

An annual financial review is as important to your overall well-being as a physical exam. And it should shoot to the top of your must-do list if you've undergone any major life events or changes. A divorce, relocation, inheritance, or stock market plunge, for instance, could upend your finances and significantly alter your retirement goals.

Don't shortchange your retirement. The dictionary defines a goal as an aim or desired result. If you're like most people, your "desired result" is a retirement free from money worries — whether that means having the cash to buy your favorite latte every morning or affording a dream vacation. But do you have a plan? Are you doing anything to reach this goal, or are you just wishing for it?

And that's why this first step in your yearly financial checkup is so important. You must identify your financial goals so you can turn those wishes into a reality. After all, as Eleanor Roosevelt said, "It takes as much energy to wish as it does to plan."

If you already have defined financial goals, congratulations. You're ahead of the pack. Here are some staggering statistics from a survey conducted by the Transamerica Center for Retirement Studies.

- A whopping 42% of retirees don't have a financial strategy for retirement.

- Of those that do have a strategy, only 18% have it in writing.

- Almost 1 in 4 retirees still carry mortgage debt.

In addition, Fidelity Investments reports that most people will need about 45% of their retirement cash flow to come from savings. But surveys show that 25% of workers have less than $10,000 in their retirement accounts. And 10% don't have any money saved up for their golden years.

Don't spend your retirement wondering where your gas or grocery money will come from. Grab a pencil and sit down with your partner. It's time to plan smart.

A simple tool puts your goals back on track. The concept of SMART goals began in the mid-1900s as a project management tool to help businesses perform more effectively. But in the last 40 years, this idea, that a goal should be defined by very precise criteria, has grown beyond the boardroom into other areas of everyday life. The kitchen — for healthier eating. The gym — for targeted weight loss. And the home office — for better money management. It's a versatile strategy anyone can use.

Each letter in the word SMART stands for a quality or feature that will help you define a goal.

- **S**pecific. You must be very clear and precise on what you are trying to achieve. Focus on the details so you can apply the rest of the criteria.

- **M**easurable. How will you know when you've reached your goal? You need a way to measure your progress.

- **A**chievable. Make sure you have the resources necessary to attain this goal. If not, decide if the goal is important enough for you to acquire new tools. Be realistic or you're setting yourself up for frustration and failure. You might need to do some math to set a goal you can honestly reach.

- **R**elevant. Your goal should align with your values and objectives. Otherwise, you won't have an incentive to work toward it. Add in the key benefit of your goal to keep yourself motivated.

- **T**ime-bound. When should you achieve this goal? Again, crunch some numbers so you can set a reasonable deadline.

To better understand the SMART concept, see how a very common but general wish easily becomes attainable.

Wish: I want to get out of debt.

Specific: I want to *pay off my credit card* debt.

Measurable: I want to pay off *$5,000* in credit card debt.

Achievable: I want to pay off $5,000 in credit card debt *by doubling my payments every month*.

Relevant: I want to pay off $5,000 in credit card debt by doubling my payments every month *so I can stop stressing over bills and use any extra money for a vacation.*

Time-bound: I want to pay off $5,000 in credit card debt by doubling my payments every month *for the next year* so I can stop stressing over bills and use any extra money for a vacation.

> Short-term goals are priorities that you can accomplish within two years. Mid-term goals take two to five years. Long-term financial goals are achievable in five or more years.

SMART steps to reach your retirement goals. Now it's your turn to try this out. By answering the questions for each section, you can fill in the blanks and transform one vague wish into a SMART goal. Do this for every goal that impacts your finances and you're on your way to making true progress in achieving them.

Wish: _____

Specific: _____
What exactly do you want to achieve? What details are important for arriving at this goal?

Measurable: _____
What's a number you can attach to your goal? Is it a certain percentage? A dollar amount?

Achievable: _____
Is it possible, with effort and commitment, to reach this goal?

Relevant: _____
Why are you doing this? Why is this important to you? Does this goal align with your values and financial mindset?

Time-bound: _____
What is your deadline? Is it realistic?

Net worth workout: A formula for financial fitness

Do you think the term "net worth" only applies to millionaires? Not at all. Along with your credit score and the balance in your retirement account, it's one of the most important numbers you need to assess your financial health.

But it's also an amount that changes, depending on your age, your earning power, the stock market, the housing market, and a whole host of other factors. At any given time, your net worth is simply a snapshot of where you are on your financial venture. So updating that number every year will help you stay on track. It's part of knowing where you want to go and how you're going to get there.

Don't estimate, calculate. Remember those goals you just identified? Well knowing your net worth will make it pretty clear where you stand in reaching them. Let's say you're trying to decide on a financial move. Maybe you want to retire. Or perhaps you're already retired but have your heart set on owning a lake house.

Just having a steady income or a cushy savings account balance doesn't necessarily mean you can afford that big dream. Believe it or not, some people who look like they're worth a cool million or two have so much debt that they're called "all flash, no cash."

Computing your net worth removes all assumptions with some very simple math — what you own minus what you owe.

Net Worth = Assets - Liabilities

Your personal balance sheet begins with assets. Basically, assets are things you own that have value — cash value, that is. You list them, add up the numbers, and voila! You have a figure representing your total assets.

But hang on. Sometimes the monetary value of an asset is not cut and dried. Take your home for example. You know what you paid for it, but its worth is based on what you could sell it for right now. Real estate usually appreciates — or increases in value — but not always.

Automobiles, on the other hand, usually depreciate — or decrease in value. That means you must analyze every asset according to how much you'd get if you sold it for cash today.

Ready to calculate your assets? Keep these tips in mind as you get started so that you get the most accurate estimate of the value of your possessions and other resources.

- A little research online will give you fair, conservative market values for your home, other real estate, cars, boats, and other possessions.

- If you're still carrying a mortgage or making car payments, you will take the outstanding amount of the loan into consideration later, when you start to list liabilities. For now, stick to the market value of these assets.

- Don't overinflate personal property. You may think certain collectibles, antiques, jewelry, or family items are more valuable than they really are.

- It's smart to leave some possessions off the asset list because you might have a hard time selling them for the amount you want.

Use the following table to map out how much your assets are worth. Add the numbers to get your total asset amount.

Asset	Dollar amount
Savings account	
Checking account	
Certificates of deposit (CDs)	
Money market account	
Emergency fund	
Investments	
Annuities	
Retirement fund	
Life insurance policy	
Pension equity	
Employer savings plan	
Vehicle 1 market value	
Vehicle 2 market value	
Home market value	
Other real estate market value	
Personal property	
Other	
Total assets	$

Liabilities offset your financial progress. Think of liabilities as debt. Just as you acquire and sell assets throughout your life, you will also incur and, hopefully, pay off debt. This ever-changing financial landscape is why an annual checkup is vital.

So the next step in assessing your net worth is itemizing the exact dollar amount currently due to each creditor. Add these numbers up to get your total liability, or total debt.

> Understand that listing your liabilities here is not the same as working up a budget, although the two are closely related.
>
> - A liability is a financial obligation you must meet over a certain period of time, like a 30-year mortgage. It can, and should, go away at some point — when you pay the debt off.
>
> - Not surprisingly, each liability is also a budget expense. For instance, a recurring house payment will become a line item in your monthly budget, until you pay that mortgage off.
>
> - But other monthly expenses, like groceries, gas, utilities, and clothing, are not liabilities. These are not amounts you owe to a creditor and are not considered debt. They will factor into your monthly budget, but not your net worth.

You'll notice that certain things — such as a home — can be an asset and a liability at the same time. It's important for your financial balance sheet to acknowledge both sides. You don't have an accurate sense of your true net worth unless you do. And that's why someone owing $900,000 on their $1 million home is not in as good financial shape as you might think.

Liability	Dollar amount
Credit card	
Home mortgage	
Other real estate mortgage	
Vehicle 1 loan	
Vehicle 2 loan	
Other installment loans	
Outstanding lines of credit	
Medical bills	
Judgments	
Personal loans	
Student loans	
Taxes	
Home equity loan	
Home equity line of credit (HELOC)	
Accrued alimony and child support	
Loans on cash value life insurance policies	
Loans against pension accounts	
Total liabilities	$

Crunch the numbers for a clear-cut wealth assessment. Now for the moment of truth. Take the number next to "Total assets" and subtract out the number next to "Total liabilities." And there you have it, your net worth.

If the result is a number greater than $0, you have a positive net worth. Congratulations, you own more than you owe. A negative number means just that, a negative net worth. You owe more than you own.

Don't be completely discouraged if you're in the second category. There are certain times in life when your assets are naturally less than your liabilities — in your early years as you're starting to build equity in your home and during retirement as you spend down your investments, for instance. But for everyone else, turning around a negative net worth should be a priority. To accomplish this you must do three things.

- Know exactly where your money is going. A big picture perspective helps you see how you spend. And since you can't change what you don't understand, setting up and following a budget is key.

- Save consistently. The goal here is to accumulate assets that don't come with liabilities. So purchasing a house with a mortgage doesn't accomplish this. But putting more money into your emergency fund or your investments does.

- Pay down debt. Without loans, mortgages, or credit card debt, you have no red in your ledger — nothing that subtracts from your assets. Just imagine what that could do to your bottom line.

Understanding your net worth is vital information to have when making financial decisions.

Tally your wealth scorecard. So how do you feel about your net worth? It may be a positive number, but is it a "good" number?

That's an important question with no one-size-fits-all answer. Mostly you want your net worth to allow you to reach your financial goals. So as you calculate it every year, keep your personal objectives in mind — especially your retirement needs. To set a net worth goal for this phase of your life, account for your anticipated expenses, like housing, utilities, and food. Then add in expenses for the lifestyle you want to have, like travel or entertainment.

You'll use your most liquid assets to pay for these expenses. Which means you'll need a balance in cash, stocks, bonds, mutual funds, and retirement accounts to tip your net worth far enough into the positive to cover the outlay.

Want to compare yourself to others? If so, take a look at data from the Federal Reserve's latest survey. In 2019 the average net worth of families in the U.S. was $748,800, but the median — or exact middle number out of everyone surveyed — was $121,700.

Or you can use a calculation that involves your age and your income to come up with a target net worth. Remember, your net worth tends to increase throughout your career. So the figure a person comes up with at age 25 will probably be much lower than the one found at 65.

$$\text{Target Net Worth} = \frac{(\text{Your Age x Pretax Annual Income})}{10}$$

Tame the money madness with a debt check

"Never spend your money before you have it." Good advice from Thomas Jefferson. But it seems most Americans aren't taking it to heart — total household debt in the U.S. has risen to $14.6 trillion. That's trillion with a "t." To put that staggering amount into perspective, it's enough to pay an average year's salary to almost 225 million teachers.

Unfortunately, debt is a way of life for many people. It's become second nature to buy with a credit card. To take out a new car loan. To carry a first, or even a second, mortgage. If you have debt and don't yet grasp the impact it can have on your retirement, consider another bit of wisdom — this time from the Financial Industry Regulatory Authority (FINRA). This organization, whose mission is to protect people from investment fraud, points out that spending less on debt leaves you more money for saving and investing in your future.

> Ideally, you'd be debt-free. That way all your extra income could be put toward investments, an emergency fund, and simply living well in retirement. To get to this happy place, create a budget designed to pay down debt quickly and efficiently.

Think about that. You may be funneling hundreds of dollars in monthly interest payments to banks and credit card companies instead of using it to build your retirement or emergency fund.

And that's why the next step in your annual financial checkup is finding out your debt-to-income ratio — the percentage of your monthly gross income that goes to paying debt.

How to eat an elephant — the surprising power of two numbers. When you calculated your net worth, you figured out your total debt — the sum of everything you owed everybody. Even if it's not a stomach-dropping number, it can seem like a lot.

Don't despair. You can get out of debt the same way that the old joke says to eat an elephant — one bite at a time. So take that first bite-sized piece by calculating your total monthly debt payment.

Make a list of the exact amount you send to creditors every month. If you don't have a predetermined payment, enter an average. Use the list of liabilities from earlier to get started.

Creditor	Monthly payment
Credit card	
Home mortgage	
Other real estate mortgage	
Vehicle 1 loan	
Vehicle 2 loan	
Other installment loans	
Outstanding lines of credit	
Medical bills	
Judgments	
Personal loans	
Student loans	
Taxes	
Home equity loan	
Home equity line of credit (HELOC)	
Accrued alimony and child support	
Loans on cash value life insurance policies	
Loans against pension accounts	
Total monthly debt payment	$

The next bite of information you need is your gross monthly income, or the amount of money you earn each month before taxes and other deductions are taken out.

Got it? Now you're ready to do some simple math.

Money in, money out — are your finances in harmony? Want to know your debt-to-income (DTI) ratio? You can bet your bank does. Lenders use this number to determine how well you manage debt payments and to judge if you'll be able to repay a loan. The concept is simple — do you make enough to cover what you owe?

Divide your gross monthly income into your monthly debt. Then multiply the results by 100 to determine the percentage of your income that goes toward your debt each month. That percentage is your DTI ratio. The lower this number, the better.

$$\text{Debt-to-Income Ratio} = \frac{\text{Total Monthly Debt Payment}}{\text{Gross Monthly Income}} \times 100$$

Let's say your monthly debts total $2,000 and your gross monthly income is $6,000. Divide the two and you get 0.33. Multiply that decimal by 100 for your DTI ratio — 33%.

This ratio can impact you in the world of finance. If you were trying to qualify for a mortgage, for instance, you typically couldn't have a DTI ratio higher than 43%. Lenders prefer that the number isn't above 36%. They believe borrowers with higher ratios are more likely to have trouble making monthly payments. But you can and should use your DTI ratio as a gauge of your own financial health, even if you have no plans to apply for a mortgage or other loan.

You can use these general categories of DTI ratios as benchmarks. Actual lenders and mortgage programs will have their own specific requirements. Remember, the best way to improve your DTI ratio is to pay down your debt.

- 35% or lower — excellent

- 36% to 49% — adequate to marginal

- 50% or higher — poor

It's math, not magic — how to create a budget that works for you

When you hear the word "budget" do you immediately start to sweat, picturing the end of all that is fun and fabulous in life? Nonsense. You're not living in a Dickens novel. You're trying to build financial security. And the best way to do that is to take control of your money — knowing and regulating how much comes in and goes out. Creating a budget is more about finding power and strength than living in hardship.

Remember, at the end of the day, you budget so you can have a fun — and fabulous — retirement.

Budgets reflect the changing landscape of your financial life. Setting up a budget will take a little time and effort. But once you have it structured to fit your lifestyle, you won't have to create a game plan for spending and saving again. However, you should revisit your budget periodically to allow for certain developments.

- Adjust your income according to life changes such as promotions, retirement, or divorce.

- Remove specific expense line items as loans and other debts are paid off.

- Adjust entries when services, like cable bills, have a price increase.

The manner you choose to budget is up to you. Some may prefer the old-school method of taking a pencil to ledger paper. Others might want to download a budgeting template off the internet — search for "free budget template." Perhaps you're comfortable working in a spreadsheet program on your computer. You could also get started with budgeting software and apps.

Whatever your choice, you must understand the three basic components of a budget — income, fixed expenses, and variable expenses — and how living within a budget impacts your life.

Nothing but net — base your math on take-home pay. For your budget to reflect the real world, many experts advise using "net" instead of "gross" income. In other words, you want your budget to be based on your take-home pay — the amount that goes into your bank account after taxes and other deductions.

For example, if you lived in Mississippi and received a yearly salary of $40,000, you would pocket only $32,410 after paying federal and state taxes, Social Security, and Medicare. That would be your annual net income, which you'd divide by 12 to find the amount to put on your monthly budget worksheet.

You have many options when it comes to choosing a budgeting method. Consider these tips as you determine which approach works best for you.

- If you decide to use gross income in your budget, you'll need to include line items for taxes and other payroll deductions and subtract that amount.

- Some budgeting guidelines advise you to spend certain percentages of your income on different expense categories — like 20% on savings. Before you follow one of these budgeting philosophies, understand if the percentages are based on net or gross income.

Fixed expenses are your budgeting backbone. Expenses come in two flavors — fixed and variable. Payments that don't change from month to month are considered fixed. They're easy to plug into your budget and include items like these.

- monthly payments on debts or loans that, for the most part, never change until they are paid off, such as a mortgage or auto loan

- set fees for phone, satellite or cable, internet, garbage, and recycling services

Variable expenses can be tough to pin down. You're naturally going to use your gas furnace more in the winter than summer. Your grocery bill might spike the month you have family visiting. And car repairs are notoriously tricky to predict. These are all reasons why certain expenses are considered variable. But you have to take them into account for budgeting purposes.

One solution is to harness the tools you may already have at your disposal. Many banks and credit cards offer automatic tracking features. Keep tabs on where every dollar is spent using preset categories or create your own. Gather paper statements or log in to your account online for monthly snapshots as well as year-end totals. Line graphs, pie charts, and summaries are good visual aids to help you review where you're spending and what percentage of your money goes to each variable category.

Of course for a tool like this to be accurate, you must use one account exclusively for these variable expenses. And remember, a good rewards credit card with a spending tracker can be a powerful asset when looking for ways to manage your finances — but not if you regularly carry a balance.

A low-tech alternative is to do all this tracking yourself, manually. Monitor your variable expenses for several months to a year, and calculate an average. Then enter that amount into your budget.

Here's a sample of a worksheet for averaging your variable expenses.

Variable expense	Jan	Feb			Nov	Dec	Average
Groceries							
Restaurants							
Electricity							
Natural gas							
Water							
Doctor							
Dental							
Vision							
Medicine							
Fuel							
Car maintenance							
Entertainment							
Clothing							
Personal care							
Pets							
Travel							
Gifts							

Don't simply track spending — budget. Let's say you do all this work calculating averages, inputting expenses, recording your spending — but nothing more. The truth is that's not really budgeting. A true budget is a plan. It's not enough to know how much you're spending each month. You must get to the point where you pay only what you want or need to each month.

To begin your plan, figure out where you are financially. You now know your fixed monthly expenses and a monthly average for your variable expenses. Post these numbers to the sample budget worksheet on the following page or into a budgeting template of your choice. Tally up your total monthly expenses.

When figuring your total monthly income, don't forget to include pensions, disability, Social Security, annuity payouts, and investment income. Now subtract expenses from income to determine your monthly net. A negative result means you're spending more than you're making. A positive number means you have money left over.

The 50/30/20 budget: A simple plan you can stick to

An easy and popular budgeting "rule" is one that divides your after-tax income into three buckets.

- Spend 50% on needs. These are generally categorized as bills you must pay and items you need for survival. Examples include housing, utilities, transportation, food, insurance, health care, and minimum debt payments.

- Spend 30% on wants, like entertainment and travel. Because these are usually unnecessary expenses, you'll want to look here first when it's time to cut back.

- Spend 20% on savings, investments, and additional debt repayments. Without funding this bucket, you'll never get ahead, so most experts say don't fall behind here.

Budget worksheet

Monthly expenses

Housing

Mortgage / rent	$
Property taxes	$
Maintenance / repairs	$
Other	$

Insurance

Auto	$
Health	$
Homeowners / renters	$
Long-term care	$
Life	$
Other	$

Food

Groceries	$
Restaurants	$
Other	$

Utilities & services

Electricity	$
Natural gas	$
Water / sewer	$
Cable / satellite	$
Internet	$
Phone	$
Trash / recycling	$
Other	$

Debt

Credit card	$
Loans	$
Alimony / child support	$
Other	$

Transportation

Auto loan	$
Fuel	$
Maintenance / repairs	$
License / taxes	$
Public transportation	$
Other	$

Personal

Entertainment	$
Clothing	$
Personal care	$
Pets	$
Travel	$
Gifts	$
Charity	$
Subscriptions	$
Membership fees	$
Other	$

Medical

Doctor	$
Dental	$
Vision	$
Medicine / drugs	$
Other	$

Savings

Emergency fund	$
Investments	$
Other	+ $
Total expenses	$

Monthly income

Net income	$
Investment income	+ $
Total income	$

Monthly summary

Total income	$
Total expenses	- $
Net	$

A budget tuneup keeps you on course

Now is the time to put the plan into your budget. Bring together the elements you've gathered so far in your financial checkup.

- your SMART goals

- your net worth

- your debt-to-income (DTI) ratio

Your goals should give you a good idea of where you want to go on your financial journey. And now you know, based on your net worth and DTI ratio, if you have the funds to get there. If you do, make the appropriate tweaks to your budget to turn those goals into realities. Maybe allocate more to debt payoff or boost your savings category.

If you're falling short, figure out where your money is going and what you can do to decrease your spending.

The 5 W's of a bulletproof estate plan

It's on your to-do list. Or maybe your do-someday list. Make that your do-when-I-have-absolutely-nothing-else-to-do list.

Estate planning isn't anybody's idea of a good time. Regardless, it needs to be on your do-now list since it can't wait. If you die without your affairs in order, you add an additional burden to your already grieving family. They must not only hunt for vital information and documents, but make decisions on their own when they cannot determine your wishes.

It's a sad fact, but only about half the seniors polled for the Transamerica Retirement Survey of Retirees said they had a will; less than a third had a living will — also known as an advance directive — or power of attorney for health care; and 30% had none of these important documents in place.

So bite the bullet and get organized. Then revisit your arrangements every year. Because estate planning is a shifting process, not a once-and-done deal. Bits and pieces of your life change from one year to the next. You buy and sell things. Perhaps you get divorced or remarried, have more grandchildren, or move. Each change could mean new decisions and new paperwork.

So hopefully now you understand three of the five W's of estate planning.

- Who — that's you

- When — immediately

- Why — to record your wishes, protect your assets, and safeguard your family

Read on to discover the What and Where.

Establish your estate with vital documents. In addition to paperwork that details your net worth, a calculation of your debt-to-income ratio, and a current budget showing regular bills, gather these physical documents.

- Social Security card
- divorce documents
- adoption records
- HIPAA authorization
- power of attorney
- bank account statements
- trust agreements
- last will and testament
- marriage license
- birth certificate
- citizenship papers
- advance health care directives
- tax returns
- vehicle titles
- funeral arrangements
- real estate titles or deeds

- investment statements
- bond certificates
- military records
- stock certificates
- current insurance policies
- military discharge papers

Important info connects the dots. Whether it's a bank, investment, email, or social media account, your survivors must have access to details — like numbers and passwords. Create lists or spreadsheets to record specifics that might otherwise fall through the cracks. This will allow family to quickly and efficiently make contact, close accounts, and generally follow through with your wishes. For each category, include information under the suggested headings.

Family and beneficiaries

A lawyer or third party may not know how to contact your Uncle John or cousin Fred to pass on a legacy. Make everything simpler with legal names and current phone numbers.

Full name	Contact info	Date of birth	Relationship	Notes

Financial accounts

Collect information on any organization that holds your money. Include bank accounts, brokerage accounts, IRAs, health savings accounts, annuities, and pensions.

Name	Account number	Contact info	Beneficiary

Liabilities

You've examined your liabilities in several contexts already. Now you simply need to record them. Include credit cards, mortgages, vehicle loans, lines of credit, and all other installment loans.

Name	Account number	Contact info

Digital accounts

This is the category most people forget about, but leaving your online accounts inaccessible is a huge mistake. On average, a single email address is linked to 130 accounts, according to a leading online security company. Tracking all these down and securing your personal and financial information would be a nightmare to someone without a list.

Name	User ID	Password

Insurance policies

Whether it's life, home, auto, long-term care, disability, or some other type of coverage, be sure to record each policy.

Insurance firm	Policy type	Policy owner	Policy number	Beneficiary	Amount	Contact info

Collect and protect — final step safeguards your plan. Obviously, you need to keep all these documents in a secure place where you, your family, your executor, or an attorney can find them. For more information on where you should and shouldn't store certain documents, turn to the *Emergency planning* chapter.

Make all the copies you need of these documents and give them to people they relate to. Here are just a few examples.

- your living trust to each beneficiary

- health care directives to your primary care physician and local hospital

- a durable power of attorney for finances to your attorney

While you'll find having copies of these important papers helpful, never, ever make duplicate originals. These are separate but identical legal documents that are signed and witnessed. So instead of a photocopy of your original will, for instance, you would have two or more legally binding wills with the same wishes on them. If you later wanted to make changes to your will, you'd have to make them on all the duplicates or you could end up with conflicting legal documents.

> Passing away without a will is known as dying intestate. If this happens, your assets are frozen until the laws of your state determine how they will be distributed.

Protect your assets — and peace of mind — with insurance

You've had insurance policies in place for years — possibly decades, so you're feeling pretty protected. And maybe you have good insurance. But do you have the right insurance?

The definition of "right" will be different for every person. And — surprise — it could be different for you this year. After all, circumstances change.

You should never put an insurance policy into a mental drawer and shut it away forever. It's vital that you review these contracts routinely, not only to make sure everything is correct, but to check that you still have the correct level of coverage. Having too much or too little insurance will cost you money.

You just made a list of all your insurance policies when tidying up your estate plan. Now you need to critically review each one. Read on to understand how certain life changes can impact different types of insurance.

Age. You're a year older. Hurray. But you'll find that penalties as well as perks come with every candle.

- Once you're into your 60s, your auto insurance rates may go up each year. Budget accordingly.

- Does a birthday this year mean a term life insurance policy is about to expire? If you want to renew your policy, you must reapply and complete another medical exam. In addition, renewing now will cost you a pretty penny because life insurance rates increase with age. As another option, if your term policy came with a built-in term conversion rider, you could change it into a permanent insurance policy. Converting has both pros and cons, but you must make this switch while your term policy is active.

- If you haven't yet purchased long-term care (LTC) insurance, don't delay. It gets more expensive every year you wait.

Marital status. If you lost a spouse, became divorced, or married this year, you have some decisions to make and possibly some paperwork to take care of.

- Automobile insurers say married drivers file fewer claims, which generally translates into lower rates. If you've recently tied the knot, share that with your provider.

- Spouses don't have to be on the same health insurance plan. Although sometimes it's cheaper to share, you may save more by customizing with separate plans if, say, your new spouse has a chronic health condition and you don't.

- Are new family members depending on you financially? You may need more life insurance. On the other hand, if you're now single and without dependents, you might want to cancel your policy.

- Take this time to review whether or not you should remove or add a beneficiary on life insurance policies you plan to keep.

- You may not need LTC insurance if you're now single and can, for example, sell your house to finance your future needs. But if you're married, an LTC insurance policy may be the better option to fund care. That would likely be the case if one spouse needed the care of a nursing facility while the other remained at home.

Health. So how are you feeling? Have you licked a thorny health issue or are you facing some new challenges?

- During Medicare's open enrollment period between Oct. 15 and Dec. 7 each year, make sure your plan still covers the doctors and hospitals you'd like to use and the prescription drugs you require. Examine the fine print and decide, based on your health needs now, if you should add, drop, or switch any coverage.

- Did you quit smoking? Maybe you got control of your high blood pressure. Congratulations. Not only will you feel better, but you may be able to save money on life insurance, too. Talk to your provider so she can adjust your policy.

- Buy a long-term care policy before you need it. If you wait until you're ill, this type of insurance may not be available or it could be much more expensive.

Residence. Changes to where you live and the kind of home you reside in can make a difference to certain policies.

- Recently moved? Certain states and even specific cities carry lower auto insurance premiums than others. Don't delay in updating your address.

- A new house or major improvements to your existing home, like additions or upgraded materials, require tweaking your homeowners insurance so you have adequate coverage.

- If property values in your area have risen lately, double-check that your homeowners policy will truly cover the cost of repairing or rebuilding your home if it is damaged or destroyed.

- Are you now a renter? Your landlord's insurance policy will only pay for damage to the dwelling, not to your possessions. Get your own renters insurance policy.

- In some states, if you rent, you could pay as much as 5.5% more for car insurance than a homeowner. That's according to the most recent analysis of over 83 million car insurance rates. If switching to another provider doesn't remedy this bump in premiums, make sure you adjust your budget.

Job status. You're not always required to let insurers know if you're working or retired. But sometimes telling them is in your best interest.

- If you just retired and no longer have to commute to work, you're probably driving fewer miles. In insurance terms, this means less risk and maybe lower premiums. On the flip side, perhaps you've changed your mind about retirement. If you're back to working full time, believe it or not, this could knock several dollars off the annual cost of your car insurance in some states.

- Transitioning into retirement when you're not yet eligible for Medicare means doing your homework on health insurance. Possible solutions? Sign up for COBRA coverage or a policy through the state or federal health insurance exchange.

- When you're working, life insurance is a safety net for your family. It replaces your income in case something happens to you. But after you retire, this coverage may not be necessary because your children are more likely to be living on their own and you may have paid off big debts like mortgages and auto loans.

- Still working full time because you or your family need the money? Then don't risk a loss of income due to injury. Consider long-term disability insurance.

Finances. Feeling flush? Perhaps your ship finally came in and your golden years are looking truly golden. Extra cash here and there prompts a different outlook on some insurance policies.

- If you have an emergency fund in place — enough to cover between three and six months of living expenses — think about taking a higher deductible and lowering the premium on your homeowners, health, and auto insurance plans.

- Paying your bills on time often leads to a better credit score, and that could mean lower premiums on auto insurance.

- In 2020, the annual average cost for long-term care ranged from $19,240 to $105,850. If you have sufficient funds and assets to pay for this care, you may not need an LTC insurance policy.

- Many experts recommend umbrella insurance — a type of liability coverage that covers claims beyond what typical homeowner, auto, and boat insurance policies pay — for anyone with significant assets.

Policy type	Life change					
	Age	Marital status	Health	Residence	Job status	Finances
Auto	✔	✔		✔	✔	✔
Home or renters				✔		✔
Health		✔	✔		✔	✔
Life	✔	✔	✔		✔	
Long-term care	✔	✔	✔			✔
Long-term disability					✔	
Umbrella						✔

5 little-known types of insurance you might need

Your wallet doesn't like surprises. And there's nothing more financially shocking than an expense from left field. It could come in the form of a scam, a scrapped vacation, or a stolen wedding ring. Don't let misfortunes like these drain your bank account.

With each new year, examine your lifestyle and ask yourself, "Where am I vulnerable?" Then look into special types of insurance that protect against the unexpected. Before you commit to any coverage, however, check out policy details such as deductibles, copays, monthly premiums, and limitations.

- **Identity theft protection.** Cover fees needed to repair the damage from ID theft, such as the cost of restoring your credit reports.

- **Cellphone insurance.** Repair or replace a damaged, lost, or stolen cellphone.

- **Personal article insurance.** Secure valuable items, like expensive jewelry, fine art, collections, or electronics with a separate personal article policy or a floater attached to your existing homeowners policy.

- **Pet insurance.** Offset expensive veterinary visits and treatments.

- **Travel insurance.** Protect against cancellations, lost baggage, emergency medical situations, and even accidental death.

Banking on Social Security? Smart ways to check your benefits

Already receiving Social Security benefits? Or maybe you're still a few years away from collecting. Either way, your annual financial checkup should include a look at your Social Security statement.

It's a quick and easy way to check for errors and budget for your future.

Older adults should get on top of this sooner rather than later. After all, roughly half of seniors in the U.S. depend on their monthly check for 50% or more of their income.

Create an account for peace of mind. Signing up for a "*my Social Security*" online account does more than help you manage your payments and get an estimate of upcoming benefits. Doing so also prevents a thief from setting up an account in your name and then directing your payments to his checking account.

So why not get started today? Here's how.

1. Go to *ssa.gov/myaccount* and select the *Create an Account* button.

2. Click Create *New Account.*

3. Read and agree to the Social Security Administration's (SSA) terms of service before clicking *Next.*

4. You'll be asked to provide personal information to verify your identity, including your name, Social Security number, date of birth, home address, and email address. After filling in the data, click *Next.*

5. The SSA will send you an activation code. Electing to receive the numbers by text or email will allow you to finish creating your account immediately.

6. After submitting the activation code, choose a username and strong password that contains a mixture of symbols, numbers, and uppercase and lowercase letters. You'll also have to select three security questions and answer them.

First things first — review your earnings record. You probably know that the amount of your benefit is partially based on the SSA's record of your lifetime earnings. Unfortunately, employers sometimes report that information incorrectly or not at all. When that happens, the SSA can't ensure that you'll receive all the benefits you're entitled to, and you could miss out on thousands of dollars in payments. That's why it's so important to verify that the SSA's earnings record accurately reflects your work history. Luckily, accessing that info is just a few mouse clicks away.

1. Go to *ssa.gov/myaccount*, click *Sign In*, and enter your username and password.

2. The SSA will send you a unique security code by text or email. Key in that code and follow the prompts to get to your "*my* Social Security" account homepage where you can find out what's in your confidential Social Security report.

3. From the homepage, select the link titled *View Earnings Record* or click the tab titled *Earnings Record*.

You'll find earnings for all your work years, along with the total amount of Social Security and Medicare taxes both you and your employers have paid.

Does something look off? Perhaps you see "$0" next to the year 2019 but you're sure you worked during that time. If that's the case, contact the SSA at 800-772-1213 after gathering proof of your earnings. A pay stub, tax return, or W-2 will do just fine.

Don't have any of that? Then before calling, write down the name and address of the employer, the dates you worked, and the amount you earned that year.

Plan for your retirement with benefit estimates. Thinking of giving up the daily grind but don't know how much you can expect from Social Security each month? Well, the amount also depends on the age at which you begin getting benefits. But don't worry. The SSA provides you with an estimate on that, too. Here's how to find it.

1. Go to *ssa.gov/myaccount* and click *Sign In*. Enter your username and password, input the security code that the SSA sends you, and follow the prompts.

2. From your "*my* Social Security" account homepage, select the *View Estimated Benefits* link or click the *Estimated Benefits* tab.

You'll land on a page telling you how much you'll collect monthly if you start getting benefits at age 62, at your full retirement age, and at age 70.

Not sure what your full retirement age is? Use the following chart.

Year of birth	Full retirement age
1943-1954	66
1955	66 and 2 months
1956	66 and 4 months
1957	66 and 6 months
1958	66 and 8 months
1959	66 and 10 months
1960 or later	67

Remember, the SSA provides only estimates. The exact amount of your payments will hinge on several factors, including cost-of-living adjustments and future increases or decreases in your earnings.

Got all the information you need from the SSA? Don't forget to log out of your account after each use by clicking the *Sign Out* link at the top of the page.

Cents and sensibility: Get your investment portfolio in fighting shape

You've been socking money away in your IRA or 401(k) for years. That's great, because building a retirement nest egg is a lot easier if you start early.

But have you looked at your investments lately? If not, make it part of your annual financial review. You'll want to evaluate how your portfolio has been performing and correct any weaknesses that could threaten your economic freedom. After all, Social Security isn't meant to be your sole source of retirement income. Here's a guide to keeping your investments on track.

Reassess your tolerance for risk. Ever hear of asset allocation? It's a fancy term for how your investment portfolio is divvied up.

- Stocks, for example, have historically had the greatest risk and highest returns.

- Bonds are generally more stable than stocks, but they offer more modest returns.

- Cash — such as the money you might have deposited in a money market, savings, or certificate of deposit account — tends to be the safest, but offers the lowest return.

The mix of assets that works best for you hinges largely on your time horizon — the months or years between now and when you'll need to tap into your portfolio — and your ability to weather a turbulent stock market.

An aggressive investment strategy, in which 80% of a portfolio is invested in stocks, is fine for someone in their 20s. But that game plan won't necessarily work when you're near or in retirement. That's because older folks need to access their funds sooner rather than later, giving them less time to recover from sharp drops in stock prices.

One solution? As you prepare for and move through your golden years, consider shifting to a progressively more conservative approach that scales back on the equities in your portfolio. Here's an example of how your investment combinations might transform as you near retirement.

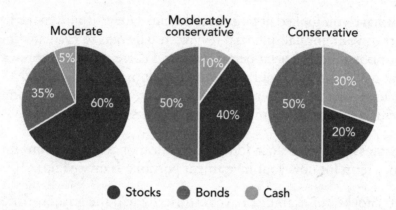

Moderate · Moderately conservative · Conservative

● Stocks ● Bonds ● Cash

Look into increasing your contributions. Approaching retirement and haven't saved up as much as you'd like? Cutting down on nonessentials will leave you more money for your investments. Just look at what contributing a few extra bucks to your IRA can do.

Let's say you're age 60 and your IRA is valued at $30,000. Assuming a 7% annual rate of return, you'll have more than $50,000 in your account when you're 65 if you put $25 a week — roughly the price of a movie ticket, popcorn, and soda — into your IRA over the next five years.

And the more you squirrel away, the bigger the potential gains. So each year, look up the annual contribution limits for your retirement accounts and evaluate whether it's a good idea to up your additions.

- For tax year 2022, you could stash a total of up to $6,000 a year in your IRAs. That figure went up to $7,000 annually if you were age 50 or older. Bonus — a joint-filing, working spouse may be able to contribute to a spousal IRA on behalf of a partner who earns little or no income. That essentially doubles the normal contribution limits.

- Got a 401(k)? You could contribute up to $20,500 a year in 2022, plus an additional $6,500 if you were 50 or older.

Review the fees you're paying. A recent *Traders Magazine* survey found that a large majority of investors don't know how much they're paying in investment fees. And that lack of knowledge can be downright costly. Fees — whether they're maintenance charges or costs that stem from buying and selling a stock or mutual fund — don't just reduce the current value of your portfolio. Once the money has been deducted from your account, you've also lost the opportunity to earn a return on it.

In fact, paying an additional 1% in annual fees can add up to tens of thousands of dollars in lost retirement income over the decades.

So what can you do? Look at your account opening documents, statements, and other related papers to see the types and amount of fees you're currently paying. Of course, there's no one-size-fits-all fee amount that will make everybody happy. But if you don't feel as if you're getting value for what you're paying, keep in mind that, in some cases, you can negotiate fees. Talk to your financial professional about reducing costs. If that doesn't work, it may be time to look at other options.

Before moving to a new account or firm, evaluate tax consequences and fees for closing or transferring your current account to ensure switching makes sense for you. Always shop around before you invest. When choosing a financial professional or a particular investment, request information on all the costs related to the account and how often you'll be charged. These are just a few of the questions you'll want to ask.

- Do I need to keep a minimum balance to avoid certain fees?

- Can I lower fees if I open a different kind of account?

- If I gave you $5,000, how much would get invested and how much would go to costs?

- After all the fees are paid, how much does my investment have to increase in value before I break even?

Conquer your credit report in 3 easy steps

Your credit report — a historical record of your relationship with debt and how well you pay it off — is more important than you might think. Lenders, utility companies, landlords, and even some prospective employers look at this information when deciding whether or not to do business with you.

But what if your report contains an error? It could be something as simple as an account that's mistakenly flagged as delinquent. Blunders like that can cause your credit score to plummet, and you may find yourself unable to get a loan or rent an apartment.

So make sure to view your report at least once a year. It just takes a few simple steps. And best of all, it's free.

Go online for instant access. You can get a copy of your credit report every 12 months from each of the three national credit reporting companies. You have the option of ordering them all at once or requesting one at a time throughout the year. The fastest way to review your free report is to head online.

1. Go to *annualcreditreport.com* and click *Request yours now!*

2. Click *Request your credit reports* and fill out the required information. You'll be asked for your name, birthday, Social Security number, and current address.

3. Request a report from any or all of the credit bureaus — Equifax, Experian, and TransUnion.

4. For each report, you'll be asked security questions to verify your identity. You may have to recall loans you've taken out or accounts you've opened.

5. Once you've correctly responded to the questions, the credit agency will generate your report. You can save it to your desktop or print it out.

Check for incorrect information. Now that you have your report, make sure your name and current and former addresses are accurate. Search for accounts that are incorrectly marked as late, or have the wrong balances or credit limits. And see if any closed accounts are listed as open.

Additionally, you'll want to confirm that all of your open accounts are marked as such. Your credit score could take a hit if your account has a balance and it's reported as closed.

Check that you recognize each account listed, too. Do you see a credit card that you don't remember opening? Maybe a loan that you never took out? If so, you could be a victim of fraud or identity theft. You'll also want to verify the legitimacy of any "hard" inquiries. Those are credit checks that companies make after you apply for credit or a loan.

Fix any errors. If you find an inaccuracy in your report, contact the lender or business that supplied the incorrect information. Same goes if you believe someone opened an account in your name. If that's the case, close the account and have it flagged for fraud.

You'll also want to initiate a dispute with any of the credit agencies that reported the error. You can contact them online, by phone, and by mail.

If you opt to get in touch via the postal service, the Federal Trade Commission says your letter should include your name and address, the mistakes you want fixed and the reasons why, and copies of documents that support your claim. You can also circle the errors that need fixing on a copy of your credit report and send that along, too.

Send the info via certified mail with a "return receipt" request so you have proof that the credit reporting company received your letter.

However you decide to file your dispute, the credit bureaus have 30 days to investigate your claims. They must also give you their results in writing.

Here's how to get in touch with each of the three credit reporting companies.

Equifax Information Services LLC P.O. Box 740241 Atlanta, GA 30374	*equifax.com/personal/ contact-us*	866-349-5191
Experian P.O. Box 4500 Allen, TX 75013	*experian.com/contact/ personal-services-contacts. html#content-02*	number on your credit report
TransUnion Consumer Solutions P.O. Box 2000 Chester, PA 19016-2000	*transunion.com/credit- disputes/dispute-your-credit*	800-916-8800

Tips from the pros: Tax moves that save money and time

Income taxes might be the single largest expense of your golden years. That's because the federal government imposes a levy on most forms of retirement income, including withdrawals from a traditional IRA or 401(k), pension payments, annuity interest, and the sale of stocks and bonds. And let's not even get started on Social Security — up to 85% of your benefits can get taxed.

You probably can't avoid paying income taxes in retirement. But with proper planning each year, you can steer clear of unwelcome surprises and even reduce your bill.

Review your withholding. Did you send Uncle Sam a big check last year? Perhaps you received a refund. If so, you may need to adjust your withholding — the portion of your wages and other types of taxable income that is automatically deducted and sent to the IRS on your behalf. Not having enough taken out could leave you with an unexpected bill in April. And having too much withheld means you've extended the government an interest-free loan.

Not sure how much should be debited? The tax withholding estimator at *irs.gov/individuals/tax-withholding-estimator* can help if you're still on the job or collecting a pension. This webpage also provides instructions on how to change the amount of tax that gets taken out. Just click the *To Change Your Withholding* heading in the expandable menu to access the info and forms.

If a large portion of your income isn't subject to federal withholding — think rental income, dividends, and capital gains — you'll need to make quarterly estimated tax payments throughout the year. To figure out how much you owe, go to *irs.gov/forms-instructions* and download Form 1040-ES.

It's time for a tax break. Know the difference between deductions and credits? It's really pretty simple. Deductions — like the kind you get for charitable donations or paying interest on your mortgage — reduce your taxable income. The value of the deduction depends on your tax bracket, but you'll pay less in taxes because your income is lower.

Credits, on the other hand, directly offset the amount of tax you owe. That's what makes them so valuable. So if your tax bill totals $1,200 but you have a credit worth $1,000, you'll have to fork over only $200. And some credits are "refundable," meaning that Uncle Sam will issue you a refund if you're eligible. Many lower-income people who don't owe taxes miss out on this refund because they don't file a return.

Don't overlook such important money-saving opportunities. Prepare for tax season by reviewing these potential boons to your budget at *irs.gov/credits-deductions-for-individuals*. You may also want to talk with a tax adviser for help lowering how much you have to pay.

Get an "A" in organization. Do you stress out at tax time trying to find your documents? No need. Set up a filing system as part of your financial checkup.

- As you receive tax-related documents in the mail, place them in a single, easily accessible folder. The idea is not to mislay the papers.

- If you itemize your deductions, you'll need to save receipts reflecting things like medical costs, self-employment expenses, and property tax payments. Make sure you also have records supporting any tax credits you might be eligible for.

- You may want to use paper clips or envelopes to categorize the documents as income, deductions, and credits.

Of course, the best way to get organized is finding out what works for you. The key is to get started now so that you're not rushed at tax time.

Once you've filed your taxes, how long should you hold onto your supporting documents? In most cases, the IRS has three years to audit a return after it has been filed. So keep all your records for at least that amount of time. Exceptions include employment tax records, which should be kept four years after the date that the tax becomes due or is paid, whichever is later.

And your returns? Keep them. They can help you prepare future returns and make computations if you have to file an amended return.

Decluttering 101 — when to shred or store your financial docs

Have papers and bills scattered on countertops or stuffed into drawers? Cutting the clutter will make life easier and lower mess stress. Use these ground rules to prune your overgrown financial files.

Keep your ATM, credit card, and bank deposit receipts just long enough to ensure that they match your monthly statements. You can shred your cellphone, cable, and utility bills once you've verified that the payment was processed — unless you're self-employed and need the documents for tax purposes.

You'll want to retain active insurance policies, and hang onto car titles and home deeds for the entire time you own the property. Place them in a safe-deposit box, along with these nine documents you should never destroy.

- birth and death certificates and adoption papers
- marriage licenses and divorce decrees
- Social Security cards, passports, and citizenship papers
- military service records

Don't delay — annual security review safeguards your estate

A whopping 75% of Americans over the age of 65 use the internet. In fact, it's practically impossible to function in today's world without an online presence — to communicate, shop, bank, and even learn. No surprise, that means it's likely some of your personal information is out there whether you like it or not.

Of course, you're careful. But as with every other aspect of your finances, you must address digital security at least once a year — if not more often.

Poor password practices leave you vulnerable. Did you know March 15 is National Password Day? That's right — being password-vigilant is so important it has its own spot on the calendar. But even if you choose some other day of the year to take care of this urgent business, don't skip any of these tips the Federal Trade Commission (FTC) has on its must-do list.

- Make every password long and complex.

- Use different passwords for different accounts.

- Opt in on multifactor authentication whenever it's offered for an extra layer of protection.

- Use a password manager to store and secure your passwords.

- When setting up an online account, select and answer security questions only you know the answer to. Don't choose those that can be answered with information readily available on the web.

- Change passwords frequently, and always do so immediately if a company says you may be the victim of a security breach.

Examine every one of your online accounts for strong password etiquette. Then waste no time in shoring up your digital defenses.

For the record — pass on in-play passwords. You've protected your bank, email, and credit card accounts by following good password protocol. Now take the next step and bring your documentation up to date. It's critical your heirs can access your latest login IDs, passwords, and answers to security questions, so revise the list that's part of your estate planning packet every time you make changes.

Check out all the other ways to keep your information and your finances safe online by turning to the *Digital security* chapter.

> The FBI says victims of identity theft lost over $200 million in 2020. And the number of people reporting this type of crime more than doubled from the previous year. The threat is real. So take your digital security seriously.

2 | Debt & budgeting

Dig yourself out of debt with the simple method that saves you money

Buried under a mountain of debt? You need a smart strategy to tackle those payments. Otherwise you'll end up shelling out hundreds — or even thousands — in interest. A $10,000 credit card debt with a 16% interest rate, for instance, could rack up $12,700 in interest if you only make the minimum payments. Great Scott!

If you're carrying multiple kinds of debt — like a car loan, credit card dues, and medical bills — it can be hard to determine what to pay down first. To save the most in interest and maybe even pay off your bills faster, turn to the avalanche method.

How does it work? Start by calculating how much extra you can put toward your bills each month. Continue making the minimum payments on all of your outstanding debts, and put the extra cash toward the account with the highest interest rate. When you pay it off, move on to the bill with the next highest interest rate. Keep it up until you're debt-free.

If you have trouble staying motivated, you could try the snowball method instead. You'll start by tackling your smallest loans first, so you can get the satisfaction of watching your open accounts shrink. However, you'll wind up paying more in interest over the long run.

Debt relief rip-offs: How to spot the signs before you get fleeced

When you're deep in debt, any offer that promises to help you sort out your money troubles seems like the perfect lifeline. But look before you leap.

While legitimate organizations will help you manage your debt, scammers often pretend to help while draining the little cash people have left. Here's how to spot the signs of a scam.

- They ask you to pay cash upfront.

- They won't tell you about their services and resources unless you give them personal info, such as credit card account numbers.

- They attempt to enroll you in a debt management program without reviewing your financial situation and going over basic budgeting skills.

The U.S. Trustee Program maintains a list of approved credit counseling agencies. Search the database online at *justice.gov/ust/list-credit-counseling-agencies-approved-pursuant-11-usc-111* to find reliable services.

Surprising way to pay off credit cards faster

American households with credit card debt spend an average of $1,155 a year on interest payments alone, according to a recent survey from NerdWallet. If only you could drop your interest rate to zero. Then your payments would go straight toward your balance so you could dump that debt pronto. Well, you may be able to do just that without changing the amount you pay each month. The trick? Use a balance transfer.

"A balance transfer card is almost like refinancing a mortgage," says Sara Rathner, a credit card expert at NerdWallet, a company that offers online tools to help people make smart financial decisions. "You're taking on a new loan with better terms, using that loan to pay off your old loan, and then making payments to that new loan."

But before you rush out and start applying for balance transfer cards, you need to know the whole story. First, you must have good — or even excellent — credit to qualify for these terms. Also be aware that transfer card issuers typically charge 3% to 5% of the total debt carried over. That means moving $5,000 to a new card could generate a $250 fee.

Finally, read the fine print. These cards boast 0% interest, but only for a limited time. The promotional period usually ends within 12 to 18 months, so make sure you have the income to pay it off by then or your debt will start to gain interest at the card's regular rate. Plus the regular interest rate may kick in for new purchases.

If you don't have the funds to cover these payments after a year, or good enough credit to get one of these cards, you may still have low-interest alternatives. "Personal loans are potentially an option for consumers who don't have the credit score needed to qualify for balance transfer cards," says Rathner.

Negotiate new terms to keep creditors off your back

Delinquent. Not a word you want associated with you. But if the late bills are stacking up, you have a delinquent debt on your hands. What can you do? Many creditors would rather have a small settlement than nothing at all. With a little knowledge, you may be able to negotiate better terms.

Start by figuring out how much you can realistically repay. Most lenders want a lump-sum payment. Research the creditor's settlement policy, then call and explain your situation. You may be able to settle at 40% to 50% of the balance, but begin by lowballing the offer. Also discuss how the settlement will show up on your credit report. An account marked as "paid in full" will minimize the damage.

Get your agreement in writing before you make any payments to the company. Lastly, keep in mind that forgiven debt of $600 or more is considered taxable.

8 useful apps to manage your budget

You'll find a wide variety of budgeting apps available, and they all provide similar options in terms of managing household accounts. Some can also be linked to your online bank accounts, making it easier to monitor and include them in your overall money management.

Most household budget apps have a free version. But if you want to expand the app's functions, you'll pay a fee. Mint, Pocket-Guard, Goodbudget, and YNAB (You Need A Budget) are among the highest-rated apps. Fudget, Emma, Spendee, and Yolt are also popular options. And they're all available on iPadOS, iOS, and Android.

Don't let these budgeting blunders sink your retirement

You've spent your entire career scrimping and saving for retirement. But without a solid budget in place, all that hard work could be for nothing. Avoid these three retirement-ruining mistakes when budgeting for your golden years.

Forgetting to factor in semiregular expenses. When you're drafting a budget, it's easy to remember the bills you need to pay every month. But you might get a nasty surprise if you overlook payments that are only due once or twice a year.

If you own a home, for example, you'll need to set aside money to pay your property taxes annually — a colossal $2,471 on average. And don't forget about smaller expenses, like subscriptions, lawn maintenance, car registration, and homeowners association dues.

Tally up the total of these costs for the year, divide the amount by 12, and factor it into your budget each month. That way, you won't have to take a big chunk out of your savings when it's time to settle the bills. Also keep track of when these payments are due to dodge late fees.

Not budgeting for your entire retirement. Before you hang up your hat, reflect on how each phase of retirement will affect your ever-changing budget so you keep your spending in proportion with your nest egg.

- Early retirement (62-70). Tempted to spend more on vacations and hobbies now that you don't have to work? If you're not careful, you could drain your bank account.

  Think about what you want your early years in retirement to look like. Then take a look at your entire portfolio and other income streams to determine if these new spending patterns will work with your overall financial retirement goals.

- Middle retirement (70-80). By this point you'll be claiming Social Security, but don't exhaust your funds and bank on this money to pay your bills. Social Security will likely cover less than half of your retirement spending, so decide ahead of time how you will bridge the gap.

- Late retirement (80+). As you approach the last phase of your retirement, you may have health issues or need help around the home. And those costs add up. Plan to spend more on health care, assisted living, or other expenses.

Always planning for the best case scenario. Does your budget leave wiggle room for changes in the economy? If you assume that the market is going to be in great shape, you might find yourself in trouble during a recession.

Adjust your budget for current market conditions, keeping various performance outcomes in mind. Have a plan in place in case the stock market doesn't give you the expected return each year.

Streamline your household accounting with Quicken

Doing the household accounts and balancing your home budget is not the most glamorous of activities. However, keeping a check on income and expenditures will ultimately save you money. If you need some help, you'll find that Quicken is one of the most comprehensive household budget products available.

Quicken software is designed to be used primarily on Windows or Mac desktop computers or laptops. But once you have the program, you can find companion apps to use with iPadOS, iOS, and Android devices. To start using Quicken, follow these steps.

1. Go to the Quicken website at *quicken.com*.

2. Click on *Quicken for Windows* or *Quicken for Mac* on the homepage.

3. Quicken offers a 30-day trial so you can decide if you want to buy it. This is in the form of a 30-day money-back guarantee. Select the product plan that meets your needs, and click the *Buy Now* button.

4. Create an account with an email address and password. These will be your account login details.

Ins and outs of the Quicken program

Want to create a budget, manage your bills, and see how much money you have — all from a central location? Quicken works by linking to your financial accounts so that you can better manage your hard-earned cash. Here's how to connect one of these accounts to Quicken.

1. Open Quicken, and click on the + button on the homepage.

2. Enter the details of the account to be linked to Quicken. The account has to be with a bank that supports the Quicken software.

3. Once the account has been linked, Quicken will automatically assign categories for your spending, such as Groceries, so that you can see at a glance where your money is going.

4. When viewing an account, use buttons on the top tool bar to access different functions for working with the account.

5. The details of the account are listed in the left-hand panel of the account window. This includes categories for Cash, Savings, Credit Card, and Investing.

Entering expenditures. To keep an eye on your expenses, you just have to link your bills to an account in Quicken. Here's how.

1. Click on the *Bills* tab on the top toolbar within an account.

2. Select the bill provider to show how this bill will affect your overall costs.

Balancing the budget. To ensure that your income and spending are as balanced as possible, follow these steps.

1. Select the *Planning* tab on the account homepage, and click on the *Budgets* button on the toolbar below the *Planning* tab.

2. Click on the *Budget Actions* button, and select *Create new budget*.

3. Enter a name for the budget, and click the *OK* button.

4. The budget will be created based on your income and expenditures.

Finances on the go. You can also use the desktop computer or laptop version of Quicken with a companion mobile app to view your financial information when you are away from home. Setting it up is pretty simple, too.

1. In the standard version of Quicken, click on the *Mobile & Web* tab on the top toolbar.

2. Click on the *Get Started* button.

3. Select the accounts you want to use on the companion Quicken app, and click on the *Done* button.

4. Download the Quicken app from either the Apple App Store or the Google Play Store.

5. Once you have logged in with your Quicken account details, you will be able to see the account information that has been synced from the desktop version.

3 | Long-term care

> "I believe that through knowledge and discipline, financial peace is possible for all of us."
>
> Dave Ramsey

Get the best deal when you follow this expert advice

Nowadays Americans are living years longer than they were just a half-century ago. The current average life span in the U.S. is about 78 years, and plenty of adults are living past that marker, too. But that extended time comes at a cost in the form of long-term care. So what's a senior to do?

"Having some long-term care insurance enables your loved ones to care about you but not have to care for you," says Jesse Slome, director of the American Association for Long-Term Care Insurance, a leading advocate in planning for future care.

This type of insurance helps pay for expenses that aren't covered by regular health insurance or Medicare, such as help with daily activities like dressing and eating. The cost of this coverage goes up as you get older, though, which is why it's important to start shopping early.

According to Slome, the shopping sweet spot is between age 55 and 65. Generally, health tends to worsen as you age, and you may be considered uninsurable if new screenings unearth medical problems. Early planning gives you more options and increases your likelihood of being accepted. Not to mention a better price tag.

Take this example. A 55-year-old man may pay about $950 for an annual premium. The cost for that same policy jumps up to $1,700 — a $750 difference — if he waits to buy at 65. That difference could be greater depending on the policy.

But don't just look for the best price when you shop. The biggest mistake people make is not considering their health, says Slome. Before you apply, make sure your health conditions don't disqualify you. The insurance company will have access to your medical records, so there's no hiding your status. And a rejection will make it harder or impossible to get coverage somewhere else.

"Being declined by one insurance company can result in an automatic decline from others," says Slome.

Just one more reason to do it right the first time. Another? Slome also points out that it rarely pays to switch policies because your health is typically not going to improve and allow you to get a better deal.

 Ask these questions to avoid getting suckered by an agent

"Let's just apply," says the agent helping you shop for coverage. "I think you qualify for preferred rates — a 15% discount."

Sounds OK, but once you submit an application, he's locked in as your designated agent at that insurance company and you might not even get that discount.

Don't ever get pressured into a decision you're not comfortable with, and don't work with an agent without the right qualifications. Expert Jesse Slome recommends asking these screening questions.

- How long have you been selling long-term care insurance? Work with an agent who has at least three to five years under their belt.

- How many insurance companies are you appointed with? Consult with an agent who is appointed, or authorized, to sell policies from multiple companies, rather than just one.

- Are you knowledgeable in both traditional and linked benefits? Policies that link other benefits with long-term care are becoming more popular. You want an agent who can help evaluate all your options.

This policy option can lower your premiums

Long-term care policies can be a hefty expense — especially on a fixed income. But you can pay less each month if you choose a longer elimination period.

The elimination period is like a deductible. It's a specified length of time you must wait after triggering your benefits before your insurance company begins to pay for care. An insurance company may lower your premium rate if you pick a longer wait time, like 90 days rather than 30, for instance.

This could keep money in your pocket each month and save you about 20% on your premiums annually, says the American Association for Long-Term Care Insurance. But proceed with caution. The entire financial burden of care will be on you until the benefits kick in. So don't just pick the lowest premium and assume you can afford the rest of the care.

3 crowd-pleasing features that could save you pain down the line

You don't want to crack your nest egg with reckless spending. But when it comes to long-term care, don't cast off an insurance plan just because it's a little more pricey upfront. Weigh the cost of these three plan features and see if one is worthwhile for you to have greater flexibility in the future.

Double the life span of your plan for less. You could get extra years of coverage without paying top dollar by getting a shared policy. You and your spouse will each have your own plan, but you can pool your benefits.

Say you both buy four-year policies. With a shared plan, you'll have a total of eight years available that either spouse can use. Although this option is more expensive than simply having two separate four-year policies, it's less than both spouses buying their own eight-year plan.

You can also find some shared policies that are set up to keep one person from using all of the benefits. For instance, each spouse has their own coverage, and there's an additional third pool of benefits they can both dip into.

Protect against rising inflation. Say you buy long-term care insurance at age 55, expecting it to cover costs you face at 85. That's a whopping 30-year gap in which the cost of medical care can dramatically change — at an even faster rate than the general cost of living, too. That's why some people protect themselves with an inflation rider.

A popular choice is 3% compound interest. You can choose a smaller percentage to save on premiums, but you risk your benefits losing value and not keeping up with future costs.

Hybrid insurance gives the best of both worlds. Worried about paying for a long-term care policy, only for the money to evaporate if you don't use it?

A hybrid policy, also called a linked-benefit plan, may be right for you.

These plans have been around for a while, but they've recently become a more popular option than traditional long-term care insurance. A hybrid policy links long-term care coverage with a life insurance policy or annuity. Unused care benefits are paid out to your beneficiaries.

This plan can be significantly more expensive than a traditional long-term care policy, so you will have to weigh the additional cost against the possible benefits.

Mine Medicare for assistance in your golden years

You've just turned 65 and are all set up for Medicare. Now you don't have to worry about getting health care help for the rest of your life, right? Wrong. This government program covers many tests and services, but it won't pay for long-term care. However, you may be able to get some other assistance through Medicare Part A. Just make sure you meet the requirements so you aren't left footing the bill.

- Medicare will only cover medically necessary home health care, and a doctor must certify that you are homebound. You must also require skilled nursing care or therapy, such as physical or speech. That means it won't pay for a home health aide if it's the only assistance you need.

- Medicare covers up to 20 days of skilled nursing care if you have a qualifying inpatient hospital stay lasting three or more days, and your doctor says you need daily skilled care. For days 21 through 100, you'll be on the hook for coinsurance. After 100 days, Medicare won't pay for any of the care.

4 | Wills & trusts

> The perfect amount to leave children is "enough money so that they would feel they could do anything, but not so much that they could do nothing."
>
> Warren Buffet

Seal in the specifics to keep the peace after you're gone

Mary's family had always been tightknit, so she thought nothing of it when she left her estate to her oldest to distribute among the others. Unfortunately, even close siblings can end up at odds with one another, and after Mary passed, her kids paid a small sum to have their family dispute mediated by a lawyer.

"This isn't going to happen to my family," you may think. "My child will do the right thing." Letha McDowell, president of the National Academy of Elder Law Attorneys (NAELA), has heard it before. And she warns that things don't always work out the way you plan.

It may seem easier to leave everything to one child, but this move essentially disinherits the other children and allows the one child to divvy up the estate. It may leave them in an awkward position. And you can't go on the assumption that they know or respect your wishes. Instead, take these often-overlooked steps that can help ensure your estate goes to the people who matter most.

Specify in your will how you want your wealth split up, and explicitly tell your heirs about your plans. How you divide your money is up to you, but keeping everyone in the loop may help their relationships in the future. You could also attach a letter to your will or trust explaining your decisions.

Having a joint will, a single will for two people, was popular back in the day. But it can put you in a pickle. After all, you can't change a joint will after the death of your spouse. A better alternative may be mirror wills, separate but almost identical wills. They're great if you have similar wishes for your estate. They offer more flexibility to change terms later on, and may save you money.

So now you have an airtight plan for your financial gifts. But what about your grandfather's pocket watch? Your aunt's china cabinet? Write a personal property memorandum. Here's how.

- It allows you to make a list of tangible possessions and single each one out for a specific person. Just identify the item on your list, write the recipient's name next to it, and sign the document when you have everything sorted.

- The property you're allowed to pass on this way includes furniture, jewelry, and household items. Make these decisions now to help prevent conflict in the future.

- You don't need a lawyer to make or update a personal property memorandum, so changes are easy. In order for it to be valid, you must reference it in your will. Check with your state laws because these documents aren't always considered legally binding.

Passing probate: Keep more of your estate out of the government's hands

You may think your well-organized will can save your loved ones from any trouble after you pass. But your possessions may still get tangled up in probate court, sometimes for longer than a year, while they're divvied up.

That could cost your heirs a big chunk of change. About 5% of your estate's value can get eaten up by attorney and executor fees, court charges, and more.

But there are a few ways to avoid probate altogether. So pay attention — you won't learn this from the IRS.

Put your trust in this plan. You can help your heirs skip probate and get quick access to your assets with a trust. A revocable living trust is a common choice, and unlike irrevocable trusts, it gives you the flexibility to change the terms later on. You title your assets so they're "owned" by the trust, then they'll be transferred to your designated beneficiaries upon your death.

Trusts can be confusing to set up on your own, so you may want to seek out a lawyer who can provide specialized assistance. And you'll still want a will for things like assets that weren't titled to the trust, or naming guardians for minors.

Bank on this step to save heaps of hassle. Whether you have a trust or not, you can ensure that your checking and savings accounts never go to probate. Just do one thing — name a payable-on-death beneficiary. This way your funds will be directly inherited by whomever you choose.

So don't wait — it's simple all around. You have total control over your accounts while you're alive. And your heir only has to confirm their identity and present a death certificate to the bank to receive whatever you've left behind.

Don't play name games with your nest egg. Worried about your stocks and bonds ending up in the right hands after you're gone? Fret not. Simply choosing a beneficiary allows them to bypass probate and go straight to whomever you named. Doing the same for your life insurance plan and retirement accounts — pension, 401(k), and IRA — will also make sure they end up in the right place.

Don't forget, you can't give away assets like these in a will. That's because the beneficiary designations trump instructions left in your will or trust. For example, if you try to leave your IRA equally to your kids in your will, but you've only designated one of them as the beneficiary, just the one gets the windfall.

For most of these assets, naming the beneficiary is part of the initial paperwork. So double-check that the form is filled out, and keep it updated.

Protect your heirs from losing their inheritance

Naturally, your estate is used to pay off your outstanding debts after you pass. But what if one of your heirs has their own creditors? In this circumstance, you may not want to leave them assets directly.

"You want to look at the situation of the beneficiary to determine what is the best way to make sure they get the full benefit of whatever you're trying to leave them," says Letha McDowell of NAELA.

Say your son owes money. One of his creditors sues him, and a court judges he must pay off his debt using his inheritance from you. Depending on your state's laws, you may have protected him by leaving assets in a spendthrift trust.

Divorce can cause a similar hiccup. Inherited money is often considered separate property, but state laws vary. Discuss with a legal expert ways to keep assets from being jointly owned by your heir and their spouse.

Make your own will — free of charge

Want to prevent lawyers from siphoning off your hard-earned estate? Then seriously consider writing your will yourself.

It's perfectly feasible to create a do-it-yourself will that holds up in court, using easy technology. And it will save you a boatload of money.

Just search for "free will templates" on the internet, and use one to create your will. You'll see a lot of advice about completing the process. Since state requirements differ, be sure to also include your state in your search phrase. This should bring up templates with wording specific to where you live.

But don't skip this next step. Once you have created your will, get a pro bono lawyer to review it for you and check that it is legally binding.

Getting advice from a professional is essential because it's easy to mix up unfamiliar lawyer jargon. Those seemingly small mistakes could end up throwing off your whole plan, says attorney Letha McDowell. If your documents are insufficient, they may not be accepted for probate, and it'll be like you died intestate — without any will at all. That could open a whole new can of worms for your heirs and cause fights that could have easily been avoided.

5 times you should review your estate plan

You set up your will four years ago and feel safe and secure now that you never have to touch it again. That's a dangerous mindset. Experts often recommend reviewing your estate plan every three to five years. You'll especially want to do a checkup under these circumstances.

- Moves. Your decision to retire to a different state should come with a review of your estate plan. Laws about how wills and trusts work, including those about property, vary by state.

- Situation shifts for beneficiaries. If your adult children were kids the last time you revised your will, for example, it's time to give it another look. You may want to alter certain restrictions you previously imposed.

- Market swings. If you allocated specific assets because of their worth, you'll want to reevaluate their current value.

- Big life events. Divorce or family deaths may also radically change how you want to distribute your assets.

- Relationship changes. Also called a trustee, your fiduciary is in charge of managing your trust in the best interests of the beneficiaries. You'll want to change your fiduciary if you're no longer close to the person you've named or they have passed away.

Simple steps protect your digital assets

In addition to your financial affairs, it's vital to inform your heirs about your online accounts — such as banking, investments, subscriptions, and more. But don't put passwords and usernames for these in your will. It becomes a public document after your death so anyone can get access to the information in it.

To ensure your heirs don't lose valuable assets, create simple lists of your financial and online accounts, usernames, and passwords.

Store these in a secure place, such as a home safe, and let your executor and family members know the location. Your beneficiaries will thank you for taking these important steps.

Shield your savings from medical setbacks with a special trust

Don't let a catastrophic illness drain your savings. Long-term care is pricey, and it can quickly snatch away the money you plan to pass on. But you can protect yourself by using an irrevocable trust to qualify for Medicaid, which generally covers care in nursing facilities and your own home.

To meet Medicaid requirements, you must have little asset worth — in some states just $2,000. That's where a trust comes in. Since assets in irrevocable trusts are controlled by a trustee, not you, they aren't counted as yours when qualifying for Medicaid. Any income from the trust will go to paying for your care, though, if you move to a nursing home.

Keep in mind there are a few risks, including a five-year look-back period for asset transfers. That means if you transfer to your trust fewer than five years before you start care, you'll be ineligible for Medicaid for a penalty period.

5 | Advance directives

> "Plan ahead: It wasn't raining when Noah built the ark."
>
> Richard Cushing

Take control of your future by filling out these 2 documents

You probably have a will in place to help take care of everything after you're gone. But are you prepared for what could happen now if you become unable to make your own decisions? You'll place the burden of figuring out how to handle your health and your money on your loved ones. These two documents make sure they can honor your wishes if you're ever out of action.

- **Durable power of attorney for finances.** If you become incapacitated or disabled, somebody needs to manage your money. The only problem? If you don't have this important document, your family members may have to make a trip to probate court to sort out who's in charge of your estate. Not only will that put a heavy load on your loved ones during an already trying time, but those legal fees could wind up costing them hundreds — or even thousands — of dollars.

- **Durable power of attorney for health care.** You can't predict sudden health changes, but you need to be prepared for them. "The important thing is to identify someone to be a surrogate for you if you can't speak for yourself," says Lori Bishop, vice president of palliative and advanced care for the National Hospice and Palliative Care Organization. Completing this form to name a surrogate, also known as a health care proxy, allows someone you trust to make medical choices on your behalf.

Regrettably, most folks don't have these plans in place. "Some people may be intimidated by the process of going to a lawyer or are worried about the expense," says Bishop. Fortunately, you can start the process from the comfort of your own home. Go online to *nhpco.org/advancedirective* or *eforms.com* to download power of attorney forms for free.

If you still need a bit of help getting everything in place, you can reach out to your local area agency on aging. They may have resources or information to help you get started.

Proxy powwow: 3 moves to ensure your health is in the right hands

Experts estimate that nearly half of seniors who are admitted to the hospital are unable to make major medical decisions on their own. But if you're like most Americans, you haven't chosen a health care proxy to make sure that you have someone to speak for you and get the treatment you want if the unthinkable happens.

"A lot of people are just putting it off. They don't want to deal with it. They don't want to think about it," says expert Lori Bishop. "What they don't understand is that it is a way to give yourself some control when you may have lost complete control."

Choosing your proxy may seem intimidating. But these tips can help you start the conversations with your loved ones and get your plans in place.

Identify someone you can trust to honor your wishes. Your proxy needs to be somebody who can make tough decisions and won't be weighed down by the emotional burden. This can be your spouse, a family member, or even a close friend.

Ask yourself if this person will be able to stick with the treatment you want, even if it goes against their own wishes. Pick someone who will stand up for you and is comfortable talking to doctors.

Check to see if your proxy is on board. You can't just assume that someone is willing to make decisions on your behalf. Be clear that you're asking someone to be your proxy, and tell them that they can say no if they don't think they'll be able to do it.

If you need help finding exactly what to say, you can go online to *theconversationproject.org* to download hand-outs and guides designed to help you work through these uncomfortable topics.

Talk about your plans so you're both on the same page. Once you've found a health care proxy, you need to discuss the kind of treatment you do or don't want. This information is spelled out in a legal document generally referred to as a living will. In some states, the living will is combined with the durable power of attorney for health care into a single form, often called an advance health care directive.

When reviewing your wishes with your proxy, identify the circumstances in which you would or wouldn't want treatment. Share what is important to you as you talk through different scenarios.

Get your forms to the proper people to avoid unwanted treatment

"Having the advance directive is one thing, but if you lock it in a vault it does you no good," says Lori Bishop of the National Hospice and Palliative Care Organization. After all, you could wind up spending tens of thousands of dollars and suffering through medical care you don't want if your doctors don't know what kind of treatment you prefer. "Completing the directives is one step. Widely distributing them and making everyone aware of them is another," Bishop says.

After your forms are filled out, here's who needs to know about your advance directive.

- Your health care proxy. The person you chose to make decisions for you needs to know your wishes. Otherwise they'll never be able to properly speak on your behalf.

- Your physicians. While your doctors may know a lot about you, they don't necessarily know what kind of treatment you'll want if you're ever incapacitated. Reach out to your doctor's office and ask them to attach a copy to your medical file.

- Your local hospital. If you're rushed to the emergency room, you'll want the hospital to know your treatment preferences. Contact them and ask if they'll keep a copy of your advance directive on file. At the very least, take a copy with you if you have to visit the hospital.

- Your family. You don't necessarily need to hand out a copy of your advance directive, but let them know what your plans are. "It's important that you share the conversation with your whole family so there isn't dispute or disagreement," says Bishop.

Smart strategies for sidestepping financial abuse

Handing over control of your money and assets to someone else could go horribly wrong if you put your trust in the wrong person. Unfortunately, some people take advantage of the situation if they're granted financial power of attorney (POA). Follow these simple steps to help protect yourself.

- Put boundaries in place. A limited POA form includes language that specifies what can be done with your money. For example, you may allow someone to use your bank account just to pay off bills. A springing POA goes into effect only after certain conditions are met, like incapacitation.

- Ask for another set of eyes. You can require the agent, the person acting on your behalf, to provide receipts and other accounting details to another person for review. That way they can catch any fraud or suspicious activity.

- Revoke the POA as soon as you are able to manage your affairs again. If the agent won't relinquish control of your money, contact a lawyer.

When to change your advance directive

Health directives aren't set in stone. And that's a good thing. Your attitude toward treatment options evolves over the years, so you'll need to go back and make sure your plans still reflect your wishes. Follow this expert advice to help you identify when you need to tweak your advance directive.

- Whenever your situation changes. "Depending on where you're at in life and where you're at in health, your perspectives change," says Lori Bishop, a nurse executive who focuses on care for people with serious illnesses. Revisit your advance directive if you get a new diagnosis, and at different phases of life. Marital changes, for example, may mean it's time for a new health proxy.

- Make your plans early if you have Alzheimer's disease or dementia. You can't modify your advance directive if you're not of sound mind. "You are likely going to lose decision-making capacity at some point, so you'll want to have discussions earlier on rather than later," Bishop says.

Split your time between two states? Experts don't generally recommend you make two advance directives. State laws and legal lingo vary, so one could nullify the other if they're not absolutely identical. Instead, consult an attorney or representative at a hospital in the second state to find out if your current form will be valid there. You'll also need to meet the signature requirements for both states since witnessing and notarization rules differ.

- Revisit your plans every 10 years. Even if your health hasn't changed, you may not want the same kind of end-of-life care that you did a decade ago. Take the time to talk with loved ones and your proxy to be sure that everyone is still on the same page.

If you decide to make changes to your plans, start by creating an entirely new advance directive. Give out updated copies to your doctor, hospital, and loved ones, and ask them to destroy the outdated paperwork. Revocation requirements may vary by state, so check your local laws to see if there are any other steps you need to take.

6 | Life insurance

> "Fun is like life insurance; the older you get, the more it costs."
>
> Kin Hubbard

Calculate your coverage to avoid sky-high premiums

Nearly half of all Americans don't have life insurance. And if you count yourself among them, you may at least want to consider it. After all, it's a way to make sure your loved ones will be financially stable if the unthinkable happens.

But before you go out and buy a policy, determine how much coverage you really need. Paying for a plan that's too expensive will eat away at cash that could be stowed away in retirement accounts.

So first off, examine your expenses. That's the most important thing to do, says Les Masterson, managing editor of Insure.com, a consumer guide that offers tools like coverage calculators and rate comparisons.

"Think about how much you're paying each month and what kind of assets you have," he says, "and that will help you figure out how much coverage you actually need and whether you need a term life or a whole life policy."

- Take a look at any major debts. If you still have 10 years left on a mortgage, you might want to consider a term life policy that can help cover those payments if you pass away.

- Factor in your income. If you still work and have dependents, a good rule of thumb is to multiply your salary by the number of years you have left until retirement. For example, if you make $35,000 a year and will retire in 10 years, a term life policy that will pay out $350,000 could fit your needs.

- Don't forget about other expenses. Smaller, whole life plans may fit the bill if you want to cover end-of-life costs like a funeral.

Must-ask questions to evaluate your policy and rescue your savings

A lot can change in 30 years. So if you bought a life insurance policy a few decades ago, you may find that your needs are no longer the same. Don't pour money down the drain by paying for unnecessary coverage. Ask yourself these three simple questions to help you decide whether or not you should change or cancel your policy.

Does my policy have a bigger payout than I need? When you chose a plan years ago, you may have opted for life insurance that could pay off your mortgage and other debts. But if your mortgage is paid off and you have money set aside for funeral costs, you might decide you don't need insurance anymore or don't require such a large policy, says insurance pro Les Masterson.

Will I outlive my life insurance? You can't predict the future, but if you're nearing the end of your plan, think about the next steps. "A lot of policies allow you to convert a term life to a permanent life policy," says Masterson. The benefit — you won't have to reapply for a new policy, which usually means you skip the health exam. Plus if you require a lower payout, you might score lower premiums.

Do my loved ones still need help paying the bills? If you're an empty nester with no one depending on you for financial support, consider switching to a cheaper plan or look into canceling it altogether.

Prep like a pro: How to get a clean bill of health to snag the best rate

Insurance companies hate taking risks they can't afford. Before they offer you a plan, they're going to cross every t and dot every i. And that means you have to take a medical exam. If you don't ace it, you might wind up facing hefty premiums. With a little preparation you can get the best deal possible.

The day before. Avoid salty snacks and fatty foods. These can drive up your cholesterol and blood pressure measurements. Instead, opt for meals with plenty of leafy greens. You should also take the day off from any strenuous exercise and rest your body as much as possible.

The night before. Steer clear of alcohol. Drink plenty of water and stay well hydrated. You may need to start a fast, too. Ask your doctor if you have to follow any specific instructions. Aim to get a good night's sleep.

The morning before. Ditch the coffee. Too much caffeine can raise your heart rate and

Experts estimate that billions of dollars in life insurance benefits go unclaimed. If you suspect that a loved one has named you as a beneficiary of a lost policy, you may be able to track down details through the National Association of Insurance Commissioners policy locator. Go online to *https://eapps. naic.org/life-policy-locator* to get started.

cause your blood pressure to spike. If you can't go without it, a small cup may be OK.

Wear comfortable, lightweight clothes to help tip the scales in your favor when it's time to weigh in. And stave off the stress by remembering to take the essentials — your list of medications and other health info, your ID, and application paperwork.

 Sidestep policy-switching scams that put your payout on the line

Who doesn't want to lower their monthly payments? So when you hear that you can get a cheaper deal, you might be tempted to pull the trigger.

But be careful. Under the guise of lowering your premiums, some agents will switch you to another policy — usually from term to permanent — that doesn't offer the same coverage.

Make sure you know exactly what type of deal you're getting before you make any changes to your policy. Opting for a different plan may save you money in the short run, but an agent earning commission may downplay the consequences.

Is a return-of-premium rider worth the extra cash?

You can spend thousands on life insurance premiums over the course of a policy. But if you outlive your plan, you'll have nothing to show for it. So some companies offer an add-on known as a return-of-premium rider, which guarantees you'll get your money back at the end of a policy. But is it worth the price tag?

Take a look at Matthew. He bought a 20-year life insurance plan when he was 50, and it cost him $842 in premiums each year. That adds up to $16,840 over the course of the policy.

If he decided to opt for a return-of-premium rider, he would double his total costs and spend $33,680 on premiums. But he would get it all back at the end of the policy. Seems like a great deal, right?

Not so fast. Instead, Matthew stuck with a basic term life policy and invested $842 annually in a Roth IRA. With a 7% growth rate, his balance totaled $36,934 after 20 years.

Run the numbers before you decide, though. If you're not willing to take on the risk of investing, you might decide that a return-of-premium rider is an easy way to guarantee a payout.

Price out the perfect policy with one simple step

"For any kind of insurance, it's always best to get quotes from multiple companies. Don't just rely on one," says expert Les Masterson. "Insurers differ on how they gauge someone's risk."

For example, one company may make smokers pay more in premiums because they see them as a bigger risk than another company. The same is true for health status.

Compare different types of coverage, too, says Masterson. You may find that a $300,000 plan isn't much more expensive than one with a $200,000 payout.

Use a brokerage or rate comparison website, or get the quotes straight from the insurers. Either way, evaluate the policies carefully to ensure they have the features you want.

7 | Funerals

> "The song is ended but the melody lingers on."
>
> Irving Berlin

Don't overspend on funeral trends

You want to save money and the environment, so a green burial seems like just the ticket. But don't fall for the hooplah of businesses trying to cash-in on this trend.

"Green burial is simply a new name for a very old thing," says Josh Slocum, the executive director of Funeral Consumers Alliance. "What we call green burial is what our late 19th-century ancestors called burial."

The term refers to eco-friendly funeral options — biodegradable materials, fewer chemicals, and other ways of minimizing environmental impact. But take it too far and you may find yourself shipping your body to another coast to a special "green cemetery" just because it bans pesticides. So carefully think through your plan. Otherwise you may not end up helping nature or your bank account.

After all, shipping leads to more truck or plane emissions and may require embalming, which involves harsh chemicals. Plus transport can cost several thousand dollars, and green cemeteries often charge more for a plot — around $1,000 to $4,000.

Luckily, you can go with the more practical, and frugal, route of a direct burial and still be eco-conscious. For instance, instead of buying a casket made of recycled materials that has to be shipped to you, choose a simple wood casket or use a shroud, like a sentimental quilt.

You can also see if a cemetery near you offers natural burials, where the body is laid directly into the earth rather than a concrete vault. If not, maybe the vault can be installed upside down without its cover for a faster return to the earth. Skipping those unnecessary products and services will also save you big bucks.

Put a stopper in a funeral cost flood with these 3 steps

Funerals cost around $9,000 on average. Talk about sticker shock. But what may be more upsetting is the emotional hurdle that makes you feel like you're not allowed to pay less.

"With funerals we're afraid to talk dollars and cents because we equate how much we spend with how much we love the person," says consumer advocate Josh Slocum.

Remove this stumbling block, and you can focus on planning a meaningful funeral that won't break the bank. Just follow these steps to avoid overpaying.

Assess your own expectations. You wouldn't go to a car dealer without setting a budget, so why would you do it for a funeral? Slocum says people disempower themselves by accepting the cost they're told rather than choosing how much to spend in advance.

Stay alert for unexpected costs like crematory fees —
which may be added on top of a quoted cremation cost
— and cemetery costs, which are separate from the
funeral price.

Also keep track of big-ticket items, like caskets, which
are easy to overspend on. Research in advance, so
you're not swindled by costly but unnecessary features
like casket seals.

Make your shopping trip count. Just like you wouldn't
buy a car without a budget in mind, you also wouldn't
use a certain dealership just because your grandparents
bought a car there, right? Well, the same is true of funeral
homes. Instead of choosing one that another relative
used, shop around to get a good deal.

As Slocum explains, the biggest thing people don't
know about funerals is that prices vary widely between
funeral homes — even in the same town. "We're talking
about a 200% or 300% difference," he says. "One direct
cremation in town might go for $900. You go to the next
funeral home, it's $2,000 or $3,000."

When shopping around, also compare a la carte and
package options. Yes, funeral homes are required by law
to offer a la carte and share full itemized price lists.
Slocum recommends only buying packages that have
services you would have bought separately anyway.

Review your options. Some items on your checklist may
hit your wallet harder than expected. If your budget isn't
balancing, consider alternatives.

Think $500 for a print obituary is outrageous? You can
run it in the digital version of a newspaper for a more
reasonable cost — about $50 to $100. Or consider having
your family post it online, like to social media or your
funeral home's website.

You may be able to ditch some services altogether.
Embalming, for instance, can cost $700, but isn't
required under most circumstances unless it's in-house
policy at the funeral home.

Plan now, pay later: Keep your family's needs first

Prepaying may settle your mind when it comes to your funeral. But despite your best intentions, it could make matters more difficult for your family after you pass.

Life is bound to throw a wrench in the plans. What happens if the funeral home goes out of business, for instance? What about if you die in another state or your kids don't know the details of your purchase?

Josh Slocum of Funeral Consumers Alliance says prepaying may not accomplish your goal of taking care of everything beforehand. But, he says, "There's no way you can go wrong by planning ahead."

Add a national veterans cemetery to your list of final resting places if you're an honorably discharged veteran. Some vets may also get an allowance for funeral, transportation, and burial costs. And ask your funeral director about military funeral honors, which include the attendance of at least two uniformed military persons, the presentation of the United States burial flag, and the playing of taps.

Planning ahead means having tough conversations with your family about what is and isn't important for your funeral. Slocum recommends asking your loved ones what their needs are, rather than telling them your wishes. That way you can best plan for their comfort and protect them from distressing circumstances where they could only have fulfilled your wishes at great expense.

If you still think prepaying is right for you, make sure you know exactly what you're paying for and how protected your money will be, including features like a refund policy. Then make a physical copy of your entire contract and deposit slips, and give them to your next of kin so they have the essentials they will need.

More resources

American Association for Long-Term Care Insurance	aaltci.org	818-597-3227
American Savings Education Council	asec.org	202-659-0670
Compassion & Choices	compassionandchoices.org	N/A
Consumer Financial Protection Bureau	consumerfinance.gov	855-411-2372
Eldercare Locator	eldercare.acl.gov	800-677-1116
Federal Trade Commission	consumer.ftc.gov	N/A
Financial Finesse	ffcalcs.com	N/A
FindLaw	findlaw.com	N/A
Funeral Consumers Alliance	funerals.org	802-865-8300
Green Burial Council	greenburialcouncil.org	888-966-3330
National Academy of Elder Law Attorneys	naela.org	N/A
National Consumer Law Center	nclc.org	202-452-6252
National Credit Union Administration	ncua.gov	800-755-1030
National Elder Law Foundation	nelf.org	520-881-1076
National Foundation for Credit Counseling	nfcc.org	800-388-2227
National Hospice and Palliative Care Organization	caringinfo.org	703-837-1500
The National Consumer Voice for Quality Long-Term Care	theconsumervoice.org	202-332-2275
U.S. Department of Veterans Affairs	va.gov	800-698-2411
USA.gov	usa.gov/legal-aid	844-872-4681

STEADY CASH FLOW

How to make your wealth last a lifetime

8 | Social Security

> "The question isn't at what age I want to retire, it's at what income."
>
> George Foreman

Dial in the perfect retirement age to max out your paycheck

Who doesn't want to get the most from their Social Security account? And one of the best ways to do that is to tap into your Social Security benefits at the right time.

Easier said than done. In fact, a new survey shows that 39% of seniors don't know when they're eligible for their full retirement benefits. Hint — age 66 to 67, depending on the year you were born. But if you decide to claim too early, you could lose out on thousands of dollars over your lifetime.

Wait to hang up your briefcase to boost your benefits. Eager to claim Social Security as soon as you're eligible? Not so fast. Waiting until full retirement age to claim your benefits could get you a 43% larger check than if you had claimed at age 62.

And every little bit counts. Take Geoff for example. If he claims Social Security at age 62, he will get $1,479 each month. But by simply waiting until his full retirement age of 67, his benefits jump to $2,113 every month. Just think of what he could do with that extra $634 each month.

What's more, you can postpone your retirement longer to build up an even bigger check. You earn delayed retirement credits every month you hold off on claiming beyond your full retirement age, up till age 70. And these credits increase your bottom line.

To claim or not to claim? How to determine your ideal retirement age. Experts estimate that the average household will lose out on a whopping $111,000 over a lifetime by taking Social Security at the wrong time. So how do you know when you should claim your benefits?

- When in doubt, wait longer. Many seniors are better off waiting until age 70, when they've earned all their delayed retirement credits.

- Consider claiming early if you're in poor health. If you don't think your retirement will last 20 or 30 years, you may want to go ahead and get your benefits. After all, getting something is better than nothing. Examine this option carefully, especially if you're married. Cashing out early could decrease your spouse's survivor benefits.

- You need cash now to cover living expenses. Just retired and need a bit of extra money to make ends meet? Taking your retirement benefits as soon as possible could help you enjoy your golden years while you're at your healthiest.

Started Social Security too soon? How to snag a redo

More than half of all seniors take Social Security too early. And they regret this mistake big time a few years down the road. If you count yourself among them, don't worry. You can undo this decision and get a bigger paycheck from Uncle Sam. Here's how.

- Withdraw your claim. Once you claim Social Security, you get a year to undo that decision. The only catch? You have to pay back all of the benefits that you've received so far. That includes any spousal benefits or additional payments you may have gotten. If you choose this route, go online to *ssa.gov/forms/ssa-521.pdf* to download the application. Send the completed form to your local Social Security office to find out how much you will need to repay.

- Suspend your benefits. Suppose you've reached your full retirement age and are already receiving Social Security, but now you want to start earning some of the delayed retirement credits that come with claiming at a later date. You can temporarily pause your benefits to increase your payout when you turn 70. Reach out to your local Social Security office to request a suspension of benefits.

Family ties — overlooked bonuses put more cash in your pocket

Nobody wants to miss out on savings. But when it comes to Social Security, it can be all too easy to pass over benefits. With a little help from your family, you can take advantage of these three commonly forgotten provisions.

Spousal benefits. Did you spend most of your marriage out of the workforce? You might still be eligible for Social Security benefits. While benefits are usually calculated based on your own earning history, you may be able to base your paychecks off of your spouse's wages.

If your husband or wife is already collecting Social Security and you're at least 62, you can get benefits that equal up to 50% of their full retirement amount. So for example, say your spouse has a benefit worth $2,000 a month. You might get a check for $1,000. Claim before your full retirement age, though, and your benefits will be reduced.

However, if you were born before Jan. 2, 1954, you may be eligible for a little-known provision that can help you upgrade your monthly benefits. You can claim your spousal benefits while holding off on taking your own. That means you earn delayed retirement credits on your record while getting a check from the government.

Divorced? You may still be able to claim spousal benefits if you haven't remarried. If the marriage lasted 10 years or longer, your ex-spouse is eligible for benefits, and you are at least 62 years old, you can file for these perks.

Survivor benefits. A recent Social Security audit found that nearly two-thirds of the beneficiaries sampled were eligible for survivor benefits. Unfortunately, only a small number of them had claimed the extra income.

When a spouse passes away, the survivor may be eligible to receive up to 100% of their late spouse's benefit. Widows and widowers may claim these benefits as early as age 60, though the amount will be reduced according to age. If you need to report a death or apply for survivor benefits, call the Social Security Administration at 800-772-1213.

Dependent benefits. Do you still have children — or even grandchildren — that live with you? Each qualified dependent could receive payments of up to half of your full retirement benefit.

Your dependents may qualify if they are younger than 18, are under age 19 and still in elementary or secondary school, or were diagnosed with a disability before age 22. For grandchildren, eligibility also depends on the Social Security status of their parents. Talk to an adviser for more info.

Retirement prep secrets help you squeeze extra bucks out of Social Security

Preparation is one of the best ways to set yourself up for success. But planning your retirement isn't something you can do a few months before you're ready to leave your job, especially if you want to get the most out of your Social Security benefits. Use these tips in the years leading up to your retirement to get more money in your golden years.

Max out your earnings now for a payday later. Your future benefits are based on the wages you earned during the highest-paying years of your career. And that means the more you earn, the more you'll get from Social Security.

Try to get a raise or seek out a higher-paying job. Or consider taking on a part-time gig to help supplement your income. Not only will you boost your future earnings, but you'll have more money you can sock away in your retirement savings accounts.

Make sure to get your years in to avoid scuttling your benefits. Social Security also looks at 35 years of employment history when calculating your benefit amount. That means any year you didn't earn income gets counted as a zero. And that can really bring your average income down. Aim to get at least 35 years of employment on record before claiming Social Security.

3 Social Security scams that threaten your bankroll

You know how important your Social Security number is. So do scammers. And they will go to considerable lengths to obtain it. Here are three scams that can have hackers running to the bank with your Social Security money.

- Phone scams, where the crooks claim to be from the Social Security Administration and say your benefits will stop unless you provide certain information, including your Social Security number.

- Email or text cons — called phishing scams — that ask for the same details as a phone scam.

- Mail scams, where you receive a flyer offering additional Social Security services, such as a security check, if you fill in and return the attached form, which includes a request for your Social Security number.

Protect yourself and send those scammers scurrying by hanging up on the call, deleting the email, and throwing away the mail flyer. If you are contacted in any of these ways, report the scammers on the Inspector General website at *oig.ssa.gov.*

Don't let your retirement job cost you thousands

Thinking about taking up a retirement job? If you haven't reached your full retirement age but you're already collecting Social Security, you might be surprised to find out that the government will reduce your benefits according to how much dough you bring home.

For every $2 you earn over the income limit, your payout decreases by $1. So if you made $4,000 a year more than the $19,560 limit in 2022, you got $2,000 less from Social Security. The year you reach full retirement age, the deduction changes to $1 for every $3 you earn over the limit, which was $51,960 in 2022. After full retirement age, you're free and clear to make as much as you like.

Take note — Social Security won't subtract the cash from your checks bit by bit. Instead, entire monthly payments may be withheld until you've paid off the reduction. For a better idea of how much your benefits will drop, go online to *ssa.gov/OACT/COLA/RTeffect.html* and plug your estimated earnings into the calculator.

You can name somebody to manage your Social Security benefits in the event that you become incapacitated. To do this, you need to fill out an Advance Designation request and file it with the Social Security Administration online, at a local office, or by calling 800-772-1213.

While you do earn some of that money back after hitting full retirement age, experts estimate that it might take up to 15 years to make up those lost benefits. Consider withdrawing your claim if you're still working while collecting Social Security.

Sidestep the tax trap with these 3 tricks

Up until 1983, Social Security recipients didn't have to pay a dime on their benefits. Unfortunately, that's not the case anymore. If your combined income is more than $25,000 as a single filer, or $32,000 as a joint filer, at least half of your Social Security benefit can be taxed.

So how do you figure out your combined income? Add half of your yearly Social Security payments to your yearly adjusted gross income and nontaxable interest. If that number is greater than the income thresholds, you'll owe money to Uncle Sam. Now for the good news — with a little know-how, you can keep your tax bill low.

Take advantage of Roth accounts. Traditional retirement accounts let you sock away money before taxes and pay the piper later. That may sound great at the time, but withdrawals from these accounts could eat into your Social Security benefit by increasing your combined income.

Roth IRAs and 401(k) plans, on the other hand, are taxed before the money is stowed away. And that means you get to keep every cent you withdraw. Even better? That money won't count against your combined income for Social Security purposes.

Take cash out of your traditional accounts first. Don't have any money stashed in Roth accounts? You can still soothe the tax strain by taking more cash out of your traditional, tax-deferred retirement accounts before you claim your Social Security benefits.

The reason? You'll front-load your tax burden before those distributions count toward your combined income. That way, when you claim Social Security, you won't need to take as much money from your 401(k) or IRA. And that could help keep your tax bill low.

Plus, as a bonus, this move may allow you to postpone claiming Social Security. So you earn delayed retirement credits and increase your benefits when you finally do apply for them.

The earliest you can start making these withdrawals penalty-free is at age 59 1/2. And by the time you turn 72, the government mandates a minimum amount you have to pull out every year. Take these required minimum distributions into account while calculating how much to pull out and when.

Consider an annuity to offset interest. Investing money in certificates of deposit (CDs) is a nice way to ensure modest, but safe, gains. The only problem? Interest from a CD is factored into your tax bill the year it's earned, whether you spend it or not.

If you find yourself with leftover cash, look into purchasing a deferred annuity instead. With this type of insurance product, you invest money in exchange for guaranteed payments at a future date. It works a lot like a CD except you don't have to pay taxes on the interest until payments begin.

And that's the key. The interest won't count toward your Social Security tax liability until it is withdrawn. And by then, your combined income may be lower due to retirement.

Mull over all these options carefully since there's no one-size-fits-all solution. Before you take one of these methods for a test drive, it's a good idea to talk with a financial adviser to determine the best strategy for your situation.

The fastest way to get your proof of income letter

Planning to take out a loan or mortgage? Maybe you're applying for housing assistance? In the past, you'd use your pay stubs to prove that you meet income requirements. But if you're on Social Security, you'll need a benefit verification letter.

This form — also called a proof of income letter or a budget letter — will list out the benefits you receive from Social Security, Supplemental Security Income, or Medicare. To get a copy, you can call the Social Security Administration. Or for instant access, simply sign into your "*my* Social Security" account online at *ssa.gov/myaccount*. Under the Benefits & Payments section of your account homepage, select *Get a Benefit Verification Letter*.

Get free money each month from this little-known program

Need extra cash to help pay your bills? If you're over 65, blind, or disabled, you may qualify for Supplemental Security Income (SSI), a program administered by the Social Security Administration.

Most seniors on SSI get around $5,000 a year from this program. But you have to meet strict income limits before you can be considered for these benefits. And you can't have assets — such as stocks, bonds, or rental properties — that are worth more than $2,000 for single filers or $3,000 for married couples. However, the home you live in and one car are not counted against these limits.

Use the Benefit Eligibility Screening Tool online at *ssabest. benefits.gov* to find out if you qualify for benefits.

---

9 | 401(k) plans

> "There are no secrets to success. It is the result of preparation, hard work, and learning from failure."
>
> Colin Powell

Reach your retirement goals with the best mutual fund fit

Mutual funds are no doubt the most common investment options offered by 401(k) plans. They're made up of a pool of shareholder money invested in stocks, bonds, and other assets. The benefits — a diverse portfolio with professional management. But how do you decide between them?

Barbara O'Neill, CEO of financial education company Money Talk, recommends looking at these factors.

- **Objective.** Before choosing a mutual fund, you need to know what your goal is — growth, income, or preservation of capital. This goal will dictate the kinds of investments in your portfolio. For example, a fund with a goal of growth may invest in more stocks to provide better returns. On the other hand, if the goal is to preserve the initial investment value, the fund will include lower risk options such as certificates of deposit. Before you invest, read about the mutual fund's objective in its prospectus to ensure it matches your goals.

- **Performance history.** Don't let a fund's recent success suck you in. Check its track record from the last decade before you commit. And even then, past performance doesn't guarantee you a great outcome in the future. That's why you shouldn't let the state of the market turn up your willingness to take risks.

  You should also take a look at the fund's volatility — how much its value rose and fell in the last year. If you have a low risk tolerance, you may want to choose a mutual fund that fluctuates less.

- **Expense ratio.** Every year a slice of your investment goes to the operating and administrative expenses of your account, called the expense ratio. These fees seem small at first, typically running at 0.5% to 1% of the managed funds. But they dramatically add up over time and could snatch thousands of dollars away from your retirement piggy bank.

  You can usually find lower expense ratios — under 0.5% — among index mutual funds, the type designed to match the investments of a market index. But don't choose a mutual fund based solely on its expense ratio.

"You want to weigh all three of those key factors," says O'Neill. "Ideally, what you want to have is a fund that meets your investment objective, with a history of good performance relative to market indexes, and a low expense ratio. Then you've hit the trifecta."

The inside story on costly contribution blunders

Yippee, your employer has made it easy on you and automatically enrolled you in its 401(k) program with a default contribution rate of 3%. Not so fast. Sticking with that rate could be a big mistake, says financial education entrepreneur Barbara O'Neill. Experts recommend squirreling away 10% to 15% of your income into a retirement account, so the default percentage won't cut it.

Even if you can't hit those high percentage markers, though, there's one thing you should always max out — your employer's contribution match. You're leaving free money on the table if you're not doing this, says O'Neill. Say you make $40,000 a year and your company matches up to 5% of your salary. If you put in the full 5%, your employer adds $2,000 to the $2,000 you already contributed. Good deal!

How to bypass early withdrawal penalties

You know the drill. Withdraw money from your 401(k) before age 59 1/2, and the IRS will slap you with a 10% penalty. The Coronavirus Aid, Relief, and Economic Security Act (CARES Act) of 2020 waived the penalty for qualified individuals who took a financial hit during the coronavirus pandemic. With some caveats, of course. Folks had to spread the tax burden or pay back the money within the next three years.

The CARES Act provided some much-needed relief for many people. But if your financial situation is looking bleak now, what can you do to dodge penalties if you absolutely must tap in to your 401(k) early?

- Rule of 55. It sounds like the name of a Sherlock Holmes mystery, but it's really a rule that lets you withdraw funds from your 401(k) without penalty if you are laid off, fired, or simply quit your job during or after the year you turn 55. However, if you have more than one 401(k), only the one from your most recent employer qualifies, and only if the employer supports these withdrawals.

- Rule 72(t). Through this loophole, you are able to avoid penalty by taking at least five substantially equal periodic payments (SEPPs). You can calculate the size of these payments through one of three methods. To find out which is best for you, visit *irs.gov* and search for "substantially equal periodic payments." The sticker is that you're required to follow the payment plan for five years or until you turn 59 1/2 — whichever comes later.

- Hardship distributions. This method allows you to withdraw money early to pay for immediate, significant expenses like medical charges. Qualifications and definitions of hardship vary, and some plans don't offer this provision at all, so be sure to check yours in advance.

Distribution decisions: 3 smart tips prepare you for RMDs

You spent years scrimping and saving to put money in your retirement account, and now it's time to get that wealth back in your hands. The required minimum distribution (RMD) is the minimum amount of money the IRS requires you to take out of your 401(k) each year. To do it right, follow this advice.

Make sure you stay in the know. Recent law changes mean required minimum distributions now kick in at age 72. Plus the IRS has just adjusted its formula for calculating

RMDs, so be sure you look at the most recent Uniform Lifetime Table available at *irs.gov*. Otherwise you could take out more money than required and miss out on potential account growth and tax advantages.

Keep in mind, if you have more than one 401(k), you must calculate an RMD for each account and take that amount from it.

Don't let Uncle Sam throw off your plan. You didn't pay tax on money that went into your traditional 401(k), so it counts as taxable income when withdrawn. The amount you pay the taxman will depend on your tax bracket, and you don't want the distribution to push you into a higher bracket. So look into drawing out money before you're required to — as early as age 59 1/2, when you become eligible for withdrawals. That way your RMD, which is partly based on your account balance, will be lower down the line.

That's also why you may not want to take the extension you're offered on your first RMD. If you do, you'll end up taking two RMDs the next year — the first by April and the second by the usual December deadline. All that extra cash flow could bump you into a high tax bracket.

What to do with your withdrawal windfall. "If you can plan ahead and come up with an RMD distribution plan then it'll make it easier when you have to take that money out," says financial educator Barbara O'Neill. You can spend it, gift it to family or a charity, or re-save it, she says.

Use your budget to determine if you need your distribution for current living expenses. If you don't, you have lots of options. Although you can't reinvest in a tax-advantaged retirement account, you can park that cash somewhere else it will grow, such as a taxable brokerage account. Some seniors prefer to consolidate their assets to avoid extra fees and make rebalancing simpler. If you're one of them, adding the money to an investment account you already own is easy.

10 | Pensions

"Money is only a tool. It will take you wherever you wish, but it will not replace you as the driver."

Ayn Rand

Pension payout: Pick the best method for you

You've planned your retirement savings like a marathon, annually putting a high percentage of your salary into your pension. But when it comes to taking out your cash, you're not sure which way to go — lump sum or annuity payments. You don't want to put in all that work just to falter at the finish line. So take these tips into consideration when choosing your path.

Support yourself with a lump sum. A million dollars sounds like a lot of money, but is it enough to last the rest of your life? That's the risk you take with a lump-sum distribution. If you already have enough income to pay for essentials during retirement, getting a wad of cash upfront may be the right road for you.

You can continue deferring taxes by rolling the funds into an IRA account. This gives you the flexibility to withdraw more one year and less another. And with control over your assets, you can make your own investment decisions. But don't let the promise of potential income sway your decision. You can invest your lump sum, but you're not guaranteed a high return.

Amplify your account with monthly paychecks. Taking your pension as an annuity gives you regular monthly income for years. Two common payout options are single-life, which pays you for the rest of your life, and joint-and-survivor, which pays out less each month but will give your survivor a percentage of your pension for the rest of their life.

Annuity payments are a good choice if you have a long life expectancy and are less concerned about passing down funds to your heirs. You also don't have to fret over making investment decisions. However, your income may be worth less over time because of inflation.

> You may be entitled to pension benefits without knowing it. A government agency called the Pension Benefit Guaranty Corporation (PBGC) pays benefits for some defunct private pension plans. Find out if yours is included by searching for your plan's name at *pbgc.gov/search-all* or call 800-326-5678.

Social Security gotchas that all pension earners should be aware of

When Carolyn worked as a public school teacher, she contributed part of every paycheck to her pension plan. Upon retirement, she began receiving her pension and went to sign up for Social Security to collect the much-needed income. That's when she got the news — her monthly Social Security benefits would be reduced by $480.

It seems like everyone gets Social Security, so what went wrong? Well, rules may differ if you have a pension. That's because in 15 states, pension-earning public employees don't pay into Social Security.

The good news is you can receive Social Security if you earn 40 hours of "credits" — about 10 years of work — at a job that pays Social Security taxes. Hours you collect at that job stay on your record. So even if you didn't earn enough before you started your pension-only job, you can add more credits later. However, the Windfall Elimination Provision may reduce your benefits like Carolyn's. Check if this adjustment applies to you before making budget plans.

11 | IRAs

Slow and steady or all at once: Find the best way to fund your IRA

The name says it all — you can open individual retirement accounts (IRAs) on your own. Unlike 401(k) plans, they aren't linked to an employer. That gives you a leg up with access to a larger pool of investment options.

You can maximize your IRA savings by investing as much as you can up to the annual limit. In 2022, that was $6,000, or $7,000 for those older than 50. So what's the best tactic for depositing that cash?

Many people wait until they're filing their taxes to contribute to their IRAs for the year prior. But Jeff Levine, chief planning officer at investment advisory firm Buckingham Wealth Partners, says the best approach may be to drop the whole sum in at one time on Jan. 1.

"The sooner you can fund those accounts, the better off you are," says Levine.

That's because the more time your money has to generate earnings that are then reinvested, the more return you build. Waiting until tax season of the following year robs you of about 15 months' worth of tax-deferred growth. Over the course of many years, contributing the same amount of money, just earlier in the year, can make a meaningful difference in your savings.

Even if you can't reach the maximum contribution limit, starting small is better than not starting at all. Say depositing a lump sum at the beginning of the year doesn't work for your budget. Try making automatic monthly payments of equal value throughout the year.

Called dollar-cost averaging, this approach takes the emotion out of investing since you're not being biased by the dips and rises of the market. Over the long term, the cost per share usually evens out with what you would've paid by attempting to time the market.

Your top IRA questions answered

Only 34% of Americans are confident about their IRA knowledge, according to a recent survey by the LIMRA Secure Retirement Institute. If lack of knowledge is preventing you from investing in an IRA, check out the answers to these common questions.

Which type of IRA do I choose — traditional or Roth?
With a traditional IRA you defer paying taxes until you start withdrawing money. That's beneficial if you expect to be in a lower tax bracket in the future.

A Roth may be your best fit if you expect to make significantly more money in the future than you make at the time of deposit. By paying taxes now, you'll save yourself from higher tax rates you anticipate down the road. You can also withdraw Roth contributions, but not earnings, early without penalty. Plus there isn't a required minimum distribution (RMD).

"The winner of the game when it comes to tax planning is not the person who pays the lowest tax bill in any one year," says Jeff Levine, a certified financial planner. "It's the person who pays the lowest lifetime tax bill." That's important to keep in mind when deciding which tax break, and therefore which type of IRA, will help you most.

Should I have multiple IRAs? You may have heard the phrase "don't put all your eggs in one basket." As Levine explains, this approach is about putting your money in a range of investments, like stocks and bonds. But gone are the days when you needed to have multiple Roth or traditional IRAs to diversify your investments. You can get all you need in a single account and avoid overcomplicating the process and upping your fees.

However, you may want one of each type of IRA to balance their benefits. For instance, you may withdraw from your Roth in a year you have a higher income to avoid bumping up tax brackets. And in a lower earning year you can pull from the traditional, and you won't pay high taxes. Having both gives you the flexibility to take out whatever funds best fit your circumstances.

What recent changes might throw off my investment plans? Thanks to the SECURE Act, retirees aren't required to take RMDs from their traditional IRA until age 72 rather than 70 1/2. Plus contributions to these IRAs are no longer capped at 70 1/2, and you may add funds for however long you continue to work.

The SECURE Act also eliminated "stretch" IRAs. Previously, inherited IRAs could be paid out over the life of the beneficiary, but now the funds must generally be withdrawn in the 10 years following the owner's passing.

HSA triple threat outplays run-of-the-mill retirement accounts

A health savings account (HSA) might be the best retirement account you never knew you had. If you have a high-deductible health insurance plan, you're probably familiar with HSAs. You can fund these accounts to pay for qualified medical expenses like copays, Medicare deductibles, and dental and vision services. What may come as a surprise is that you can also use an HSA like an IRA to fund your retirement.

"In terms of prioritizing where dollars should be saved," says Jeff Levine, chief planning officer for Buckingham Wealth Partners, "you likely would actually prioritize the HSA over the IRA for a few reasons."

Levine is referring to HSAs' threefold tax breaks. You don't have to pay income taxes on your contributions, your earnings grow tax-free, and you don't have to pay taxes when you withdraw, either, if you use the money to pay for medical expenses.

After you turn 65, you can even spend the funds on nonmedical costs without penalty. In this circumstance, you do have to pay tax on the cash, like you would a traditional retirement account, but you'll never face a required minimum distribution. And unlike other health accounts, like a flexible spending account, HSAs are portable and stay with you if you change jobs or stop working.

> Want to hit the jackpot with creative IRA investments? Think again. Restrictions ban investing in life insurance and collectibles, borrowing from your IRA, using it as collateral for a loan, and more. Make one of these mistakes and your account will no longer be considered an IRA. Instead your money will be treated as a distribution. That means you'll have to pay income tax on it.

Because of the versatility and tax-free medical cash, you may want to max out HSA contributions before funding an IRA. In 2022, limits are $3,650 for self-only high-deductible health plan coverage or $7,300 for family coverage. And don't overlook the $1,000 limit increase for those age 55 and up. Since you can't make any contributions after you enroll in Medicare, typically at age 65, every dollar counts.

 ## The mistakes that could wipe out your retirement savings

Rolling money from one retirement account into another doesn't usually raise your tax bill. You're in the clear with these direct rollovers because the money never touches your hands. However, with indirect rollovers, you're in control of the funds. That makes them helpful as a short-term loan, but miss your deposit deadline and things get dicey.

"Moving retirement money incorrectly — either not understanding things like the 60-day rollover rule or the once-per-year rollover rule — those types of things are absolute killers for retirement accounts," says investment expert Jeff Levine, "because if you get it wrong you could effectively lose your entire retirement account."

Deposit the rollover money into the same or different account within 60 days. Otherwise it's considered a withdrawal and subject to income tax and, if you're under 59 1/2, a 10% early withdrawal fee. Make only one indirect rollover every 12 months or you'll be slapped with even more penalties.

---

12 | Annuities

"You are never too old to set another goal or to dream a new dream."

Les Brown

It pays to delay: Postpone immediate annuities to bag big benefits

Which would you rather get — a $500,000 windfall when you retire or $2,700 deposited into your account every month for life? More than 60% of participants in one survey said they'd take the monthly income. Why? People are worried about outliving their savings. Enter the annuity.

When you purchase an annuity, you give an insurance company a lump sum or series of payments. In exchange, they provide regular paychecks for the rest of your life or a certain period of time, starting immediately or at some point in the future.

The most basic type, immediate annuities, are usually funded by a lump sum and allow withdrawals to begin within a year. Financial planners say younger retirees may want to wait as long as they can before buying one. Here's why.

- **Score a higher payout.** When's the purchasing sweet spot? Early to mid-70s, say experts. For example, a 65-year-old man who invests $185,000 in an immediate annuity could get about $897 a month for as long as he lives, but a 75-year-old man could get roughly $1,269 per month. An extra $4,464 a year.

- **Have longer access to your nest egg.** And that can be good news in case of an emergency because immediate annuities are notoriously inflexible when it comes to accessing your money. That's why advisers don't often recommend putting more than 25% to 30% of your savings in one.

Before you take the leap, consider how your annuity payouts will be affected by life expectancy, inflation, interest rates, and other factors that could make it a bad idea for you.

"The prospect of saving enough money to last through a potentially long retirement can be overwhelming, even for those who feel financially secure in their pre-retirement life," says Ron Pressman, former chief executive officer of institutional financial services at TIAA. "The more you know about annuities, the better you can evaluate your options and select the investment products that best suit your financial needs and goals."

 The sneaky sales trick that could shortchange your savings

Switch to a new annuity, suggests the salesperson. You'll get the latest features without incurring taxes. Hold up — salespeople make a commission, so when it comes to annuity swaps, known as "1035 exchanges," they may not tell you these must-know facts.

- Make the swap within the first seven to 10 years of purchasing the first annuity and you may have to dish out a surrender charge. That fee is often 7% of your balance or more. Cha-ching. Plus a new annuity means you'll begin a new surrender period.

- If you exchange a variable annuity that has a payout guarantee, you'll take the actual account value rather than the guaranteed value — the initial premium amount unaffected by market performance. A bummer for your bank account if the guaranteed value is higher, say, in a down market.

When salespeople encourage these swaps for financial gain, it's known as churning. Protect your money by weighing the costs and benefits.

Low interest rates? Hedge your bets with a ladder

You're set on buying an annuity now. But interest rates are at an all-time low, and you don't want to be locked into reduced monthly payments for life. If you can't wait until rates go up, consider this smart staggering strategy.

Instead of putting all the funds in one annuity, split the money and build a ladder. You do this by making smaller annuity purchases periodically every few years. So you'll increase your chances of being able to cash in on rising interest rates.

You can structure your annuity ladder in many ways, and your choice will depend on your goals. Whether you choose a simpler fixed-rate annuity ladder that works similar to a certificate of deposit (CD) ladder or a more complex deferred annuity ladder that suspends payment until later in life, be sure to read the fine print.

And pay attention to the financial standing of the insurer. Consider the scores from two or more respected rating companies like AM Best, S&P Global, Moody's, or Fitch Ratings. Some experts suggest you purchase from more than one firm to spread out the risk.

The SECURE Act: 3 perks you don't want to miss

A recent retirement law, called the SECURE Act, delivers new opportunities for annuities within 401(k) plans. Take action to cash in on these changes.

- See if your employer now offers in-plan annuities. The new law takes away some of the legal risk for business owners, making annuities within 401(k) plans more likely.

- Evaluate your options. These annuities are now portable. So if you purchase one within your 401(k), you can roll it over to another 401(k) or an IRA without surrender charges and fees.

- Estimate potential rewards. Workplace retirement plans will have to provide a disclosure statement to illustrate how much money you might get if you use your balance to purchase an annuity.

Contract loopholes: How to withdraw annuities without penalty

Need to withdraw some or all of your annuity money earlier than expected? That's going to cost you. But before you panic, take a peek at your contract. You may uncover some ways to reduce or sidestep the fees.

For one, take advantage of the free-look period. Most new annuity contracts give you 10 to 30 days to back out without paying surrender charges. If your initial purchase was many moons ago, keep in mind surrender charges usually go down as the annuity matures. And if you can wait out the surrender period — typically seven to 10 years — you can avoid the fee entirely.

Some contracts have provisions that waive the fee in emergency situations. You may also be able to withdraw a certain amount, often 10%, annually without surrender fees or other penalties.

Remember that the IRS has a finger in the pie, too. If you can wait till you're 59 1/2, you'll avoid the 10% early withdrawal penalty on the taxable portion of the distribution.

3 beneficiary mistakes can wreck your financial legacy

Joan felt a sense of relief when her husband bought an annuity. But after he died, she got the unhappy news — the payments would not continue. Avoid these mistakes to make sure your future is secure.

Choosing the wrong annuity type. Each kind of annuity has many variations, but these are the main three to mull over.

- A single-life annuity offers the largest monthly payment, but, as Joan discovered, the paychecks stop coming when the annuitant dies.

- A period-certain annuity offers payments for a specific number of years. If the annuity holder dies during that time, a beneficiary will receive benefits for the remainder of the term.

- A joint-and-survivor annuity continues to provide regular payments as long as one spouse lives. This is a good option if the couple wants the surviving spouse to keep the initial payment schedule and avoid the fees that come with beneficiary payouts. As with all annuity perks, it comes at a cost.

Misunderstanding death-benefit options. Review your contract to see if your chosen annuity includes a death benefit. You don't want any surprises down the road.

Annuities commonly come with a standard death benefit that pays beneficiaries the value of the contract, less any fees and payments already made to the annuity holder. But don't count on it. If needed, you can add riders like the "return of premium" provision so that the remaining value of the annuity goes to a beneficiary. Examine the benefits of such a rider versus the added fees it could cost.

Not naming a beneficiary. After sifting through all your options and choosing the right annuity, you may be ready to kick back and relax. But don't forget one of the most important steps — actually naming your beneficiary.

If you don't pick one, the death benefit becomes part of your estate and goes straight into probate. Protect your heirs from this time-consuming and expensive legal process by naming beneficiaries and contingent beneficiaries right away.

Ease the inheritance tax burden with this little-known strategy

Tax havoc. That's what could happen if you leave money in an annuity to nonspouses. Think about it. The popular options of taking all that dough as a lump sum or payments over five years may bump them into a higher tax bracket. That said, if you are the recipient of an annuity, don't sweat your payout pick. Chew over this underused option instead — the annuity stretch.

It may be a good choice for nonspouse beneficiaries of nonqualified annuities, which are funded with after-tax dollars as opposed to pre-tax money from qualified accounts like IRAs. The idea is that you spread out the payments based on your life expectancy, and therefore reap smaller annual tax bills. Plus the money in the annuity continues to grow tax-deferred, so you could ultimately pocket more cash.

Of course, no one method is best for everyone, so consider your situation before taking the plunge.

13 | Employment

Discover your second act in 3 simple steps

You're ready to set out on a new career path. But with so many questions running through your head — Should I explore a new field? What's the easiest moneymaker? How do I even find part-time work? — you don't know where to start. Fortunately, retirement coach Nancy Collamer has a map to guide you. Just follow these three steps.

Find yourself to find the best fit. "The first step is the process of hitting the pause button and spending some time on introspection and self-reflection," says Collamer.

She recommends asking yourself a few key questions. What do I love to do, what do I do well, and what do I find most meaningful at this point in life? Where the answers to these three questions overlap is where you can start digging for opportunities that match a need in the marketplace.

Keep in mind lifestyle goals, too. What's most important — income, community, flexibility, or something else?

Investigate your options. This step is all about exploration. Do some research to find out what opportunities are out there. Downshifting from your full-time job into a consulting role, for instance, is a common and potentially easier way to transfer your skills to a new position. But consider interests you haven't invested time in before, too. You may discover a new passion.

Don't underestimate the impact of a new line of work. You may end up committing your next decade to it, so you want something that feels meaningful.

Take your change for a test drive. Once you've found a few leads on your road to a second act, it's time to try out the diverging paths.

"Experiment often and experiment in the smallest ways possible," Collamer suggests. That may be a small project or getting your feet wet with volunteer work.

With the popularity of side gigs, you can find some real money-makers to try out in your spare time. How does an extra $300, $500, or even $1,000 a month sound? Increase your cash flow by working part time as a receptionist, school bus driver, or nanny. Or look into experience-driven positions like transcriptionist, tutor, bookkeeper, or paralegal.

Don't waste your time on false promises of easy money, though. You should be wary of virtual personal assistant, mystery shopper, and envelope-stuffing scams that run rampant among work-at-home offers.

Want to make your search easier? Visit the website *sidehusl.com*, recommends Collamer. This site reviews and ranks job posting platforms to help weed out poor opportunities.

Snow job: Expert tips to dodge work-at-home scams

Paying to work? It sounds ridiculous, but that could happen if you fall victim to a work-from-home scam. Some shady business might promise you money for assembling products at home — all you have to do is invest in their kit. But when you finish, the company won't pay up. Now you've wasted time and money.

Fortunately, remote work is increasingly popular, and there are plenty of legitimate opportunities you can carry out from your couch. Try narrowing your search by looking for "remote job" or "virtual job," not "work from home," recommends expert Nancy Collamer.

Ask yourself if the offer makes sense, she says. Never pay upfront expenses, and don't hand out financial info during the application process.

Outsmart resume-screening software to get ahead of the pack

Now more than ever, writing a resume and cover letter can feel like trying to solve a sphinx's riddle. That's because nitpicky computer software, called an applicant tracking system (ATS), may boot you out of the candidate pool before a real person even sees your application.

An ATS can parse through docs submitted online for keywords that match the job description and then rank all applicants by closest fit. This is efficient for larger employers because it narrows down applications to a select few, but you could slip between the cracks.

Avoid early elimination by looking at the specific terms the job description uses. The more often you see a keyword, the more weight it should have in your own documents. Tailor your application for each opening, and follow these additional tips to beat the bots.

- Job titles are an easy way to highlight relevant keywords, so list yours accurately. For instance, if a recruiter searches for "assistant editor" and you previously held that title and listed it correctly, your resume won't be filtered out.

- Emphasize applicable hard skills, like marketing and computer troubleshooting, within your previous experiences or in a separate skills section.

- Both write out and use acronyms for common keywords, including credentials.

- Avoid using tables, columns, or headers, which can confuse an ATS.

- Stick to standard bullet points and simple fonts, like Times New Roman and Arial.

- Always input your resume data into an application's text field if it's requested. This may even give you room to add details that didn't fit on your one-page resume.

Need some organizational tips? Search online for resume and cover letter templates to get inspiration.

Invest in yourself for improved professional prospects

Decades of work experience is often the core of your application as you prepare for your second act. But you can make your application stand out even more by brushing up on old skills or adding new tools to your belt.

"It's important to be willing to invest in yourself a little bit," says Nancy Collamer, founder of *mylifestylecareer.com*. For example, taking one quick course in some sort of new technology might really boost your marketability, she says.

Besides advancing your computer skills, take time to research what best suits your line of work. You may even want to take an online certification training program. Think long term since you could be working in this field for the next 10 or 15 years.

Collamer recommends setting aside a couple of hundred dollars each year to take a course or workshop as they can both help you grow and expose you to new and interesting concepts. You can access these resources through industry trade associations, your local community college, and the professional networking website LinkedIn.

Keep your LinkedIn profile updated because recruiters look around on there. "You never know when somebody might reach out to you," says Collamer.

📱 More resources

American Institute of Certified Public Accountants	*360financialliteracy.org*	N/A
Annuity Guys	*annuityguys.org*	877-679-0829
Annuity.org	*annuity.org*	855-995-1277
Center for Retirement Research	*crr.bc.edu*	617-552-1762
ConsumersAdvocate.org	*consumersadvocate.org*	N/A
Employment For Seniors	*employseniors.org*	614-863-1219
Financial Literacy and Education Commission	*mymoney.gov*	N/A
FINRA	*finra.org/investors/have-problem/helpline-seniors*	844-574-3577
Pension Benefit Guaranty Corporation	*pbgc.gov*	800-400-7242
Pension Rights Center	*pensionhelp.org*	888-420-6550
Retired Brains	*retiredbrains.com*	N/A
Senior Community Service Employment Program	*benefits.gov/benefit/89*	877-872-5627
SeniorLiving.org	*seniorliving.org*	855-241-1699
Social Security Administration	*ssa.gov*	800-772-1213
Supplemental Security Income	*ssa.gov/ssi*	800-772-1213
TIAA	*tiaa.org*	800-842-2252
U.S. Department of Labor	*careeronestop.org*	877-872-5627
U.S. Securities and Exchange Commission	*investor.gov*	N/A
USA.gov	*usa.gov/retirement*	844-872-4681

END THE MONEY DRAIN

Smart strategies keep more dollars in your pocket

14 | Credit score

> "You cannot escape the responsibility of tomorrow by evading it today."
>
> Abraham Lincoln

How to keep your credit strong in retirement

You've retired, paid off your mortgage, and are sitting comfortably on your nest egg. So you may be wondering, "Why should I worry about my credit history? I'm not actively applying for credit anymore." But making that assumption could be a big mistake.

Your credit score, which is primarily based on reports supplied by the credit bureaus, is used to predict the likelihood you'll pay your bills on time. A lower score may lead to changes in interest on your credit cards or insurance rates. A good credit score, however, can help you land a top-tier travel rewards credit card for your bucket list vacations, accessible credit for unexpected medical bills, and better terms if you decide to get a home equity loan.

"Maintaining a credit history will help ensure that you have that credit available to you, not necessarily to take on debt, but to take advantage of the financial advantages it can give you," says

Rod Griffin, senior director of public education and advocacy at Experian, one of the three major credit bureaus.

One way to get your credit score up is with Experian Boost. This free program allows you to add on-time payments that don't usually factor into your score to your Experian credit report. Think utilities, streaming services, and phone bills. Griffin recommends this program to everyone as it gives you credit where credit is due. After all, you're already paying on time, so get rewarded for it.

"Two out of 3 people are telling us they're seeing improvements in their credit scores immediately," says Griffin. That score lift averages about 12 points, and it hops up to 19 points for people with a thin credit history.

"For seniors and retirees, that can be a fantastic tool to help make sure there's activity in their credit history," says Griffin. Other ways to maintain a high credit score include paying all your debts on time, not maxing out your cards, and not closing old credit accounts.

Fact-check 4 common credit score myths

It's tricky enough trying to get a good credit score without misinformation muddying the waters. Find out the truth about these commonly held beliefs to score a better number.

Myth 1. Carrying a small balance month to month is beneficial. Sara Rathner, a NerdWallet credit card expert, explains that this advice you may have received from well-intentioned friends is false.

"The theory is that it helps you seem responsible to lenders, but you can maintain and improve your credit score by paying your bills in full," she says. "Doing that has the exact same result, but it costs you nothing because you're no longer paying interest on a small balance. So if you have the money, there's no reason to carry a small balance from month to month."

Myth 2. Not using your credit card helps your score. In order for a credit account to count toward your credit score, it must have activity for several months in a row — three to six, typically. And no activity could actually hurt your score. If you want to keep your card swipes to a minimum, financial educator and Experian spokesperson Rod Griffin recommends using it at least once every couple of months on something small you can easily pay off.

Myth 3. You must have a credit card account to have a good credit score. "There's no magic number about how many credit cards you should have," says Griffin. One or two is enough, but you can build up your credit score without paying by plastic.

Paying your auto loan, personal loan, and mortgage on time and in full is an alternative way to uplift your score. However, using your credit card responsibly is one of the easiest ways to pump up your credit score because you have control over how much you spend each month.

Myth 4. Being a day late on your bill will destroy your credit. Miss the due date for your credit card payment by a day or two? Expect to be hit with a late fee and an uptick in interest from the card issuer. But don't worry about your credit score — yet.

Late penalties aren't recorded by credit bureaus until you've missed a full payment cycle, meaning the next bill comes due before you pay off the first. Often that's about 30 days.

"If you've missed the due date by a bit, you can still protect your credit history," says Griffin. Do that by paying back what you owe quickly. The longer you wait, passing the due date by 30, 60, or even 90 days, the more damage your score will face. Keep in mind partial payments won't protect you.

2 smart tricks snag your credit score for free

One of the best ways to detect identity theft is to check your credit score regularly. Make a habit of it, and you can tell if there are any unexplained changes that could indicate fraud. A dramatic shift in your credit score could be a sign of illegal activity connected to your finances.

Remember, a credit report and your credit score are two different things.

- Credit report. This is a statement that has information about your credit, such as payment history, amount of debt, and amount of new credit.

- Credit score. This is a number between 300 and 850, calculated based on the information in your credit report. A higher score means you have a good history of repaying loans and makes you eligible for lower interest rates.

You can have several different credit scores depending on which credit reporting agency provided the information, the scoring model they used, the type of loan you are applying for, and even the day your score was calculated. In addition, you may see a FICO score or a VantageScore, two separate businesses that create and sell credit scores to lenders and other financial companies.

To get a clear picture of your credit standing and keep an eye out for fraud on your accounts, you should check both your FICO score and VantageScore. But don't think you have to shell out a single dime for this information.

Fringe benefits let you score a free score. Many credit card companies, banks, and credit unions offer free FICO scores as a perk of doing business with them. Look for your score when you log in to your online account or view your latest paper statement. You can always call their customer service line for assistance.

Take advantage of no-charge online services. If you don't mind signing up for free with a new online account, you can get your FICO score through the Discover Scorecard at *discover.com/ free-credit-score*, and your VantageScore from Credit Karma at *creditkarma.com* or Credit Sesame at *creditsesame.com*.

 Watch out for hidden costs of this new trend

"Buy now, pay later" (BNPL) options, often offered by major retailers at checkout, are like the flip side of layaway plans. Instead of paying installments and getting your purchase later, you receive the item upfront and then pay it off. That flexibility makes BNPL appealing, but be cautious.

The rules on credit reporting and inquiries can vary widely between providers, and that could make or break your credit score. Take these popular BNPL services for example.

- Afterpay doesn't run credit checks or report late payments.

- Klarna, on the other hand, runs a hard credit inquiry — which could impact your credit score — if you choose a long-term financing option instead of the standard four payments.

- Sezzle Up reports your payment history to the bureaus, which could be good if you foot the bill responsibly.

Before using these services, verify how they deal with credit reporting, inquiries, and limits.

Set it and forget it: Credit freezes make protecting your score simple

Want to stop thieves from stealing your identity? A credit freeze will stop them cold because it prevents anyone from accessing your credit report. That means schemers can't take loans or open new lines of credit in your name, which is a great way to block criminals from ruining your good credit.

To protect yourself fully, you must contact all three credit bureaus — Equifax, Experian, and TransUnion. Then you can keep your account frozen until you need it. And good news, it's free by law. If, down the line, you want to open a new line of credit or let someone perform a credit check, you'll unfreeze your account with the PIN you set up. Freezing and unfreezing your account won't affect your credit score.

The credit reporting bureaus offer their own services to protect your account in a similar way to a credit freeze. They're called credit locks, but don't mix them up with a credit freeze. Locks may come with fees, and they're not regulated by the government.

Keep in mind that credit freezes won't stop ID theft. Someone can still do damage if they steal your credit card or Social Security number. So stay vigilant about your financial safety.

15 | Debit & credit cards

"Procrastination is like a credit card: It's a lot of fun until you get the bill."

Christopher Parker

Never use your debit card at these surprisingly common locations

Think twice before you swipe your debit card at nonbank ATMs, gas stations, or public transit terminals. That's because unattended card readers are a great spot for scammers to hide devices that copy the details of your card when you pay. And since that info is tied to a checking account, crooks can get instant access to every last cent you have in the account.

Always check card readers carefully for signs of tampering. Skimmers, which criminals attach to card readers, grab data off the card's magnetic strip. Give the card reader and keypad a gentle tug before you swipe. If anything feels loose or out of place, it's best to avoid using it.

Shimmers, on the other hand, are harder to spot because they're placed on the inside of the readers in order to get info from chip cards. Just one more reason not to swipe that debit card in dangerous places. Experts often recommend you use credit cards at payment terminals instead because they offer better protection against fraud.

Check your spending statements at least once a week. Look for any unusual charges or purchases you don't remember, and report them immediately.

The simplest thing you're not doing that will thwart thieves

"Don't carry every credit card you own in your wallet," says Sara Rathner, credit card expert at NerdWallet. "Only carry the ones you use on a regular basis."

So simple, but many people think they should carry all their cards just in case they need them. If your wallet was lost or stolen, thieves would have access to every single one of your cards.

Instead, pick one or two cards that get the most use to be your daily drivers. Keep the rest locked away in a safe, secure location at home, says Rathner. And if you have a specific credit card that you want to use — say, a store charge card — take it out before you shop and remember to put it back afterward.

Bonus — keeping those extra cards at home will help you cut down on impulse buys. Win-win.

3 critical moves to make if your cards go missing

Lost your wallet? You'll want to act fast to cancel your cards before thieves can go on a major shopping spree. Take these steps to protect your money.

- Contact your bank or credit card company. If your cards are missing or you suspect fraud, reach out to the issuer at once. They'll cancel the card so new purchases can't be made, and they'll get a new one out to you so you're not strapped for cash.

- Change all your login info. If you have mobile or online banking, it's a good idea to come up with new passwords, whether it was your card or account number that was taken. That way, you'll have more protection in the future. And if you use a PIN for your debit card, contact your bank about changing that, too.

- Review your statement for bogus charges. Federal law says you're only required to pay $50 on fraudulent credit card charges. But most issuers will cover 100% of what thieves spent. Your liability on debit card losses depends on how fast you report it. Comb through your billing statement and let the company know which purchases aren't yours.

Go contactless for a safer way to pay

Have you seen the new credit card readers that simply let you tap to pay? Many new cards have the option for contactless payments, where you wave your card over the reader.

But not everyone is convinced these cards are safe. Some fear that scammers could use the touchless tech to steal their info without having to steal the card.

Fortunately, experts say those fears are largely unfounded. In fact, these cards are safer and harder to clone than old-fashioned, magnetic strip credit cards. Every time you tap your card, the payment software generates a complex one-time code that doesn't give away any of your personal info.

If you're interested in this tech, contact your credit card company to see if you can update your current card.

In dispute — when and how to challenge charges

Mary ordered a new television. But when it arrived on her doorstep, the screen was cracked. And when she tried to return it, the store wouldn't take it back.

If she'd paid with cash, she'd be out of luck. Fortunately, Mary had used a credit card and was able to dispute the charges with her credit card company to get her money back.

Disputing charges can also help protect your wallet from billing errors, fraud, and faulty products or services. But if you do it for the wrong reasons, or too often, your credit card company may close your account. Here's how to know if you should get your credit company involved.

- You can't resolve the problem with the original merchant. Before you dispute the charge, talk to the merchant. Take photos, keep receipts, and get other forms of evidence to show that the product was faulty and the store won't take it back.

- You spotted a billing error. If you ordered a TV but were charged twice, point out the mistake promptly.

- You suspect foul play. If you think somebody is using a stolen card, report the fraudulent purchases.

To dispute a charge, contact your credit card company and tell them about the issue. For nonfraudulent charges, you typically have 60 days after receiving your statement to send a letter to the company's billing inquiries department. The letter should highlight the charge, explain your reasons for disputing it, and include any evidence you have.

If you need a sample letter, the Federal Trade Commission has one online at *consumer.ftc.gov/articles/sample-letter-disputing-credit-and-debit-card-charges*.

5 steps to pick the perfect card

Deciding on a new credit card can be overwhelming. How do you know if you want to get a card that offers cash back or points? Or would you rather opt for something that provides travel rewards? Advice from credit card expert Sara Rathner can help you choose the best card for you.

Think about what you can qualify for. "Some cards are available to people in a wide variety of credit score ranges," says Rathner. "Other cards, especially your really high-end rewards cards, are reserved for consumers who have good or excellent credit."

Consider the cost of the cards. Tally up annual fees, the interest rate, and other dues. Then compare that to the value of perks offered by the card. "Ideally, you are not spending more on the card than you're getting back in rewards or benefits," she says.

Ask where you spend your money. Some cards will give you more points or cash back if you shop at certain stores, buy groceries, or use your card to travel. "You want to pick cards that reward you more where you spend more money," says Rathner. "That way you're going to maximize every dollar you spend."

Decide how you want to redeem rewards. Looking for a card with perks? Think about what kind of benefits you want. If you're a frequent flyer, a card that gives you airline miles may be the best choice for your wallet. Otherwise, cash-back cards come with the most flexibility. And those aren't your only redemption options. Gift cards, store merchandise, and cryptocurrency are often available, too.

Determine how much effort you want to put in. Some cards offer simple ways to redeem your rewards and earn benefits. But others may have better bonuses for certain spending categories that rotate quarterly, or have separate portals for each redemption option. "Those are more complicated, but if you are up to the task then that could be worthwhile," says Rathner.

What to do if you get this common call

A phone call to let you know that your credit card was over-charged seems like a great alert, right? Not so fast.

Scammers may pretend to be from your credit card company, and though they might address you by name and promise to get you a reimbursement, they're really only after your account details.

Don't engage in unsolicited calls about billing mistakes or click on any links in emails or texts. While you can sign up for smartphone alerts to let you know about suspicious purchases, you won't need to hand over personal information to resolve these charges.

Instead, contact your credit card issuer or bank directly. Call the number on your statement, the company's website, or the back of your card rather than one provided by a potential scammer.

In a credit crunch? Try these alternative options

A bad credit score makes it hard to qualify for a new card. But getting by without plastic can be tough. So if your score isn't great, consider these options instead.

Secured credit cards. If you're working on boosting your credit score, you might want to consider a secured credit card. In order to get one, you have to make a cash deposit upfront. That then becomes your credit limit. So if you put down a $300 deposit, you'll have a limit of $300 on that card.

"Oftentimes secured cards offer a path to graduation, so to speak," says financial buff Sara Rathner. "So after a few months of using the card carefully and responsibly — not overcharging, paying on time — some cards will either deem you eligible for a credit limit increase or let you move your account onto an unsecured credit card."

Alternative credit cards. Credit history plays a major factor in determining your credit score. So for example, if you recently lost your spouse and you didn't have bills and credit cards in your name, you may not qualify for the cards you want.

That's where alternative credit cards come in. Companies will consider other factors, like income, assets, and debt to determine your eligibility.

Debit cards. "If you do not feel comfortable carrying a credit card, you can use a debit card in situations where cash is not accepted," says Rathner. "That's directly linked to your checking account. The money comes out immediately, so there's no risk of getting into debt."

Some debit cards even come with reward programs, so you may not even miss having a credit card. And don't forget about pre-paid debit cards that help you set your own credit limit with the funds you load.

16 | Banking

> "Business and life are like a bank account — you can't take out more than you put in."
>
> William Feather

Don't waste your money on unnecessary overdraft fees

Would you ever take out a loan with a 17,000% interest rate? No way! But guess what? Certain overdraft fees may translate to that outrageous rate.

You get hit with these tolls when you use your debit card or ATM card to pull out more than you have in your account. And those expenses add up fast, considering the average overdraft fee costs about $34.

What bankers don't want you to know is that you can avoid the dues entirely. That's right — they can't charge you overdraft fees on most ATM or debit card transactions without your say so. If you sign up for overdraft protection, though, they'll charge you to let your transactions go through even if you don't have enough cash. Don't opt in, and your card will simply decline the purchase.

However, if you write a check or send an electronic bill payment that your account can't cover, your bank can still hit you with a nonsufficient fund fee. Budget carefully and check your bank statement regularly to avoid these charges. And use this secret alternative to overdraft protection. Set up text message alerts for when your account is running low so you know when you're in the danger zone.

Accidentally overdrafted your account? Contact your bank's customer service department and politely ask them to drop the charge or if they have a forgiveness policy.

6 must-know secrets for safe online banking

Online banking gives you great flexibility in terms of conducting financial activities. However, with this comes the inevitable risk of scam artists trying to steal your money or your financial details. Here are some things to be aware of when you sign up for online financial services.

Be cautious with all aspects of online banking. If something does not feel right when performing any kind of transaction, stop and cancel anything you have done.

Don't feel rushed or intimidated when using any aspect of online banking. This is particularly true if you are contacted and asked for any of your bank details. It could be a fraudster trying to get you to divulge sensitive information about your online banking activities.

In many cases, these scams operate by pressuring people into thinking they have to make a quick decision to stop something bad happening to their account. If in doubt, ask for more time to think about it.

Contact your bank if you think you've been approached by a scammer. If you're not sure a call or email is legitimate, contact your bank directly and tell them the details. If it was a genuine email or call they will be able to verify it.

Use a strong password for any online financial accounts you have. Also use two-factor authentication if they offer it.

Check your bank's policy on fraud. Make sure your bank or financial institution has a guarantee against any fraud you may be a victim of as a result of online banking. Read this guarantee carefully. You'll want to know the circumstances in which you will receive a full refund if you are a victim of an online fraud.

In most cases you should get back 100% of your money, but check for any situations in which you would be liable for some of the costs. Details should be on the bank's website.

Do not access your online bank account in public areas. This includes places where people can physically see your login details or access them through a Wi-Fi hotspot. Also, make sure that you log out as soon as you have finished an online banking session.

Stash your cash the right way to earn more interest

Money kept in your bank accounts is safe, secure, and easy to access. So why shouldn't you put all your savings there?

Most of the cash you put in a bank account won't earn much interest. Experts say the average savings account only gets you a measly 0.06% return each year. Here's how to calculate what you need to keep on hand so you can max out your money while making sure you don't run short.

Your checking account. This is where you'll store the money you need to pay your monthly bills and cover your daily expenses. A good rule of thumb is to keep enough in here to cover two months' worth of expenses, plus a 30% buffer in case you get hit with an unexpected bill.

That means if you need $1,000 a month, you should keep your checking account stocked with about $2,600.

Your savings account. The old guideline was to keep about six months' worth of savings stored away in case of an emergency. But now experts are rethinking that recommendation.

"A lesson the pandemic taught all of us was that six months is not enough," says Georgina Tzanetos, a writer for personal finance company GOBankingRates. Instead, she suggests people keep enough cash to cover expenses for nine to 12 months.

Other deposit accounts. If you're considering higher-interest savings options, the best fit for you will depend on how often you need to access your money.

- Certificates of deposit (CDs) earn higher interest rates than standard savings accounts. The only downside? You can't access the money for a few months — or even years — after you put it in.

- You need to put down larger chunks of change to open a money market account, but you'll be rewarded with higher interest rates on your savings. While these usually pay less than CDs, they offer more flexibly through checking account features.

Ditch your traditional savings account for this expert-endorsed option

"We've enjoyed almost a decade of near-zero inflation, but that's obviously over," says Georgina Tzanetos, a former financial adviser. "It's important for senior citizens to take that into account if they're sitting on a lot of cash because that money will start losing value."

Instead of stowing your cash away in traditional savings accounts, she recommends making the switch to a high-yield savings account. The reason? You'll build up interest faster to help protect your cash against inflation.

Say you had $20,000 socked away in your traditional savings account from your bank. With a 0.06% interest rate, you'd earn about $12 over the course of the year. But a high-yield savings account — with a much higher interest rate of 0.55% — would earn you $110.

Consider switching to an online bank or a credit union. They typically offer better interest rates than brick-and-mortar banks.

 What you should never do with unexpected checks

Got a check in the mail with a letter that says you've just won a big prize? While that may sound like great news, think twice before taking a trip to the bank to cash in on your winnings.

Scammers often send out these checks with instructions to wire them a bit of cash to cover the taxes or fees. But after you deposit the check, it turns out that it was a fake.

It can take your bank a week or two to process checks and flag fraud. And any money you send or spend in the meantime comes out of your own pocket. Avoid cashing checks for strangers or if you're not sure that the source is legitimate.

Switching banks? This careless move could cost you big time

You might decide to find a new bank if you want to save on fees or get better interest rates. But when you make the switch, avoid this costly mistake — closing your account too early.

If you have automatic bill pay or direct deposit set up, make sure you've moved all your payments to your new bank before you close up shop. Forgetting about recurring debits and credits, including annual subscriptions, can lead to fees from bounced charges, damage your payment history, and disrupt services.

Keep the old account stocked with enough funds to cover a few bills for a month or two, just in case you've forgotten to move any automatic payments over. Once you're positive that you don't have any more loose ends, go to the bank, take out all the money you still have stored there, and formally tell them you want to close the account.

2 tips to help you track down long lost treasures

It's no big deal if you misplace something small, like your reading glasses. But if you've forgotten about a safe-deposit box or bank account, you might be missing out on important documents or a pile of cash. Fortunately, you may be able to recover your missing treasure.

- Start by checking with the bank. They may have a record of the account you're asking about, but if it's not in your name you'll need to prove you can legally access it. Gather documentation that verifies you have power of attorney or that you're the legal executor of a loved one's will.

- Track down unclaimed property. After a while, banks give unclaimed property to the state. To file a claim with the government, contact your state's unclaimed property office. Go online to *unclaimed.org/search* to locate your state's official program website in just one click.

17 | Income taxes

> "The hardest thing in the world to understand is the income tax."
>
> Albert Einstein

Save big with little-known medical deductions

Can you guess the biggest money-related worry among seniors? It's not unexpected expenses, inflation, or an economic downturn. It's the ability to pay for medical treatment. That's right. More than 50% of retirees cite health care costs as their greatest cause for concern, according to a recent survey by Edward Jones and Age Wave.

That's why it's so important to take advantage of the terrific tax breaks that help you recoup some of your expenses.

If you itemize on your federal taxes, you can deduct qualifying medical payments that exceed 7.5% of your adjusted gross income (AGI). That's your taxable income minus any adjustments, such as contributions to a traditional IRA. You may be able to claim unreimbursed charges for yourself, your spouse, and dependents.

So how much could you save? Let's say your AGI is $28,000 and you paid $4,000 for health care. To calculate your deduction, multiply $28,000 by 7.5% — you'll get $2,100. Anything you spent above that amount can be used to reduce your taxable income. So all you have to do is subtract the difference between $2,100 and the $4,000 you spent. Bingo! You've got a deduction worth $1,900.

If you're thinking about going to school — whether for a degree or the pleasure of learning a new skill — look into the Lifetime Learning Credit. It's worth up to $2,000 per tax return. And if you're contributing to a retirement account, you may qualify for a $1,000, or even $2,000, Saver's Credit.

Go to *irs.gov/taxtopics/tc502* for a full list of qualified medical expenses, including these common ones you won't want to miss.

- doctor, dentist, and surgeon fees

- inpatient hospital care

- insulin and other prescription drugs

- transportation for medical care

- long-term care and health insurance premiums, including Medicare

- false teeth, hearing aids, wheelchairs, and prescription eyeglasses

Of course, you should take the standard deduction if it's higher than the total of all your itemized deductions. Along with medical costs, those include real estate taxes, mortgage interest, gifts to charity, and more. Folks who are self-employed may be able to deduct health, dental, and long-term care premiums without having to itemize.

Tap into 6 senior perks that downsize your dues

With age comes wisdom. Not to mention precious time with the grandkids. Just a couple of the fringe benefits that come with getting older. Here's another — extra tax breaks.

You'll want to take advantage of as many as you can. After all, they're a great way to slash your tax bill and boost your bottom line.

Catch-up contribution write-offs. You may not consider being 50 as anything special, but the IRS does. That's the age in which older workers can begin making catch-up contributions to their retirement savings.

You get to deduct those contributions from your taxable income in the year you make them. And you won't have to pay taxes on the cash until you withdraw it — when you might very well be retired and in a lower tax bracket. In 2022, workers age 50 and older could contribute an extra $6,500 annually to 401(k) plans and $1,000 to IRAs.

Tax Counseling for the Elderly program. Once you hit 60, you're eligible for free tax counseling. Yup. Complimentary assistance on preparing your tax return — including info about pensions and retirement benefits — is available from Jan. 1 to April 15 each year. Go to *irs.treasury.gov/ freetaxprep* to find a location near you.

Higher standard deduction. This discount is available only to those age 65 and older. If you're filing jointly with your spouse and both of you meet the age requirement, you could each claim an additional deduction of $1,400 for tax year 2022. Qualified seniors filing with single or head of household status could claim $1,750.

So how much does all that add up to? Well, a qualified married couple could take a standard deduction for seniors of $28,700. Cha-ching! To determine the amount of your standard deduction, go to *irs.gov/help/ita/how-much-is-my-standard-deduction*.

Higher income threshold. Here's another plus for turning 65. The minimum amount of income that triggers federal taxes goes up. That means you can make more money without having to file.

Credit for the Elderly or Disabled. Low-income individuals age 65 and older may be eligible to shave thousands off their taxes. To see if you qualify, go online to *irs.gov/help/ita/do-i-qualify-for-the-credit-for-the-elderly-or-disabled*. Younger people who are permanently disabled may also get the credit.

State exemptions. Along with the federal government, states also offer income tax perks to folks in their golden years. Of course, some areas of the country are friendlier than others. Georgia, for example, doesn't tax Social Security payments. For people age 65 and older, up to $65,000 of retirement income — interest, dividends, pensions, and annuities, for example — is also exempt.

So if you're thinking of moving, check with that state's Department of Revenue to see how good the tax breaks are for seniors. Your wallet will thank you.

Looking for your refund? Let's get tracking

More than $2,800. That's the amount of the average federal tax refund. Money that could be used to open a savings account, pay down credit card bills, or create an emergency fund. But what should you do if you're expecting a check and don't receive it?

The IRS normally issues refunds within 21 days of accepting an e-filing. So the sooner you send in your return, the earlier you should get reimbursed. But circumstances can delay that.

For example, mailed paper returns cause things to slow down. So do filings that contain incomplete or inaccurate information.

The IRS requires extra time if it can't match the particulars you provided with what it has on record. In a worst case scenario, you may have been the victim of identity theft or fraud.

To find out if your return has been received and if your refund has been approved or issued, go to *irs.gov/refund* and click *Check My Refund Status*. You'll need to give the IRS your Social Security number, filing status, and the refund amount as shown on your tax return.

You can start checking within 24 hours after the agency received your e-filing or four weeks after you mailed a paper return. The info is updated daily, and may include instructions or information on how your return is being processed.

Sometimes, a refund may be smaller than expected. A possible cause? The IRS had to make corrections to your return. If that occurs, you'll get a notification explaining the reason for the reduction.

The federal government can also use all or part of an expected refund to offset past-due amounts on federal and state income tax, student loans, or child support. If you suspect that's the case, the IRS advises contacting the agency that is owed the money.

Ward off tax ID theft with this easy step

You've probably heard about tax-related identity theft. It's when someone steals your Social Security number and other personal information to file a fake tax return. Why would someone want to do that? To steal whatever refund may result, of course.

You may not even know you're a victim until the IRS rejects your legitimate return because it's been flagged as a duplicate.

To battle such crimes, the agency is offering an Identity Protection Personal Identification Number (IP PIN) to all taxpayers who want one. It will give you a six-digit number — known only to you and the IRS — that will be used to verify your identity when filing a return.

To join the IP PIN program, go to *irs.gov/identity-theft-fraud-scams/get-an-identity-protection-pin* and click *Get an IP PIN*. You'll need to verify your identity to set up an online account.

Along with personal information like your name, address, Social Security number, and tax filing status, you'll be asked to provide data from a financial account — a student loan account number, for example, or the last eight digits of a credit card. Then follow the prompts to retrieve your unique PIN.

Keep the number in a safe place until it's time to do your taxes. Be sure to use it when filing with the IRS. Without the correct PIN, the agency will either reject or delay the processing of your return. Remember, this is a single-use PIN. You must get a new one each year.

Protection by the numbers: Steer clear of this phone scam

Countless people have lost millions of dollars and their personal information to tax scams. Don't be one of them. Watch out for hoodlums who call you on the phone, pretending to be from the IRS. They're only after your money.

"The callers are aggressive and relentless," says Treasury Inspector General for Tax Administration J. Russell George. "Once they have your attention, they will say anything to con you out of your hard-earned cash."

A common scenario? The scammer demands that you pay off a bogus tax bill, often through a prepaid debit card or wire transfer.

Don't do it. The IRS never calls to demand immediate payment. Nor will it threaten to have you arrested. The agency generally contacts taxpayers by mail. So hang up immediately if you get one of these calls. If you think you might owe taxes, call the IRS at 800-829-1040.

Thinking of moving? Don't miss this home sale tax break

You're probably familiar with capital gains. They're the profits you make after selling personal property that has increased in value. Capital gains are often taxable, but if you're selling your home, you may just luck out.

That's because the IRS lets you exclude a large portion of the gain from your taxable income if you've owned and lived in the home for at least two of the past five years. How much of that profit can you keep tax-free? A whopping $250,000 if you're a single filer and $500,000 if you're married and filing jointly.

So let's say you're a single filer who bought a house 40 years ago for $50,000 and sold it last week for $325,000. You'd have a capital gain of $275,000. But because of the exclusion, only $25,000 of that would be subject to capital gains tax, which is generally lower than ordinary income tax.

How much lower? Long-term capital gains tax rates are 0%, 15%, and 20%, depending on your taxable income and filing status. That compares with 10% to 37% for ordinary income tax.

Tax rate	Single	Married filing jointly
0%	up to $40,400	up to $80,800
15%	$40,401 to $445,850	$80,801 to $501,600
20%	more than $445,850	more than $501,600

What's one way to avoid paying any capital gains tax at all? If you think it's financially smart to do so, sell your home in a year in which you have little to no taxable income. In the previous scenario, you wouldn't owe capital gains tax on the $25,000 as long as your taxable income was at or below $40,400.

Be aware, though, that the capital gains exclusion disappears if you've lived in your home for less than two of the last five years. If that's the case, your entire profit will be taxed as ordinary income.

You may have heard that Uncle Sam doesn't tax inherited money. Not quite true if you're the beneficiary of a traditional IRA. Come tax time, you'll have to include any IRA distributions from the previous year with the rest of your gross income. That's because the funds in the account haven't already been taxed. Surviving spouses, however, can roll over distributions into their own IRA if the distributions aren't required.

Death and taxes: What to do when the 2 collide

Federal income taxes are probably the last thing you want to think about after a loved one dies. But the unpleasant fact remains. The IRS requires a tax return if the deceased person's gross income exceeded the standard deduction in the year he died.

The amount changes each year, but it's not a lot. In tax year 2022, for example, it was just $12,950 for a single filer under the age of 65. And for those older than that? $14,700.

So who completes and sends in the return? It's often the job of the executor of the estate. If that's you, you'll need to file Form 1040 with the IRS, writing the word "Deceased," your spouse's name, and the date of death at the top of the form.

Prepare and file the return as you would any other — the mid-April deadline still applies. Report income earned between the start of the previous year and the date of death, along with credits or deductions that the deceased was eligible for. Who knows? The departed may have been entitled to a refund. If that's the case, you can claim it on Form 1310, Statement of Person Claiming Refund Due a Deceased Taxpayer.

Of course, if tax is due, you'll need to submit a payment with the return or see if you qualify for an installment plan. Either way, you'll include with your return Form 56, Notice Concerning Fiduciary Relationship. It explains your relationship to the person who passed on.

Special rules apply to surviving spouses if they, instead of an executor, are filing with the IRS. Widows and widowers can file a joint return for the year in which their husband or wife died, claiming the full standard deduction. When signing the tax form, they should write "filing as surviving spouse" in the area below their signature.

For more complicated tax situations, it's always a good idea to work with a tax professional. They will be able to answer your questions, guide you through the process, and help you avoid costly mistakes.

More resources

AnnualCreditReport.com	annualcreditreport.com	N/A
Consumer Federation of America	americasaves.org	202-387-6121
Consumer Financial Protection Bureau	consumerfinance.gov/consumer-tools/bank-accounts	855-411-2372
Credit.org	credit.org	800-431–8157
Equifax	equifax.com	888-548-7878
Experian	experian.com	888-397-3742
Federal Deposit Insurance Corporation (FDIC)	fdic.gov/resources/consumers/money-smart	877-275-3342
Federal Reserve Consumer Help	federalreserve consumerhelp.gov	888-851-1920
Federal Trade Commission	consumer.gov	N/A
Free File Alliance	freefilealliance.org	N/A
Internal Revenue Service	irs.gov/individuals/seniors-retirees	800-829-1040
MyFreeTaxes	myfreetaxes.com	866-698-9435
National Association of Area Agencies on Aging	n4a.org	202-872-0888
Office of the Comptroller of the Currency	helpwithmybank.gov	800-613-6743
TransUnion	transunion.com	833-395-6938
USA.gov, Credit Reports and Scores	usa.gov/credit-reports	844-872-4681
USA.gov, Filing Your Taxes	usa.gov/filing-taxes-topics	844-872-4681

SAFE & SOUND

Protect what matters most

18 | ID theft

"No thief, however skillful, can rob one of knowledge, and that is why knowledge is the best and safest treasure to acquire."

L. Frank Baum

Grand theft identity: 9 no-nonsense ways to keep your info safe

Could someone steal your identity to get to your money? It happens all the time. Identity theft criminals thrive on people's personal information, so the safer you keep it the harder it is for them to operate. Here's how to protect yourself, your name, and your money.

- Protect your Social Security number at all costs, as this is one of the most valuable pieces of information you own. Don't carry your card around with you unless you have to, and don't write your number down on anything except essential official documents.

- Shred all hard copy documents that contain any personal details. A strip-cut shredder is the least secure option since it simply slices your paper into long, ribbon-like strips that are fairly readable. A cross-cut shredder chops paper diagonally from both corners, leaving you with short, narrow pieces.

And a micro-cut shredder is classified as a high-security shredder because it produces much smaller particles than strip- or cross-cut shredders. This type has downsides, however. It processes paper slower and costs more than the other options.

- Do not give out any personal information if you're approached with an unsolicited request. This could be in the form of an email, a phone call from someone pretending to be from your bank, or a text message. If in doubt, don't reply.

- One indication of identity theft can be strange transactions on your bank or credit card statements. Keep an eye on these and contact your bank if you think anything is suspicious.

- If you will be away from home for a period of time, don't let mail sit in your box just waiting for a potential thief to swing by and pick up. Ask someone to collect it for you.

- Use secure passwords on all of your online accounts, and use antivirus software and a firewall on your computer to keep the information on it as protected as possible.

- If you are getting rid of a desktop computer, laptop, tablet, or smartphone, make sure it has been reset to its original factory condition to wipe all of the data from it.

- Store important documents and items with sensitive details in a secure place, preferably in a home safe.

- Check out the government website *usa.gov/identity-theft* for a wealth of information about dealing with identity theft.

Top myths you can't afford to fall for

You may be confused by all the different information and advice you get about identity theft. Learn the truth to protect your sensitive information.

It won't happen to me. Identity theft can happen to anyone, and the more complacent you are about it, the more likely it is to happen to you.

I'll notice ID theft immediately. You may think your antivirus software will warn you of any breaches, but you can't count on it. Criminals are adept at covering their tracks, and they may wait several months until they deploy some of the elements of identity theft. Therefore it is important to regularly check all your online accounts and credit score.

I'm careful online so I'm safe. Identity theft criminals frequently operate by stealing bags, wallets, and purses to find information. They also go through trash and take unattended mail that may be lying outside a house.

I will be fully reimbursed if I'm a victim of identity theft. In a lot of cases, this will be true. However, if it is deemed that you're in some way responsible for the identity theft, such as leaving an important document lying around in public, or revealing sensitive information online, then you may be liable for some of the costs.

It's only a financial crime. While financial gain is the major reason behind identity theft, it can also be used by criminals to get jobs fraudulently, obtain medical treatment, or even evade prosecution for a crime.

Medical ID theft — it's not what the doctor ordered

It sounds like a nightmare. Someone pretending to be you has been admitted and released from the hospital. Next thing you know, the billing department is hounding you for payment. Bad dream? Nah. Just the tip of the iceberg when it comes to the trials faced by victims of medical identity theft.

This crime occurs when a scammer hijacks your personal information — name, health insurance details, and Social Security number, say — and uses it to get medical care. That includes anything from doctor visits and surgeries to prescriptions and medical equipment.

The effects can be devastating, both financially and medically. The fraudster's unpaid bills can wind up on your credit report, for example. If he falsifies insurance claims, your premiums can go way up. Not only that, the thief's medical information — his blood type, allergies, and test results, for example — can get added to your health records and jeopardize your future care.

Of course, you'll want to avoid this mess. Be sure to follow these precautions.

- Carefully guard your Medicare and other insurance cards.

- Destroy prescription labels before throwing them in the trash.

- Ask your doctor's office if you can identify yourself without having to provide your Social Security number.

- Watch out for offers of free medical equipment in exchange for your Medicare number.

- Never give health care-related information to anyone who calls, emails, or texts you unexpectedly.

Surprisingly, strangers aren't the only crooks who commit this type of fraud. You'd never suspect it, but roughly one-third of medical identity thieves are family members of the injured party. But no matter who's responsible, the warning signs are the same.

- You get calls from debt collectors for medical services you didn't receive.

- You receive mail from health care providers you don't know.

- Your health insurer says you've reached your benefit limit when you haven't.

- You find errors in your explanation of benefits statement.

- You see unfamiliar medical debt collection notices in your credit report.

So what should you do if you find out you've been victimized? Immediately file a police report and contact your insurance company. Ask your health care providers for a copy of your records and alert them to any errors.

5 foolproof steps foil phishing attacks

One of the most common forms of scams aimed at computer users is known as phishing. This is a relatively simple form of cybercrime as it does not require a complicated virus or spyware.

Instead, phishing involves asking people for sensitive financial information, such as bank account details and logins for online accounts. Why on earth would anyone willingly hand that information over? The phishing request is usually made through an official-looking, albeit fake, email. Phishing emails can pretend to come from some of the following organizations.

- banks, with a message saying your account has been suspended

- courier services, with a memo saying there is a problem with a delivery they have for you

- a cloud service, such as iCloud or Dropbox, with a warning that your account has been locked

- any organization where users have online accounts, with a notice that claims they have noticed suspicious activity or need you to confirm some personal information

Included in the phishing email are details of what the problem is and how it can be remedied. Unfortunately, the "remedy" usually involves clicking on a link, which takes you to a page where you have to enter financial details to resolve the issue. Needless to say, this doesn't fix anything — since there never was a problem — but instead provides the phishers with your crucial financial details.

Phishing emails can seem intimidating, and it may be tempting to perform the requested action. However, the golden rule is that you should not click on any links in an email you have doubts about. Instead, take a few minutes to try and discover if the email is legitimate.

Check whether you have an account with the organization mentioned in the email. Millions of phishing emails are sent every day, in the hope that users will have the service or account named in the email. Whenever you get a suspicious-looking email, take some time to check whether it is relevant to you or not. If it is, examine the email further to find out if it is genuine.

Inspect the actual address of the email. Phishing emails are usually disguised to show the name of the company they are claiming to be from. However, the email address at the top may be very different and bear little resemblance to the actual company. Click, right-click, or tap on the name of the email sender to view the full email address.

Note the language, spelling, and grammar in the email. If there are numerous spelling or grammar errors, this could be a sign the email is not genuine.

Search the web for alerts. The online community is excellent at keeping on top of scams. Other people will undoubtedly have received the same phishing email as you and posted warnings about it.

In addition, stay tuned into government watchdog sites that post consumer alerts about current exploits.

- The Federal Trade Commission (FTC) keeps their website updated on the latest scams. Go to *consumer.ftc.gov* and click on *Scams*.

- Check *us-cert.gov/report-phishing* for up-to-date information about phishing and options for reporting phishing emails.

Look up the company's actual website online. Check on the internet rather than through any links in the phishing email to see if the named company has indeed reported any problems.

No trash talk here: Prevent credit card scams with a quick call

They say one man's trash is another man's treasure. That's why you should never just toss away preapproved credit card offers. If you discard this junk mail without shredding, criminals can parse through your garbage, retrieve the contents of the envelope, and try to activate the card for their own use.

Don't even want these offers in the first place? You can stop financial institutions from sending them by calling 888-567-8688 and following the prompts. You'll have to provide personal information, including your name, address, and Social Security number, to process your request. The phone number is managed by the major credit bureaus, so you can only opt out of the credit card offers that they have prescreened.

Invasion of the wallet snatchers: How to outsmart pesky pickpockets

Numerous perils in the online world can result in you being scammed, conned, or worst of all, having your identity stolen and used for criminal purposes. However, one of the most common sources of identity theft has nothing to do with virtual misdeeds, at least not initially. It involves the old-fashioned crime of bag, wallet, or purse snatching.

A new study has found that computer fraud is only 12% of theft cases. Surprisingly, traditional ways are more common. Once a criminal grabs your purse, they have access to details from your driver's license, bank cards, credit cards, and any other personal items you carry. With this type of information, identity theft criminals could build up a comprehensive profile and start impersonating you.

> "Shoulder surfing" is where criminals simply look over your shoulder when you complete sensitive documents or use your bank and credit cards. Turn your body or use your hand or a piece of paper to shield your info.

But you can fight back. Here are some steps to take to protect the physical security of your sensitive documents when you are away from home.

- Take as few valuable items as possible with you when you go out. Only carry what you need. The fewer items you have, the less you have to worry about and protect.

- Keep bags closed. An open bag is an inviting sight for any criminal, particularly if they have their mind set on identity theft.

- Hold your bag or purse in front of you, ideally with at least one arm over it. If it is behind you, you won't be aware what is happening to it.

- Don't keep your wallet in a back pocket. It could fall out or easily be taken by a criminal. Don't keep your smartphone in a back pocket either.

- Don't put yourself in danger if someone tries to take your bag, wallet, or purse, and threatens violence. If this happens, hand over the item, and report the matter to the police immediately.

Blow the whistle on thieves with quick action

Keep an eye on all of your personal information and, if you think you may have been a victim of identity theft, act immediately.

- Contact your local police and report your concerns. This is important in terms of trying to catch the identity theft criminals, but it will also provide an official date of when you reported the potential crime. That will lessen any responsibility that could be attached to you.

- Report the issue to the Federal Trade Commission (FTC) using their website at *identitytheft.gov*. They have a range of options relating to identity theft and can issue you an identity theft report and, if needed, a recovery plan.

Theft after death — smart moves to protect your loved one's estate

It's sad to say, but death isn't the end of identity theft. Scammers steal the personal information of the dead to open credit card accounts, collect government benefits, and take out loans. And they'll often commit this crime right after someone passes away, hoping that relatives are too busy grieving to notice the fraud.

While surviving family members aren't responsible for the bogus charges and claims, this lawbreaking can add months — even years — to the estate settlement process.

So where do thieves collect details about the deceased? Sometimes at hospitals and funeral homes. More often, they find information in obituaries. So it's best to exclude things that make it easier to steal your loved one's identity, including his birthdate, middle name, birthplace, home address, and mother's maiden name.

> You're already guarding your credit card and Social Security numbers. Good. To protect yourself further, safeguard the security code on the back of your credit card. Why? A criminal who steals your credit card number — say, through a data breach — may need the code to buy things online or over the phone. So don't fall for scams where someone calls requesting this important code. Credit card companies don't ask for it.

The executor of the estate or next of kin should also contact the Social Security Administration (SSA) at 800-772-1213 to report the death. The SSA can lock the deceased's Social Security number so that thieves can't steal benefits.

You'll also want to send copies of the death certificate to the financial firms that the departed did business with. Shutting down an account? Ask that it be marked "Closed: Account holder is deceased." Don't forget to cancel your loved one's driver's license to prevent a con artist from getting a duplicate.

Finally, mail a copy of the death certificate to the three major credit bureaus — Equifax, TransUnion, and Experian — and ask that a "deceased alert" be placed on the person's credit report. A few weeks later, check the report to ensure that no suspicious activity has taken place.

19 | Scams

> "How prone to doubt, how cautious are the wise."
>
> Homer

Love or lies? Avoid swindles from phony suitors

A heartbreaking $304 million. That's how much money was reported lost to romance scams in 2020. This record amount, up 50% from the previous year, is enormous. But it makes sense, too. These schemes rely on loneliness — something lots of people felt during the COVID-19 pandemic. You don't have to be a victim, though.

The con artists behind sweetheart scams want to deceive you. They may pose as a new friend or possible love interest and build a relationship with you by chatting online. But your alarm bells should start ringing if they refuse to meet in person. The scammer usually has an excuse for not getting together, like being away for work or illness. But keep your guard up.

False romancers try to manipulate you out of your hard-earned cash, so they may be pushy with questions about your finances.

Eventually, they'll ask for money by spinning a story about costly medical needs or travel expenses. Don't fall for it. Stop communicating with the person and notify your financial institution immediately if you sent money or shared banking information.

The fraud stops here: Strategies for protecting older adults

Scammers work hard to take advantage of new situations to dupe you and your loved ones. Just look at what happened early on in the COVID-19 pandemic. Fraudsters came up with a slew of ruses, including posing as vaccine survey takers and contact tracers, to get hold of personal information.

Because of the fast-changing nature of swindles, you may worry about keeping up to date. But according to Jason Zirkle, training director for the Association of Certified Fraud Examiners, you don't need to know about every con that comes along.

"Scammers usually only want one of two things," he says. "They want you to send them money directly or they want you to give them personal information." His advice? Steer clear of anyone you don't know who contacts you for these things.

Casually dropping such helpful information is a good way to make sure your older relatives are aware of the danger but not unnecessarily fearful. Check out these other recommendations.

Stay on top of financial records. Seniors are often hesitant to get assistance with their finances, but with care and patience you can offer your support without putting them on the defensive or questioning their independence.

Work with your loved one and their bank to see if you can gain "read only" access to their online banking.

That way you can watch for suspicious activity. Remember, you don't need to take over to help out.

Take preventive steps. Reduce unwanted telemarketing calls by adding your family member's phone number to the National Do Not Call Registry at *donotcall.gov*. Consider installing a call-screening tool for an extra barrier. Advise your relative to never conduct business over the phone — all proposals and offers should be in writing.

Be good company. Scammers consider all seniors good targets, but older adults without the support of family and friends are the most vulnerable to their schemes. That's why Zirkle advises that you stay connected. "The biggest thing I see that helps in these situations is being there for your loved ones," he says.

So carve out time to drop in or give their phone a ring. Doing so can prevent them from becoming socially isolated, and lets you keep an eye out for elder abuse from a caregiver or dodgy new "friends."

4 scams you shouldn't ignore

The type and number of email scams and cons is developing constantly. You've heard about phishing, but that's not the only type of email scam you need to worry about. Be on the lookout for these as well.

Current events scams. During the COVID-19 pandemic, people endured a range of email scams for fake cures and false warnings. This can happen whenever there is a major national or international incident, so beware of any emails relating to a current crisis.

Money awaiting collection. A classic example is the Nigerian prince who has a large sum of money waiting for anyone who is willing to try and help him get it out of the country — for a fee of course.

Charity donations. Some scam emails relate to charity appeals, but the money goes straight into the scammers' pockets.

Stock market scams. Emails promoting miracle products on the stock market are usually what they seem — too good to be true.

You don't have to worry about getting hooked by scams and computer viruses over email as long as you follow a couple of very simple rules.

- Don't open any attachments in emails from senders you don't recognize. This is one of the most common ways viruses enter computing devices or criminals get hold of your personal details.

- Never click on links in suspicious-looking emails. They are designed to either trick you into giving away sensitive financial details or infect your device with a virus. If you avoid unknown links in emails, you can help stop thieves from stealing your identity as well as prevent destructive viruses.

The scary side of social media

More and more people are joining social media to stay connected with friends and family. But scammers can ruin your good time as they infiltrate these networks in large numbers.

At the top of the Federal Trade Commission's list of social media scams are reports of online shopping sites that fail to deliver the promised product. Facebook and Instagram are two common platforms where people have been lured in by these carefully curated, but phony, ads.

To protect yourself, always suss out a company before making a purchase. Search its name online paired with words like "scam" or "complaint." That way, you can get tipped off even if a con artist posing as a legitimate business has deleted negative comments that were left on his ads. You can also read reviews of a company in question.

Still not sure who you're dealing with? Take the advice of Jason Zirkle of the Association of Certified Fraud Examiners. "If there's ever a question, it's always safe to shop at the big retailers," he says.

So you can't trust all those random ads on social media. But what about your friends? Maybe not. If someone who you think is a pal messages you with offers of financial assistance, follow up with them to make sure it's legitimate. Your buddy's account may have been hacked, and you don't want to get sucked into a scam.

Scam-reporting websites are great tools in the fight against misinformation on the web. They're dedicated to reporting on a comprehensive range of email scams and also fake news reports that are making the rounds. Two sites to look at are *scambusters.org* and *snopes.com*. Use them to search for social media scams, Social Security swindles, and more.

Protect your paycheck from these risky loans

You need a little extra cash to cover your bills this month, so you're considering borrowing some money. What misstep should you avoid? Taking out a payday loan. Typically, it's a high-cost, short-term advance of a small amount of cash.

The loan — typically $500 or less — comes due right after your next payday, so you must be ready to square your account within a couple of weeks or you'll face extra fees. These charges build up the longer you have a balance due and can trap you in debt. In fact, several states have banned these high-interest loans or added safety restrictions because of their risks.

That's not the only danger you face, either. If you apply for a payday loan online, you may actually be contacting a broker who will take your personal information — Social Security and bank account numbers, for example — and sell it to an online lender. This can increase your risk of identity theft, unwanted solicitations, and even raise the overall cost of the loan.

What's more, you can get scammed by applying online. Fraudsters posing as payday lenders sometimes offer to deposit money in your bank account — but only after you've wired them a "good faith" deposit. In such cases, the con artist's check will bounce after he's got your money.

Don't get taken when you give

No one likes to be scammed or ripped off, but this seems particularly unfair when you are trying to do a good thing and donate to charity. Unfortunately, a lot of unscrupulous fraudsters try and profit illegally from people's generosity.

So with the huge number of charities out there, how do you know which are the best and safest ones to use? Thankfully, help is at hand. A number of free websites check out charities for you and provide all the information you need to be confident about donating.

Get the real scoop on any charity by taking a look at *charity watch.org* and *charitynavigator.org*. These websites help you make sure your money really is going to a good cause.

20 | Digital security

7 warning signs your computer is under attack

Computer viruses have been around for almost as long as computers themselves. They operate by infecting your devices then performing various malicious acts.

Viruses install themselves on your computer without your knowledge. When they are opened, either automatically by the virus itself, or by an act such as clicking on an infected attachment in an email, the virus then conducts its malicious mission.

Any erratic or unexplained behavior that suddenly starts happening regularly could mean your device has a virus. If this happens, you should investigate immediately. Not sure you'll know if you are under attack? Here are some danger signs to watch out for.

- The operating system fails to start. This is a serious problem since, obviously, you will not be able to access your device.

In cases such as this, look for a software security expert in your area.

- Slow performance in terms of opening apps and accessing items.

- Error messages keep appearing for no apparent reason.

- Files and folders disappear without explanation.

- Random emails are generated and sent to all of the contacts in your address book.

- Your device crashes or freezes with monotonous regularity.

- Apps launch themselves with no input from you.

The dangers of the digital and online world can appear frightening and daunting at times. However, understanding these dangers and taking steps to protect yourself is the best way to gain the confidence to carry on safely with the rest of your computing activities.

Halt the hackers: Essential steps to secure your home Wi-Fi

A wireless router lets you connect your devices — computers, tablets, smartphones, and even smart TVs — to the internet, without cables. Securing this router is an important step in keeping your personal information safe from hackers.

- Change any passwords that came with your router. This could include the Wi-Fi network password and the router admin password.

- Replace the default manufacturer's name of your router with something unique and secure.

- Turn on your router's encryption feature so any information you send over the internet is scrambled.

- Register your router with the manufacturer so you receive software updates. If your router came from an Internet Service Provider (ISP), like Verizon or Comcast, ask about automatic updates.

- Turn off any features that allow remote management.

- Set up a guest network with its own name and password. This limits the number of people with your primary password.

- Never stay logged in as an administrator.

Vaccinate your computer against damaging viruses

As with many threats in the real or online world, being aware of the problem is the first step to preventing it. The good news is that there are companies dedicated to providing excellent antivirus protection.

Unfortunately, the hackers and fraudsters are very determined and increasingly sophisticated, and you can never be 100% secure all of the time. But if you remain constantly vigilant, you will give yourself the best chance of a safe and secure computing environment. Here are some steps to protect your information and your investment.

Use antivirus software to identify any malicious attacks. This is your first and most important step. There are both free and paid versions available, and you should always use one on your device if you plan to connect to the internet.

Never open an attachment if you receive an email from someone you don't know. This includes clicking or tapping on any links in the email. It's one of the most common ways that hackers deploy viruses. If you get an email like this, don't access anything in it. Instead, delete it immediately.

Look for a Wi-Fi router with a built-in firewall. The aim is to use the router to stop viruses before they get the chance to access your devices. Check the specifications of the router before you buy it to see if it has a built-in firewall.

Windows users have a built-in antivirus option that can scan for viruses and provides a free firewall that protects against malicious software accessing your desktop computer or laptop. You'll find it within the *Windows Security* section of the *Settings* app.

Use a software firewall on your computer for detecting malicious items trying to access your device via the internet. For Windows, deploy this in the *Settings* section, and for macOS devices, navigate to *Security & Privacy* in *System Preferences*. Antivirus apps also come with separate firewalls.

Keep on top of information about new viruses. Antivirus software sites, such as *mcafee.com* and *norton.com*, usually have news about the latest viruses as well as products to protect against them. Details about particularly widespread viruses also sometimes appear in the national news.

No more money mishaps: Get free malware protection

Malware is just what it sounds like — malicious software. Its purpose is to damage or exploit a computer, server, or network or to steal your identity or other valuable information. These are the most common infectious programs you need to watch out for.

Worms. Digital worms are much more malicious than the squirmy creatures you may find in the backyard. They're a form of virus that actively works to spread itself, rather than waiting to be activated through a particular action or on a specific date. Worms flow automatically from computer to computer over the internet.

Like viruses, they perform similar destructive and irritating tasks. One of their specialties is to replicate themselves via email by accessing your computer's address book to send itself to all of your contacts.

Trojans. These get their name from the wooden horse of Troy, where a malicious force (the Trojans) was hidden inside an innocent looking gift (the wooden horse). In computing terms, the Trojans are still the malicious force, frequently hidden in apparently friendly items, such as games apps.

Trojans generally have a different purpose from viruses, which try to destroy elements of your digital world. Instead, they are more intent on gathering information from the infected device. This could be bank or credit card details, which they can obtain by creating a fake advertisement on your computer offering something that requires you to enter your bank account details.

Spyware. Particularly devious, spyware infects your computer and then looks through all the information there. Whatever it finds it then reports back to the spyware's author. Companies can track your every move online, then build a profile of you to sell to advertisers.

The information spyware finds can include details in files and folders. It can also include things like keystrokes used on websites, so the spyware can recognize login details and passwords. This type of spyware activity is known as keylogging.

Luckily, help is at hand when it comes to removing malware with a range of apps designed for this task. The large antivirus companies all have products designed to remove worms, Trojans, spyware, and more. Here are top-rated choices to look at. Free versions can usually be upgraded to more powerful, paid-for versions.

Kaspersky	kaspersky.com
McAfee	mcafee.com
Norton	norton.com
PCProtect	pcprotect.com
TotalAV	totalav.com
Panda	pandasecurity.com
Spybot Search & Destroy	safer-networking.org/products/spybot-free-edition
SpywareBlaster	brightfort.com/spywareblaster
SUPERAntiSpyware	superantispyware.com/free-edition.html

Don't let ransomware hold you hostage

Another type of malware you want to avoid is ransomware, a threat that can ruin your computer and cost you hundreds of dollars. This is frequently directed at large organizations with hundreds of computers, but ransomware can also be aimed at individuals.

Ransomware freezes your computer so you can't access anything. In effect, the computer is rendered inoperable. Once a ransomware attack has taken place, there will be a pop-up message on your computer to alert you to what has happened. This will also contain details about how you can unlock your device, usually by sending a payment to obtain a digital key. Frequently the key does not exist, and the money is never seen again.

Often the payment for a ransomware demand is in the Bitcoin digital currency, which seems in keeping with the digital nature of the crime being committed.

To avoid a ransomware attack, use antivirus software that includes ransomware protection. But if you do suffer this type of attack, try the following steps.

- Do not pay any money. Even if you do make some form of payment, there is no guarantee that your computer will be released from the ransomware.

- Try rolling back your computer to a previous state, before it was infected with the ransomware. Not all ransomware attacks will allow this but, if it is possible, it can be done on a Windows desktop computer or laptop by going to *Settings* then clicking on *Update & Security* and then *Recovery*. On a Mac using macOS, use the *Time Machine* backup app to return to a previous version.

- Take your computer to a recognized software security expert. Search online to find one in your area. As long as your files and system are backed up you should not lose any valuable documents.

3 most common security mistakes: Are you making 1 of them?

The digital world is full of potential dangers. But if you're aware of some of the common mistakes that can lead to financial fraud, you can take steps to avoid them and improve your defenses against unwanted attacks. Don't stumble when it comes to these security missteps.

Oversharing on social media. What's the quickest way to let burglars know the best time to pilfer your home? Post on social media that you're super excited about your vacation next week or share real-time pics of yourself away from home. That's right — if you tend to overshare online, your biggest security threat could be you.

And it's not just obvious info — such as credit card numbers and phone numbers — that can put your finances at risk. Details that seem harmless, like the name of your first pet or your mother's maiden name, could give hackers the answer to security questions or a clue to weak passwords. So do yourself a favor. Make your accounts private and watch what you post.

Not using two-factor authentication for sensitive websites. This security method sends you a code, usually to your smartphone, after you have signed in to a website and entered your password. This code is then the second step in verifying your identity and allowing access to the website. Two-factor authentication is used on websites that store sensitive financial information. If a website offers this, you should use it.

Not updating operating systems. If you don't have the latest version of your device's operating system, you will also not have the latest updates that offer protection against viruses and online threats. Therefore it is important to keep your operating systems as up to date as possible. For Windows, look for the latest updates under *Settings*. For macOS, look for updates in *System Preferences*.

3 simple ways to protect your privacy online

Whenever you're online, you leave a digital footprint of data. How this data is collected and used is a major consideration for all computer users, since no one likes to think of it being used in ways it shouldn't. Here are three important steps you can take to protect your privacy in the digital world.

Read the terms and conditions. When you download a new app or update an item such as the device's operating system, you'll frequently see a page of terms and conditions in relation to using the item.

It is common for people to accept this without reading it properly. However, it is worth taking some time to look at this page, so you can see any details about how your private data is going to be used.

Check the privacy settings on your devices. Get to know the privacy or security options for your computers, tablets, and phones so you can take control of how your data is used. For Windows, iPadOS, iOS, and Android, look in *Settings*. For macOS, look in *System Preferences*.

Learn to surf securely. Privacy is a hot topic when it comes to online activities. Control and manage access to your information through settings in individual web browsers.

- For the Edge browser on a Windows 10 device, look under the *Menu* for *Settings* and then *Privacy & Security*.

- For the Safari browser on a macOS device, go to *Preferences* from the Safari menu bar, and click on the *Privacy* tab. For the Safari browser on an iPadOS or iOS device, you'll have to access Safari's *Privacy & Security* from the *Settings* app, not the browser itself.

- For the Chrome browser on an Android device, start within the browser and look under the *Menu* for *Settings* and then *Privacy*.

Snoop alert: Free Wi-Fi poses security risk

Free public Wi-Fi in airports, coffee shops, and hotels is a great thing. These hotspots allow you to connect to the web when you're away from home. But you need to exercise caution when you use them. This is an insecure method of connecting to the internet, meaning criminals in the vicinity can easily hack in.

So what is the one thing you should never do in an airport terminal, cafe, or hotel room? Use public Wi-Fi to perform any type of online transaction — including shopping — where you have to enter sensitive information or financial details. As you are happily shopping away, someone nearby could be stealing your debit or credit card details, giving them access to a spending spree of their own, at your expense.

If they get enough of your account details, it could cost you your life savings. Don't take the chance. Save your shopping for your secure Wi-Fi at home.

Shop online with confidence

Stay in your pajamas and browse hundreds of sites and products. What's not to love about that? It's a great way to shop as long as you're careful. Stay safe from crooks and identity thieves — especially if you use your credit card — with these seven brilliant tips.

- Before you give out your credit card number online, be sure the website address starts with "https," as this indicates it is a secure site. Click or tap in the address bar to see the full website address.

- Also look for a locked padlock icon in the address bar. For web browsers on a desktop computer or a laptop, click on the padlock icon to see security details for the site.

- Be wary of special offers in emails. Check the email address to make sure it's really from the retailer it claims to be. Fraudsters create fake emails with special offers saying they are from online retailers, and hope they'll get your bank and credit card details once you click on the link in the email. Check the retailer's website to see if the offer is listed there.

- Keep your antivirus and firewall software up to date. This is important since online shopping involves giving out sensitive financial details such as your debit or credit card details.

- Get comfortable with certain online retailers and keep to these as much as possible. This way, your debit and credit card details will be distributed to fewer websites.

- Some online criminals create fake shopping sites, and anything you spend on them goes straight into their pockets. In addition to checking for the "https" and lock icon in the web address, avoid fraudulent sites by verifying the full website address. Sometimes these are abbreviated in a browser address bar to just the name of the company. Click or tap in the address bar to view the full website address for the page you are viewing. If it's a fake site, the address will look different from what you may be expecting.

- Create an email address just for online shopping, and never use it for communicating with family and friends. Take advantage of a web-based service, such as Gmail, and use this whenever you register for a new online shopping site. Any emails from the retailer, or anyone else who obtains these details, will go to your shopping email address, rather than your personal one.

Going cashless: Reduce contact, risk, and hassle

Shopping habits were not spared when COVID-19 wreaked havoc on the American landscape. Brick-and-mortar store closures and a desire to avoid public interaction meant online sales hit close to $800 billion in 2020. That was up 32% from the previous year. And this trend is continuing.

What that means to the average shopper is a heightened need for online security. Check out these two options that might allow you to buy with a little less anxiety.

Mobile payment systems. Heard of PayPal? What about Google Pay, Apple Pay, or Samsung Pay? These are examples of digital wallets, sometimes called e-wallets, which let you link a credit card to an app on your smartphone or computer. You then use the app to make a purchase without ever giving the vendor your account details.

The nonprofit Identity Theft Resource Center (ITRC) says digital wallets use two-factor authentication, single-use PIN numbers, and advanced encryption to protect your financial information. But you'll also want to take your own security measures.

- Engage all features on the app and your phone that restrict access — like fingerprint sensors, facial recognition, and passcodes.

- Know how to freeze the digital wallet app or lock your phone remotely if you happen to lose your device.

- Have your smartphone automatically lock after a certain amount of time it's not in use.

Prepaid cards. No need for a credit card or even a bank account when you use a stored value card. You may think of these as gift cards or prepaid debit cards, but they're a convenient and secure way to make purchases online without having to share any financial information.

You can buy prepaid cards at grocery or drug stores, online, over the phone, or from some banks and credit unions. Carefully follow all instructions for registering and activating these cards.

7 secrets to strong and secure passwords

Coming up with a password for every computing device and online account is one of the least enjoyable aspects of the digital world. Add to this the issue of keeping them all safe, and it begins to feel like a real chore.

But help is at hand. The first step is to construct passwords that are as strong as possible, and then ensure they don't fall into the wrong hands. Just remember these tips.

Aim for variety. Make passwords a minimum of eight characters long — preferably more — and use a combination of uppercase and lowercase letters, numbers, and symbols.

Avoid the temptation to choose simple passwords. You may think a simple password is too obvious to guess. Think again. Two of the first options hackers will try are 123456 or PASSWORD. Both are still two of the most common passwords in use.

Don't use easily obtained details. Hackers and identity theft criminals work at obtaining as much information about people as possible. Therefore you should avoid passwords that contain details they could have obtained elsewhere, such as birthdates, pets' names, and favorite sports teams.

Try picking words at random. You can do this from any book or newspaper. Once you have selected words in this way, mix in uppercase and lowercase letters as well as numbers and symbols.

Use a different password for every online account. This may seem like an unnecessary hassle, but it is worth doing. If one online account is hacked, your other ones will be protected as long as they have different passwords.

Change your passwords regularly. This is another chore, but it could ultimately contribute to your online security. Experts recommend you change passwords every 90 days.

Protect your password on a need-to-know basis. Unless you have a very good reason, never share a password with anyone, even family members. Once a password is known to more than one person, it can potentially be shared to a much wider audience.

Password managers are an easy 1-stop solution

Remembering dozens of different passwords can be tiresome and at times frustrating. However, it is possible to never forget an online password again. It's safe, secure, and easy. Just use a password manager.

This is an app for your computer or mobile device to remember all your different passwords. All you need to do is remember one password — the main one for your password manager — and store it in a safe place.

Use your manager to store passwords for any items that require a secure login, such as online banking accounts, social media sites, and subscriptions. Password managers will also offer to create secure passwords when you register for a new site that requires login details.

Many password managers offer a free version with limited options, as well as enhanced versions for a monthly fee. Take a look at these.

1Password	1password.com
Dashlane	dashlane.com
LastPass	lastpass.com

Password manager apps can also be downloaded from the app store for your specific device. Look for them in the Microsoft Store, the Apple App Store, or the Google Play Store.

21 | Emergency planning

"When prosperity comes, do not use all of it."

Confucius

This 1 rule will help you stay out of debt forever

You can't predict the future. But you need to be ready for the worst case scenario. If you're hit with unexpected car or home repairs, the last thing you want to do is turn to high-interest credit cards or loans to bail you out.

"Going into debt is both one of the easiest and worst mistakes that people over the age of 55 can make when presented with an emergency expense," says Georgina Tzanetos, a former financial adviser and current writer for GOBankingRates.

So how can you stay out of debt? "Having an emergency fund is really top priority for seniors," Tzanetos says. She recommends keeping around nine to 12 months' worth of living expenses saved up for a rainy day. That might seem like a lot, but even smaller amounts can help during times of financial stress.

The best place to keep the money? Tzanetos suggests a high-yield savings account so that you can earn interest and get to your funds easily.

Discover these unlikely sources of hidden cash

Don't have enough savings stowed away to handle an emergency expense? Instead of going into debt, you may have cash right under your nose that you can use to pay off medical and other types of bills incurred during a crisis.

Tap into the value of your home to make ends meet. A reverse mortgage — a kind of loan that lets you convert your home equity into cash — can be a good idea for older seniors who aren't spending as much as they used to and are close to or have already paid off their homes.

That's according to Georgina Tzanetos, a finance writer for GOBankingRates, who says reverse mortgages can be a simple way to supplement retirement income. And the best part? "You only owe what you spend," she says. "If you spend $10,000, that's the equity that you've lost and not anything more."

Learn as much as you can about reverse mortgages before signing anything. Go to *apps.hud.gov/offices/hsg/sfh/hcc/hcs.cfm* to find a government-approved housing counseling agency that will help you understand the process.

Consider cashing in on your life insurance policy. If you have universal or whole life insurance, your plan has been accumulating cash for years. And some insurers will let you withdraw those funds early. You can use the money to cover bills, pay off your home, or even invest it to earn more down the road.

However, pulling cash out of your policy could decrease the amount of death benefits your family will get. And it may cause your premiums to go up. Consider this option carefully before you go down this route.

Think before accessing retirement accounts. Consider the tax ramifications and potential long-term damage to your portfolio before you pull any cash out of your retirement savings to cover the costs of an emergency.

But if you're still working, borrowing from your 401(k) might be an option. In most cases you'll have to pay the money back within five years. You can also withdraw contributions from a Roth IRA tax- and penalty-free at any time. But remember, that money will lose the ability to continue growing tax-free. Talk to your financial adviser to find the best strategy for you.

Store 4 vital documents in your safe-deposit box now

Are you ready for a natural disaster? Even if you keep your house stocked with canned food, bottled water, and other survival gear, you may not be as prepared as you think. After all, you want to keep your important documents shielded in case your home gets damaged.

Here's one of the best ways to make sure they're protected. Stow the paperwork in a safe-deposit box. That way you'll be able to recover what you need even if your residence is destroyed. These are the most important things that should be safely stored at the bank.

- An inventory of all the items in your home. You'll need a good record of this info if you have to file an insurance claim.

- Your car title. Replacing a car title is an expensive hassle. Fortunately, you'll rarely need to access this document, so it's perfectly suited for a safe-deposit box.

- Copies of your photo ID. You may need these to apply for assistance from the Federal Emergency Management Agency (FEMA).

- Copies of your medical records. These can help health care professionals determine what medications you take or the type of care you need if your records are lost or destroyed.

Don't have a safe-deposit box? Storing electronic copies of this paperwork on a secure cloud server could provide easy access no matter where you are when disaster strikes. Or you could get a household safe, but experts warn these aren't as secure as a safe-deposit box in a bank.

> A natural disaster might keep you from getting benefit checks in the mail. And you don't want to go days — or even weeks — without that money. Make the switch to electronic deposits so you don't have to worry about receiving payments.

Grab your 'go bag' when disaster strikes

You may need to evacuate your home if a flood, storm, or wild-fire is headed your way. Chances are, you won't have time to pack every little thing you need, so it's important to keep a waterproof "go bag" stocked with these essential items.

- Cash. You may not be able to use ATMs and credit cards during a natural disaster, so it's a good idea to include enough money to cover a few days of food and lodging.

- ID. You should have your passport and a copy of your driver's license ready to go. Don't forget to add a list of your account numbers and passwords.

- Emergency contact info. Keep the phone numbers of family and friends inside the bag.

- Important records. Make sure you have copies of your estate planning documents, insurance policies, and the deed to your house.

22 | Home security

> "The ache for home lives in all of us, the safe place where we can go as we are and not be questioned."
>
> Maya Angelou

DIY security strategies that work

What's a common misconception about home security? "That it can be made foolproof and completely safe," says Lt. Marshall McCoy of the LaGrange Police Department in Georgia. All the same, you can make your home less likely to be targeted. Use these measures that come straight from Lt. McCoy's security inspection checklist to help burglar-proof your home without an alarm.

- Check all entrances. Sliding doors should have a pin or anti-sliding bolt lock, and fence gates should be padlocked shut.

- Create good visibility around the perimeter of your house by turning on outdoor lights at night. Keep shrubbery cut low around windows and doors to eliminate hiding spots for sneaky thieves.

- Going out of town for a few days or even just the night? Put your lights and radio on a timer to give the impression that someone is home.

- Establish a relationship with your neighbors and make a plan to be each other's eyes and ears. Up-to-the-minute residents may encourage you to use popular apps, like Nextdoor or Citizen, that allow users to share and discuss real-time, local crime. The trouble is, these apps can be a hotbed for misinformation, causing more anxiety. So be cautious. Luckily meeting neighbors the old-fashioned way, in person, is still in vogue.

Save bundles with these surveillance system secrets

You may think staying home for longer hours throughout the coronavirus pandemic would have made people less likely to buy home security systems. After all, being away is what exposes your home, right? But for some people, the extra home time revealed the importance of keeping their houses safe around-the-clock. If your perspective has changed, too, keep reading to discover inexpensive ways to beef up your security.

Find the features that fit you. Security systems can be dressed to the nines with expensive add-ons. But you don't have to shell out big bucks to be safe. Instead of buying everything offered, pick out only the features you need.

For instance, do you want professional monitoring? This is where a trained team keeps tabs on your system for emergencies. It's pricier than self-monitoring because of its monthly service fee, but you won't have to worry about missing a critical alert. If you go this route, ask whether you or the authorities are contacted first after an alarm goes off and if there are penalties for contract breaks. Contact your local police and fire departments to ask if you need to register with them and if there's a fine for false alarms.

Installing cameras? Don't waste money on cheap but dodgy models. Their poor image quality won't be useful. And when it comes to installation, you can cut costs by doing it yourself. Plus you can save by starting small with a few sensors or cameras and expanding later if you need to.

Don't pay full price for your services. You don't have to pay full price for a security system if you're a savvy shopper. Providers like SimpliSafe and ADT run discount sales from time to time, so keep an eye out during shopper-friendly holidays like Black Friday and Memorial Day weekend. You may be able to get a discount as a senior or veteran, too. Check for programs run through AARP or Veterans Advantage.

Offset the cost of home upgrades with surprising rollbacks. Many insurance companies will reward you when you install a home security system. Depending on the comprehensiveness of the monitoring, those savings could be as much as 20% off your normal homeowners insurance bill. This deal may be called a protective device discount.

And that's not the only money saver. If your security controls come with home automation tools like programmable lighting and temperature you can use them to lower your energy bill.

Simple ways to keep your valuables safe without a safe

More than 1 million. That's how many burglaries the FBI reported in a recent year. Avoid becoming another statistic by using these four hiding places a burglar would never think to look.

- Garage boxes. Label these boxes with mundane names like "School Projects" or "Old Clothes." Having many boxes means someone who breaks in will have to waste time searching for anything of value.

- False outlet. Regular safes are good, but you can make certain valuables like cash or jewelry even tougher to find by storing them in a small safe behind a fake wall outlet.

- Behind drawers. Don't leave valuables in your drawers. Hide them in the space behind them. Typical drawers don't go all the way to the back of a cabinet, which gives you room to tape an envelope of important documents to the back of the drawer and slide it out of view.

- Hollowed-out books. If you already have shelves upon shelves of books, slipping in a false volume won't tip off a thief. You can buy fake books that open to hide your goods, or make one yourself.

Resist concealing items in places a burglar is sure to check. The master bedroom, for example, is a hot spot for expensive goods, so never hide your valuables under your mattress. Avoid your bathroom, too. Not only can your possessions get water damage, but toilet tanks and medicine cabinets aren't beyond a thief's gaze. Skip your sock drawer, which is prime real estate for a thief. Plus valuables you leave out in plain view are easy pickings.

Sound the alarm on shifty sales schemes

The last thing you want when upgrading your home security is to fall for a scam. So if you're shopping online, search for provider names along with words like "scam" and "complaint" to see how users rate their experience.

Sometimes companies send employees door to door to pitch their systems. But watch out for scammers imitating legitimate salespeople. If you already have a security system, they may claim they're installing upgrades or that your company's been bought out and you need to sign a new contract. Always be wary of pushy people who warn of a supposed spree of burglaries nearby or advertise limited-time deals that have hidden strings attached.

More resources

American Institute of Certified Public Accountants	360financialliteracy.org/Topics/In-Crisis	N/A
Better Business Bureau Scam Tracker	bbb.org/scamtracker	N/A
Consumer Financial Protection Bureau	consumerfinance.gov/consumer-tools/fraud	855-411-2372
Facebook	facebook.com/privacy	N/A
Federal Emergency Management Agency (FEMA)	fema.gov	202-646-2500
Federal Trade Commission (FTC), ID Theft	identitytheft.gov	N/A
FEMA, Ready Campaign	ready.gov/financial-preparedness	N/A
FTC, Consumer Info	consumer.ftc.gov	N/A
Have I Been Pwned	haveibeenpwned.com	N/A
Identity Theft Resource Center	idtheftcenter.org	888-400-5530
National Consumers League	fraud.org	202-835-3323
National Council for Home Safety and Security	alarms.org	N/A
National Insurance Crime Bureau	nicb.org	800-447-6282
OptOutPrescreen.com	optoutprescreen.com	888-567-8688
Privacy Rights Clearinghouse	privacyrights.org	N/A
SafeHome.org	safehome.org	877-297-8021
Security.org	security.org	866-204-0310

HEALTHY LIVING

Get the right care at the right price

23 | Medicare

> "Healthy citizens are the greatest asset any country can have."
>
> Winston Churchill

Hot tips to shrink your Medigap premiums

Finally signing up for Medicare can feel like a huge weight has been lifted from your shoulders. However, the frightening reality is that standard Part A hospital insurance and Part B medical insurance don't actually pay for all of your health care costs. Don't get left in the lurch. You can fill in the holes with Medicare supplement insurance, called Medigap.

This type of private insurance policy swoops in after Medicare pays its share and will help cover remaining expenses like copays, coinsurance, and deductibles. So if you spend a lot on out-of-pocket costs, a Medigap plan may be right for you. Some polices even cover services not offered under Medicare, like health care if you're traveling outside the U.S.

To get these benefits, you have to pay an extra premium each month to the private insurance company of your choosing on top of the Part B premium that goes to Medicare. Use the following tips to save on those Medigap charges.

- Different plans may offer the same coverage but have widely different costs. Visit *medicare.gov/medigap-supplemental-insurance-plans* and use the policy comparison tool to find the best deal.

- Consider switching Medigap policies if your current one isn't working well for you. If you're still healthy and shortly past your 65th birthday, it may pay to change it up.

- See if you qualify for a household discount. For instance, you and your spouse might sign up for Medigap with the same company and get rewarded with a 5% discount.

- Opt for a highly rated insurance company without a big name. Same coverage, lower price.

Save on Medicare with 4 fantastic pointers

"Unaffordable care isn't just bad for someone's wallet, it's bad for their health," says Dr. John W. Scott, a health policy analyst and trauma surgeon. Fortunately, with these four tips you can keep more money in your pocket.

Get a helping hand. You can get assistance paying for your Medicare Part D prescription drug coverage through Extra Help. This program is available to people who have limited resources and income, and more than 2 million seniors qualify but don't take advantage of it. The Extra Help program is estimated to be worth about $5,000 a year and can help cover your monthly premiums, annual deductibles, and copayments.

Find out if you qualify and apply online for free at *https://secure.ssa.gov/i1020/start*. You automatically qualify and don't need to apply if you have full Medicaid coverage, you're on Supplemental Security Income (SSI), or your Medicare premiums are paid for by a state program.

If you participate in Extra Help, you also won't have to pay a late penalty if you don't enroll in a Medicare prescription drug plan when you're first eligible.

Your state could slow your spending. Some states offer assistance with paying Medicare deductibles and coinsurance for people with low incomes through a Medicare Savings Program. Call your local Medicaid office to find out if your state has one of these programs. Contact information is available at *medicaid.gov/about-us/ contact-us/index.html*.

Pay for the plan you need. "Making sure that you're still on the best plan for you, that's another good way to make sure you're getting the best possible use of your benefits," says Caitlin Donovan, senior director of the Patient Advocate Foundation.

You have options when it comes to your Medicare Advantage and Part D plans, so don't settle and pay for features you don't need. Use the Medicare Plan Finder at *medicare.gov/plan-compare* to compare choices.

Update your financial status. High earners are subject to a law that adjusts monthly premiums for Medicare parts B and D. In 2022, for example, single people with an income over $91,000 or a couple with an income above $182,000 saw higher premiums.

However, those costs could be lowered if your income has recently gone down due to a major life-changing event, like the loss of a spouse, a change in work status, or a significant adjustment in a pension plan. Make a request using Form SSA-44 from the Social Security Administration and provide documentation that verifies the event.

Increase your Social Security payments with this popular plan

Medicare Advantage plans are swiftly becoming a top choice among retirees to cover medical costs outside of Medicare's standard plan. After all, they often have cheaper premiums than Medigap, and they may cover services like eye care and dentistry.

Plus some Medicare Advantage plans come with a feature that can increase your Social Security payments.

Yes, you read that right. This benefit is known as the Medicare Part B giveback, or premium reduction. It does exactly what it sounds like — pays some or all of your Part B premium. And its popularity is making it newly available in some areas.

This is how you cash in. Part B premiums are usually subtracted from your Social Security benefits. Since the giveback reduces your Medicare Part B premium, less money is drawn out of your Social Security check. That means you receive a fatter check each month.

So who can take advantage of this offer? First, you must be enrolled in both Medicare parts A and B. And you only qualify if you pay your own Part B premium, meaning government assistance — like Medicaid or Medicare Savings Plans — can't be pitching in. Keep in mind givebacks aren't available with every plan or in all areas.

Depending on your plan's rules, the value of the giveback could be up to the full standard Part B premium amount, which was $170.10 a month in 2022. But when deciding if a Medicare Advantage plan is right for you, don't let these potential savings distract you from other important features, like if it covers your medication costs and if your preferred doctors are in-network.

Don't let medical fraudsters fake you out

When's high season for Medicare fraud? During the open enrollment period, from Oct. 15 to Dec. 7. Still, you need to keep an eye out for scams all year long.

Start by double-checking all of your receipts and statements for services you've never received.

Calls from Medicare are rare, so be on guard if you get a ring from a supposed representative. Scammers may call you and pretend they want to verify your identity to update your Medicare card. They may also offer free medical supplies or claim you qualify for a refund. Be wary. They're after your Medicare number or other sensitive details.

Only give personal information to doctors or someone you trust who's working on your behalf. You may also hear from a legitimate representative if you're a member of their plan already or you called for assistance.

To report fraud, call 800-633-4227 and be prepared to share details about the service you're questioning.

The exception that lets you delay Medicare without penalty

Arlene is turning 65 next year. Normally, someone her age would be planning their transition to Medicare. However, Arlene hasn't retired yet. In fact, she's expecting to stay at her current job for another five years and would like to delay Medicare and stay on her company's insurance instead.

You usually have a seven-month window to first apply for Medicare that opens three months before the month you turn 65.

And unless you're already receiving Social Security benefits, which will automatically enroll you, you have to sign yourself up. Enrolling for Medicare late typically dings your payout with a penalty that will continue for the rest of your life.

Arlene is the exception. As long as she enrolls in Medicare within eight months of her retirement, she won't face the steep penalty. Using COBRA after her retirement wouldn't change this eight-month timeline, though. The countdown starts when you stop working or your employer coverage ends — whichever happens first — regardless of other insurance coverage.

Two reasons you may want to delay Medicare are because you like your health insurance coverage through your job or you want to keep contributing to your health savings account (HSA). Medicare is not a high-deductible insurance plan. That means when you enroll, you no longer qualify to add funds to an HSA. However, you can withdraw funds already in your HSA after enrolling in Medicare to help cover the cost of deductibles, premiums, copayments, or coinsurance.

> Medicare is typically reserved for people 65 and older, but you may qualify earlier if you're disabled. In most cases, someone who is age 20 or older and has been receiving Social Security disability benefits for 24 months is eligible for Medicare. You'll receive notice three months in advance with an information package and your Medicare card. Then, at the start of your 25th month, you should be automatically enrolled in Medicare parts A and B.

Be sure to carefully read all the rules about delaying Medicare and your specific circumstances before making any decisions. You don't want an accidental late-enrollment penalty to mar your Medicare premiums for as long as you have coverage. A 10% increase for each 12-month period you were eligible for Part B but didn't sign up — that adds up.

24 | Medicaid

"The test of our progress is not whether we add more to the abundance of those who have much; it is whether we provide enough for those who have too little."

Franklin D. Roosevelt

Plan for the costs of care without breaking the bank

Medicaid programs require you to meet strict income limits before benefits will kick in. That may mean spending down tens — or even hundreds — of thousands in savings before you can qualify for care.

And if you spend all your savings, your spouse and loved ones may be left without enough to live on. Plus even if you do spend down the right way, an overlooked error during the application process could ruin your chances of qualifying. With a little bit of know-how, you may be able to protect your money and still get the care you need. Track down a Medicaid planning professional for help with the nitty-gritty. Here's how to find reduced-cost, or free, assistance.

- Geriatric care managers. Also called life care managers, these professionals prepare seniors for all aspects of elder care. Many — but not all — can help you plan for the financial impacts, too. This service is often cheaper than an attorney or a financial planner, but may not offer the same level of legal and financial assistance.

- Local area agency on aging (AAA) advisers. AAA offices are often staffed with counselors who offer free advice on navigating the nuances of qualifying and will help you start an application. However, they won't offer counseling if you're well over the income limits for Medicaid. To find your local AAA, go online to *eldercare.acl.gov* and search for your ZIP code or city and state.

- State Health Insurance Assistance Program (SHIP) counselors. These volunteers are trained to help people make informed Medicare and Medicaid decisions. They can provide some advice on completing applications and the criteria you need to meet before getting Medicaid, though they may not be able to offer assistance on how to qualify. To find your state's SHIP program, go online to *shiphelp.org* and click *Find Local Medicare Help*. Or call 877-839-2675 and say "Medicare" when prompted.

Use a lady bird deed to avoid this common Medicaid mishap

After someone on Medicaid passes away, the government will come after their estate to recoup the costs of health care. And that often means making a claim against their home.

If you want to leave your house to your children, you might be tempted to give it to them before you apply for benefits. But that can violate the look-back period and prevent you from qualifying for coverage.

However, people who live in certain states may be able to get something called a lady bird deed. This could allow your home to pass to your loved ones without going through probate, which means Medicaid can't collect reimbursement from it.

Lady bird deeds are generally inexpensive to set up, though not all states allow for them. Consult with a Medicaid planner or attorney if you're interested in creating one.

Denied coverage? These 2 tricks may help you get the care you need

Around 1 out of every 4 Medicaid determination letters contain errors made by the people who review applications, reports the American Council on Aging. And in some cases, these mistakes may be enough to keep you from getting benefits. If you are denied, don't give up.

- Start by requesting a reversal. If you believe that a simple mistake — like a missing bit of paperwork — is the reason your Medicaid claim was denied, write an email or make a phone call to the caseworker in charge of your file and point out the problem. Fixing the error may be all it takes to get the application properly processed.

- Submit a formal appeal. Wrongfully denied and can't get the office to reverse the decision? You will have to go through a hearing with a judge to sort it out. Consider reaching out to an attorney or a Medicaid planner to help you prepare for the process. You typically have 90 days or less to submit an appeal after being denied benefits. If possible, file the paperwork in person and have it date-stamped.

Don't toss out any of your medical bills while you're waiting on a ruling. If your appeal is successful, the benefits will be applied retroactively so you can recoup any cash you spent out of pocket.

Relocation considerations: 4 moves boost your chances of approval

Every state runs its own Medicaid program, so the rules for eligibility and levels of care differ depending on where you live. That's why some people who aren't able to get benefits in their hometown move to another state to qualify for coverage. But simply relocating isn't a guarantee that you'll be able to get on Medicaid. Here's what you need to know before you make a major move.

Consider your retirement accounts. Some states will count your IRA in their asset calculations, while others won't. That means moving could help you preserve a big chunk of your nest egg. Take a look at the local rules regarding IRAs and other retirement accounts when you weigh the benefits of a move.

Make a plan to establish residency. You can't apply for Medicaid in a new state before you're officially a resident. The good news? There are no rules for how long you have to live in the new state before you start the process. You need to be in your new home, living with a family member, or in a nursing home in order to submit an application.

Don't forget about your spouse. Some states allow a husband or wife to keep a certain amount of joint assets without affecting the applicant's eligibility. Carefully examine the rules regarding community spouse resource allowances before making any moves.

Account for the cost of your home. If you still live in your house, Medicaid won't consider it an asset. But if you move to a new state without selling it? The value of that property might just keep you from receiving benefits. Similarly, money from the sale of your home could jeopardize your ability to qualify for Medicaid. Whether it's buying a home in the new state or paying off debt, determine what you'll do with the windfall ahead of time.

25 | Prescriptions

> "The aim of medicine is to prevent disease and prolong life; the ideal of medicine is to eliminate the need of a physician."
>
> William J. Mayo

Save up to 80% with these free discount cards

Whether or not you have medical coverage, prescription medications can be pricey. If you need extra help paying for them, getting a prescription discount card is an easy way to save. These cards generally come at no cost to you, and the markdowns can be massive. In fact, SingleCare, GoodRx, ScriptSave WellRx, and Blink Health all have prescription discount card programs that boast a savings of up to 80%.

Score these deep discounts by going to the website or mobile app for your preferred program. Just search for the drug you need and then compare prices at pharmacies in your area to find a coupon card that gives you the best price. When you go to the pharmacy, simply show them the coupon card for instant savings.

For example, if you're uninsured, the average cost of Lisinopril is around $146 for a thousand 10-milligram tablets. With SingleCare, though, the price of that same blood pressure medication drops to just $4 at certain pharmacies. Obviously, the difference between applying the discount or using your insurance coverage will vary. So compare your copay with the discount value and use whichever one gives you the lowest price tag.

And look into other perks offered by discount card companies. Sign up for the Members Savings program with Single-Care, for instance, and you'll get $5 off your first prescription. Plus you'll earn an extra buck toward your medications each time you fill one after that. The best news — this program is totally free.

The Patient Advocate Foundation offers a copay relief program that can help pay for prescriptions and treatments, even if you're on Medicare. Visit *copays.org* to see if you qualify for assistance and apply for a fund that fits your needs.

Watch out for coupon-clipping limitations

Medicare and coupons are two great ways to push down your prescription costs. Unfortunately though, you can't double dip.

A law called the Anti-Kickback Statute makes it illegal for someone to use Medicare coverage and a manufacturer coupon or other drug discount at the same time. So you'll have to choose to use one or the other.

Using a discount from the manufacturer or pharmacy may make sense for you if the cost is cheaper than it is through Medicare. But always consider the long-term impact. You may think that these coupons mean you'll never need Medicare Part D to help with prescription drug payments. However, your coupon may have a limited number of uses or expire down the road. Plus you could face a penalty if you later decide to re-enroll in Part D.

1 simple step to low-cost — or free — prescriptions

Free prescription drugs sound too good to be true, but you can do just one simple thing and get free, or at least greatly reduced, medications.

Join a Patient Assistance Program (PAP), and you may be able to get prescriptions at a fraction of their original price, or for free, depending on your circumstances. These are programs run by pharmaceutical companies, aimed at helping people who can't afford the full price of prescriptions.

Here are a few ways to track down one of these programs in a jiffy.

- Check Medicare's directory of pharmaceutical assistance programs at *medicare.gov/pharmaceutical-assistance-program*.

- Use a search engine like Google. Type the name of your medication into the search field along with the phrase "assistance program."

- Call the medication manufacturer and ask them if they have an assistance program and how to qualify.

- Locate financial assistance resources at webites like *rxassist.org* and *medicineassistancetool.org*. In addition, savings finder websites like *goodrx.com* and *needymeds.org* provide info about PAPs when you search by medication.

Rx rollbacks seniors only get if they ask

Has your doctor just prescribed a new medication? Or maybe one you're already taking is becoming too pricey for your budget. "The best thing you can do if you're worried about your finances is to actually talk to your doctor about it," says Caitlin Donovan, senior director of the Patient Advocate Foundation.

That's why she recommends doing a prescription audit with your physician or pharmacist every year to assess your current medications and their cost. During the meeting, ask these questions to discover discounts you may have missed.

Is there a generic equivalent to my current medication that's cheaper? Brand-name drugs and generics are equally effective at treating your condition because they contain the same active ingredients. So before paying for a medication because of the familiar name, see if you can find a cheaper generic option. Just make sure it doesn't contain extra active ingredients or allergens that may affect you.

Are all of my current medications still necessary? Check in with your doctor about your medication regimen. Maybe a lifestyle change will mean you can lower your dose of a prescription. Or perhaps a newly prescribed drug does the same job as one you're already taking.

Is there a similar but less expensive prescription that my insurance covers? Sometimes your insurance won't cover the exact medication your doctor prescribes but will pay for a similar one. Ask your insurance provider for a drug formulary to see all the medications it covers. Then you can work with your doctor to find what combination of drugs will work best for both your health and wallet.

Can I buy this medication in bulk to save? If you regularly take a medication, buying it in a 90-day supply rather than a 30-day supply could save you money. However, you don't want to make any changes that will affect your dosage. Always consult your doctor before trying something like pill splitting, says Donovan.

Do you offer free samples of my medication? Pharmaceutical companies may give your doctor free samples of their prescription drugs, which means virtually every brand name could be available. These freebies can offer short-term savings if you simply ask your doctor for them.

What is the cash price of this medication? "People may not realize that you may pay more for your prescriptions at the counter through your insurance than if you paid in cash," says Donovan.

It doesn't hurt to ask your pharmacist what the cash price of your prescription is. If you're concerned your prescription will cost more than you can afford, you can avoid discomfort by calling your pharmacy or insurer ahead of time.

Get the benefits you deserve — for free

No one likes paying taxes, but when you do, it's nice to think you'll get something back. The good news is you can. The taxes you paid get you free info and assistance with prescriptions, rent, food, utilities, Social Security, veterans benefits, and more. Even taxes.

Simply pay a visit to the website *benefitscheckup.org*. It is run by the National Council on Aging and is a treasure trove of information just for seniors about benefits programs throughout the United States. The best news? There could be as many as 50 to 70 government programs for seniors in your state alone.

To find out what specific benefits are available in your area, enter your ZIP code into the box on the homepage, and click or tap on the *Get Started* button. There is also an online live chat option you can use for queries and information.

After looking through all the great information on this site, you may start to think your taxes have been a good investment for retirement after all.

Steps to take if your insurance drops your drug

Each year pharmacy benefit managers (PBMs) work on behalf of insurers to develop and maintain formularies, lists of drugs your insurance covers. What if your prescription doesn't make the cut? It happens all the time. In fact, in 2021 two of the major PBMs dropped nearly 200 medications from their formularies. And many people didn't even get a warning. If you find yourself at the pharmacy counter with a prescription that's not covered, don't panic.

Make sure your pharmacist has your current insurance information. If you've transferred your prescription to a new pharmacy, double-check that another pharmacy doesn't have a duplicate prescription. Also see if the pharmacy is in-network. Some plans may actually require you to fill your prescription through a mail-order pharmacy, so confirm whether or not that applies to you.

If those moves don't clear things up, try these steps to get your insurer to reconsider.

- Request an exception. Asking your doctor to work on your behalf is your best shot. That's because you have to prove that the medication is medically necessary and that the alternate drugs your insurance covers will be less effective or possibly harmful.

- File a formal appeal to the insurance company if your request for an exception is denied. If that fails then move on to an external review board. In both cases, your doctor should be leading with more details about your medical history and other research that may bolster your case.

- If you have to appeal further, consider hiring a patient advocate. Though working with one of these professionals may be expensive upfront, they're trained to help you navigate the appeals process and could save you thousands in prescription costs.

Have Medicare? The appeals process has five levels. Learn more about each stage at *medicare.gov/medicare-prescription-drug-coverage-appeals*.

Website review — 4 things you must check before buying pills online

Only 3% of online pharmacies reviewed by the National Association of Boards of Pharmacy (NABP) meet U.S. standards. Yikes. Can you tell the difference between an upstanding online pharmacy and a dud? Here's a hint — you need to scour the pharmacy's website for these dead giveaways.

- Look for the NABP's Verified Internet Pharmacy Practice Sites (VIPPS) seal. This accreditation means the pharmacy meets certain quality and safety requirements. You can also go to *nabp.pharmacy/programs/vipps* and click "Accredited Digital Pharmacies" to access the list of approved pharmacies.

- Scan the website to see if they have a U.S. state-licensed pharmacist on staff. Safe online pharmacies will have one available to answer your questions.

- Make sure they require a valid prescription from your doctor. If the site claims you don't need one, say adieu.

- Verify that they're based in the U.S. by looking for a street address. Beware of providers located outside of the U.S. These pharmacies can be dangerous. They may send you drugs with different active ingredients that can have harmful side effects or interactions with your other medications.

Once you find a reputable pharmacy, you've hit the jackpot. Ordering your prescriptions online can be cheaper and more convenient.

26 | Supplements

> "The art of healing comes from nature, not from the physician. Therefore the physician must start from nature, with an open mind."
>
> Paracelsus

Pick the perfect supplements without paying top dollar

Trendy subscription services will deliver personalized boxes of vitamins and minerals right to your doorstep. While these convenient supplements can be tailored to suit your dietary needs, the cost may leave you shaking your head. There is one thing these services got right, though. It may be time to ditch the tired old multivitamins and go with a customized regimen.

"An easy way to save money on supplements is to buy only what you really need," says Carol Haggans, a scientific and health communications consultant at the Office of Dietary Supplements, part of the National Institutes of Health.

After all, if you follow a healthy diet, chances are you're already getting most of the vitamins and minerals that come in a multivitamin. And even if you do have gaps in your diet, a multivitamin isn't a guaranteed way to fill them.

"Some seniors, for example, might benefit from a supplement containing vitamin B12 or vitamin D, while others might not need any supplements," says Haggans.

And that's where your doctor comes in. "Talking with your health care provider is the best way to get specific advice," Haggans says.

Medical professionals can run simple tests to make sure you're not running low on any important nutrients. As an added bonus, if your doctor does decide you need to take a supplement, you can get a note that will let you use the funds in a health savings account (HSA) to buy them.

4 shopping mistakes that squander your savings

Liquid minerals, microbead vitamins, bite-sized super-food squares — supplements sure have received a makeover in recent years. Product makers claim these forms are easier for your body to use, but the only thing you'll find strong evidence of is the high price tag.

Instead of buying into marketing buzzwords, focus on quality, cost, and what works best for you. Start by avoiding these four shopping blunders.

Ignoring trustworthy seals of approval. Medications have to go through rigorous tests before they can get approval to be sold at stores. Unfortunately, the same isn't true for dietary supplements. That means the vitamins and minerals you see at the store may not necessarily have all the advertised ingredients.

However, independent agencies, like U.S. Pharmacopeia and NSF International, certify supplements that pass their quality tests. So you can be sure that what's on the label is in the bottle. Look for the USP Verified and NSF mark on supplement labels.

Buying brand names. Instead of reaching for high-priced, brand-name vitamins and minerals, see if the store offers cheaper generic supplements. They may be just as effective as the more expensive options. If you're switching from a pricier brand name, verify that the new supplement contains the same ingredients and amounts per serving.

Not buying in bulk. Don't forget to consider the per-unit cost when you purchase supplements. You may find that buying a bottle of 100 or more vitamins will actually be more cost-effective than a bottle with only 30 pills. But you need to make sure you'll actually use the whole bottle before it expires. Otherwise, you may be wasting cash on pills you'll never use.

Wasting money on megadoses. You might think that the more nutrients you can pack into a pill, the better. But that's not the case. Taking too much of certain vitamins can actually be harmful in some cases. Keep your vitamin and mineral intake within the daily recommended value, unless a doctor tells you otherwise.

What to know before you buy supplements online

Online shopping is a great way to score bargains. But if you can't go to the shops and look at things before you buy them, you take a chance of getting something that doesn't live up to your expectations.

A too-small shirt or pants that don't fit quite right are no big deal. But if you buy vitamins and minerals that don't deliver on their promises, you could be wasting cash on fake — and even dangerous — supplements.

Fortunately, you can use the National Institutes of Health's recently updated online database to research supplements before you buy.

"These upgrades mean health care professionals, researchers, consumers, and others will not only have an easier time finding what they're looking for, they'll find it in the formats they need, which is particularly important when you're trying to answer questions about dietary supplements and their ingredients," says Emily Connor, lead on the database redesign.

To use this resource, go online to *dsld.od.nih.gov* and search by product name, ingredient, dietary claim, or any other term on the supplement label.

Once you zero in on a brand, it's time to narrow down the best place to buy it. Stick with websites you trust, and avoid those that claim to have supplements for next-to-nothing. Also comb through the site for the storage, shipping, and return policies.

 Never buy these 5 things at the dollar store

Heading to the dollar store to shop for supplements and over-the-counter meds? Hold your horses. You might be saving a little money, but it could come at the cost of your health. Experts say these meds and supplements may be ineffective and out of date at best, and in some cases, they could be tainted with dangerous chemicals.

And those aren't the only two things you should avoid getting from the bargain bin. Don't buy these products at the dollar store either.

- Sunscreen. The bargain store brands of sunscreen may not offer as much protection as they advertise.

- Batteries. Dollar stores often scoop up old batteries that other retailers won't carry anymore.

- Plastics. Dollar store plastic products may contain high levels of phthalate, a poisonous chemical that can lead to liver and kidney damage.

27 | Doctor visits

> "I wonder why you can always read a doctor's bill and you can never read his prescription."
>
> Finley Peter Dunne

The right questions could save you hundreds at the doctor's office

A recent study revealed that Americans owe an eye-popping $140 billion in unpaid medical bills. If you had that much cash in dollar bills, you could build a stack stretching over 9,500 miles through the sky and into outer space.

It's no wonder people will go to extreme lengths to save money on health care. A recent survey shows that nearly 1 out of every 3 Americans skip medical care, including trips to the doctor, because the cost is too steep. Instead of putting your health at risk by missing important tests, procedures, and checkups, ask your doctor these questions to avoid sky-high medical bills.

- "Do I really need this procedure?" If your doctor recommends a medical procedure and you're concerned about the cost, ask about alternatives plus the pros and cons of each option. And don't be afraid to ask more than one doctor.

"Getting a second opinion is always worthwhile, especially for a very complex procedure," says Caitlin Donovan, senior director of the Patient Advocate Foundation.

- "Are there any wellness programs I can try instead?" Making simple tweaks to your lifestyle — like starting a different diet or regularly exercising — may help you manage chronic conditions without the help of costly treatments or expensive drugs. Ask the doctor what options are available to you.

Protect your pearly whites without spending a pretty penny

A healthy mouth and a healthy body go hand in hand. But chronic conditions like diabetes, as well as certain prescription medications, can increase your risk of cavities, gum disease, and other dental problems.

That means getting routine care is crucial. The only problem? Medicare won't cover regular cleanings, fillings, or other dental procedures. You'll have to pay 100% of the costs out of pocket. And if you're on a fixed income, those bills can add up.

Luckily if you know where to look, you can get fillings, dentures, implants, cleanings, and more at a reduce cost — or even free. And the best place to get dental care you can afford? The little-known Health Center Program funded by a government agency called the Health Resources and Services Administration (HRSA). HRSA-backed health centers provide services on a sliding fee scale. In some situations, you may be able to get treatment without paying a single dime.

To find an HRSA clinic near you, go online to *findahealthcenter. hrsa.gov*. Be sure to carefully read about the services and procedures offered before you make the trip. Not all clinics provide the same perks.

Don't have a free clinic near you that has the services you need? Consider visiting a dental school. They often offer highly discounted, or even free, dental care so that the students can gain experience. Licensed dentists watch the procedures carefully to make sure they're done correctly.

Virtual visits save big bucks — here's how to make the most of them

Virtual doctor visits may sound like something out of a science fiction movie, but more and more people are using their computers instead of going to their physician's office. The reason? Telehealth visits are convenient, easy, and — most importantly — a great way to save money. Some experts estimate the average online visit costs less than $50, while a trip to an urgent care facility for the same problem would ring at $130.

And in the wake of the coronavirus pandemic, more doctor's offices are offering telehealth options. If you're new to this tech, you'll want to use these handy tips and tricks to make sure you get your money's worth from each visit.

Set up before your appointment. When you visit the doctor for a face-to-face appointment, you probably won't have to worry about background noise or computer troubles. But that's not true for virtual visits. Find a quiet, comfortable place where you can sit and talk to your doctor without worrying about being overheard. And you'll need to be able to clearly hear the doctor while they're speaking.

In addition, test your tech out ahead of time. You don't want to miss the meeting because your computer has to update or your camera isn't working. If you need help troubleshooting, consult a tech-savvy friend or family member a few hours before the appointment.

Come prepared with questions and concerns. "The most common mistake I see is that patients underestimate their complaint or their concern with the doctor," says Dr. John Berdahl, an ophthalmologist and partner at Vance Thompson Vision.

What does he suggest? Write down your concern, along with a list of questions you have for your doctor, before the appointment. "That way you won't minimize it when the time comes," he says. As a bonus, the list will help you remember your questions if the new tech experience gets you frazzled.

"Good questions to ask a doctor are anything you're worried about," says Berdahl. But when it comes to virtual visits, don't forget to make this all-important inquiry first — how you should reach the doc if you have tech troubles during the visit.

Consider looping in a friendly face. You may normally want to bring a friend or family member to your doctor's office so they can help you take notes, remember certain concerns, or interpret information from the doctor. With virtual visits, you may be able to loop these people in, no matter where they are in the world.

Before your appointment, ask if your telehealth visit can be a three-way video or phone call so that someone else can attend.

The award-winning program that offers free vision care

As you age, your eyes become more and more prone to problems. The good news? Medicare covers annual glaucoma screenings, yearly diabetic retinopathy exams, and certain macular degeneration treatments for qualified seniors. The bad news? Any vision care — like routine exams for eyeglasses — has to come out of your own pocket.

If you can't afford medical eye exams, check out EyeCare America. "That's a program to help make sure that patients and especially seniors who haven't had access to good eye care can still get it," says Dr. John Berdahl, an ophthalmologist and chair of the EyeCare America Seniors Program at the American Academy of Ophthalmology.

The Seniors Program offers free eye exams to adults age 65 and older who haven't seen an ophthalmologist in the past three years. And it will help with up to a year's worth of follow-up care for any conditions that are diagnosed during the visit.

To see if you can take advantage of the program and to find a participating ophthalmologist near you, go online to *aao.org/eyecare-america*, click on the button labeled *Patients: See If You Qualify*, and follow the prompts on the screen. You can also call 877-887-6327 for more information on the program.

3 timely tips to fend off telehealth fraud

More and more doctor's offices are offering telehealth visits. And scammers have taken notice. In fact, in the largest health care fraud takedown in history, the Department of Justice recently identified $4.5 billion in losses related to telemedicine schemes.

So how can you protect your wallet — and other important medical information — from scammers?

- Watch out for health care providers you don't know offering to set up an appointment for you. They may

call or send you an email confirmation for a supposed upcoming virtual visit, but it's actually a scam
designed to trick you into sharing personal info.

- Keep your devices and telehealth apps up to date to
patch up security loopholes.

- Check with your insurance before the virtual
appointment so you're clear on what's covered.
Then review your bill afterward for unusual charges,
like a fee for a half-hour visit if you booked a 15-
minute session.

Can't drive? This may be the next best way to get to the doctor's office

More than 600,000 seniors age 70 and up stop driving every year,
according to an estimate published by the American Public Health
Association. And if you've hung up your car keys for good, you
may find it tough to get to doctor appointments. You could end
up shelling out big bucks on a cab if loved ones aren't available to
drive you. Or you may just skip the appointment altogether.

The bright side — nonemergency medical transportation services
could help you get where you need to go. If you're on Medicaid,
your state may offer free rides to your appointments. It may
cover a taxi ride, send a shuttle, or reimburse you for ride-sharing
services like Lyft or Uber. Even if you're not on Medicaid, certain
Medicare Advantage plans offer this benefit. Check with your
insurance provider to see if this option is available to you.

You can also look for a mobility manager who can help you navigate your transportation options. Reach out to your local area on
aging, public transit authority, or center for independent living
to see if they can connect you with someone who will help you
get around town.

28 | Hospital bills

> "A hospital should also have a recovery room adjoining the cashier's office."
>
> Francis O'Walsh

No one can afford not to know this tip about free health care

Imagine getting 50%, 75%, or even 100% off your hospital bill. Thousands of Americans get all their medications, checkups, and other health services absolutely free — without insurance or Medicare. You can thank the Health Resources and Services Administration (HRSA) for that. It's a federal agency responsible for working with medical providers to make affordable health care more available.

The HRSA's Hill-Burton program is one way you may be able to receive assistance for hospital services that are not covered by Medicare, Medicaid, or a third-party insurer. People with an income at or below the federal poverty level could be eligible for free care. Reduced-cost care may be available for people whose incomes are as much as twice the poverty guidelines.

You may apply before or after receiving care, even after a bill has been sent to collections. Visit *hrsa.gov/get-health-care/affordable/ hill-burton/facilities.html* to find a participating facility, and then apply at the admissions or business office. Always call in advance to make sure the facility you have in mind still has funding and covers the service you need.

Elevate your negotiating skills to lower your hospital bills

Medical expenses can weigh down your life and wallet, but you have the power to reduce how much you owe. Use this advice to negotiate your hospital bills so health-saving treatment doesn't turn into life-crushing debt.

Compare the bill to your benefits. "Any time you get a bill, the first thing you should do is not pay it," says Caitlin Donovan, the senior director of the Patient Advocate Foundation. That's because mistakes are incredibly common on hospital bills and almost never end in your favor.

Bills from medical providers may also arrive before they've been run through your insurance. So instead of forking over your cash as soon as you receive a hospital bill, wait until your explanation of benefits (EOB) arrives. An EOB is like a receipt, not a bill, which documents the care you received and how much you were charged.

Getting your EOB is a sign the bill has been processed by your insurance. You can then compare the amount your bill says you owe to your EOB. If there's a difference, call your insurer to discuss the mistake.

Set your spending limit. Before you call the hospital billing office to negotiate, Donovan advises figuring out what you can afford to pay upfront or on a monthly payment plan. In your negotiations you want to lower your total bill and choose an approachable payment schedule.

"The last thing you want is to still be owing so much per month that you can't keep up those payments and then you wind up going into collections," she says.

Find the fair market value. Even after cross-checking your EOB and bill, you could end up owing more than you need to be paying. Instead of trusting your provider to charge you a reasonable amount, compare fair market values of procedures and services in your area with websites like *fairhealthconsumer.org.*

If your hospital has their prices published, check the negotiated rate, not the chargemaster, to see what an insurer would pay for the services. You shouldn't pay more than this amount whether or not you're insured. Use these two pieces of information as leverage when negotiating.

Call the billing office with confidence. Start by asking about the hospital's financial aid program — all nonprofit hospitals are required to have one. Then explain you can't afford their charges and suggest an amount that would work for you.

Offering cash upfront could make your offer more enticing, but you can suggest a payment plan after knocking down the price, too. This process can be intimidating, so remember it's in the hospital's interest to negotiate as well.

"Not only do you deserve to not pay too much for your health care, but also you're talking to a billing office that is set up specifically for you to do this," says Donovan. "That's what they're there for, so be confident that you can and should be doing this."

Rule change saves you from surprise billing

Many insurance companies make special deals with a group of providers and facilities to agree on payment for different services. These are your in-network providers. If you choose to visit an out-of-network provider, you're usually charged a higher amount.

But sometimes you don't know or have a choice in who treats you. Surprise billing is when you seek out services at an in-network facility, only to find out later you were treated by an out-of-network provider. The best way to avoid these bills is to ask your hospital or other facility ahead of time if they can guarantee you won't see any out-of-network providers.

It's not just the main doctor you need to worry about. Out-of-network slip-ups include ancillary providers like the anesthesiologist, radiologist, and others. And if you have an emergency, you likely won't have a say in who you receive your care from anyway. In fact, experts estimate that an out-of-network provider administers care in every 1 in 6 emergency room visits and inpatient hospital stays.

Fortunately, a recent rule change bans surprise billing for emergency services. It also prohibits out-of-network charges at in-network facilities for ancillary care and services provided without advance consent.

The hospital admission scam that could cost you thousands

You go to the emergency room with chest pain, and hospital workers decide you're not well enough to go home but not doing poorly enough to be checked into inpatient care. They decide to monitor you for a short period under observation status. Watch out.

Medicare encourages hospitals to assign patients outpatient observation status. Even respectable facilities are doing it. But the cost is your wallet. Medicare Part A doesn't include observation status, which leaves you paying a higher portion under Part B. To protect yourself, check your paperwork and speak to your doctor if you believe your status should be switched.

29 | Health aids

> "To ensure good health: Eat lightly, breathe deeply, live moderately, cultivate cheerfulness, and maintain an interest in life."
>
> William Londen

Keep an ear out for these cheaper alts to traditional hearing aids

Prescription hearing aids cost a pretty penny. The cheapest ones still clock in at nearly $1,000 dollars. And top-of-the-line models are nearly six times that much. Even worse? Medicare won't chip in and help you cover the costs of these helpful devices.

But there's good news on the horizon. The government is finally wrapping up details that will allow stores to sell over-the-counter (OTC) hearing aids. And that means big savings for those who are hard of hearing. Experts estimate that these OTC alternatives will only cost a few hundred dollars, rather than a few thousand.

Can't wait? Try hearing amplifiers. Think of these a bit like drugstore reading glasses. They're not customized to your exact needs, but they may be able to help you with day-to-day activities. If you have mild hearing loss, they're an affordable way to cut through background noise or pick up on things that you normally can't hear.

If you're a veteran, you may qualify for free or reduced-cost hearing aids through the Department of Veterans Affairs (VA). Reach out to your local VA office or call 877-222-8387. You can also contact an area agency on aging and ask if they can direct you toward programs that offer financial help.

Supply shopping: Avoid these 3 major mistakes

Need a wheelchair or scooter? Time to seek out a durable medical equipment (DME) store. But if you're not familiar with the purchasing ins and outs, it's easy to make mistakes that could turn the process into a time-consuming headache.

Avoid these all-too-common buying blunders with expert advice from Brittney Salter, director of operations at Southeastern Medical Supply Inc.

Going to any ol' supplier. Medicare only pays for DME if you get the equipment from an approved supplier. To make it easier to locate a store, Salter recommends using Medicare's supplier directory.

This recently updated resource helps you find a local supplier that sells the equipment you're looking for. Search by ZIP code at *medicare.gov/medical-equipment-suppliers*.

Coming without your paperwork prepared. Firstly, you must have a prescription from a doctor. But there's more.

"The biggest mistake is there's always an assumption made that if you have a prescription, you can immediately get whatever equipment is needed," says Salter.

You also have to get a certificate of medical necessity before Medicare and most other insurance will cover the costs. If you have an idea of what you need before you go to your doctor to get a prescription, reach out to a local DME supply store and ask them what information you'll need from your doctor during the visit.

"If you can get everything out and completed in that one appointment, it's going to make the process go much quicker," Salter says.

Not realizing how much you'll need to pay. Even if you're buying a wheelchair that's covered by Medicare, you may still have some out-of-pocket costs. "Medicare and most Medicare Advantage plans only cover 80% of the equipment," says Salter.

If you need a bit of extra help covering those out-of-pocket costs, reach out to local support groups to see if they know of any financial resources. You can also talk to employees at the supply store to see if they offer payment plans.

Use this account for an unexpected tax break on assistive devices

As you know, you didn't have to fork over a slice of your health savings account (HSA) contributions to Uncle Sam. If you spend the savings on a new house or a trip overseas, however, you'll have to give the government its share. Fortunately, you can use those dollars to cover medical expenses without taking a tax hit.

That means you can spend it on health aids — like eyeglasses, contacts, wheelchairs, or hearing aids — without worrying about the IRS. If you're not sure whether or not an expense is tax exempt, reach out to your HSA provider. You might be surprised about what's eligible. Walkers and canes, orthopedic inserts, and prosthetics make the list.

Would you like prescription eyeglasses for as low as $8? It's perfectly possible to get them wherever you live just by shopping on these websites. Try *voogueme.com*, *goggles4U.com*, and *www.zennioptical.com*.

More resources

Benefits.gov	benefits.gov/benefit/606	N/A
Center for Medicare Advocacy	medicareadvocacy.org	202-293-5760
Centers for Medicare & Medicaid Services (CMS)	cms.gov	877-267-2323
CMS, Medicaid	medicaid.gov	N/A
CMS, Medicare	medicare.gov	800-633-4227
Federal Trade Commission (FTC)	consumer.ftc.gov/health	N/A
Health Resources and Services Administration	hrsa.gov	N/A
HealthCare.gov	healthcare.gov	800-318-2596
Medicare Rights Center	medicareinteractive.org	800-333-4114
National Association of Area Agencies on Aging	n4a.org/medicareand benefitsenroll	202-872-0888
National Council on Aging	benefitscheckup.org	N/A
National Institutes of Health	ods.od.nih.gov	301-435-2920
National Patient Advocate Foundation	npaf.org/patients-caregivers	800-532-5274
NeedyMeds	needymeds.org	800-503-6897
Pharmaceutical Research and Manufacturers of America	medicineassistancetool.org	571-350-8643
U.S. Department of Health and Human Services	health.gov/myhealthfinder	N/A
U.S. Department of Veterans Affairs	va.gov	800-698-2411
U.S. Food and Drug Administration (FDA)	fda.gov/food/dietary-supplements	888-723-3366
United States Pharmacopeial Convention (USP)	quality-supplements.org	N/A

LOW-COST LODGING

Open the door to powerhouse savings

30 | Home buying & selling

Let your home take center stage with this expert advice

"When you're selling your home, you have to make it look presentable," says Shell Brodnax, CEO of the Real Estate Staging Association. "You want somebody to go out there and look at your home and say, 'This is the best house, and I want it.'"

That's where staging comes in. This process — which can involve adding lamps and lights, moving furniture around, or painting the walls — is a great way to amp up the selling price for your home.

The numbers back it up. "We just did a study in 2020 of 13,000 staged homes — 85% of them sold for 5% to 23% over list price," Brodnax says. In addition, these homes spent significantly less time on the market than unstaged properties.

Typically, getting a home professionally staged will cost around 1% of the house's listing price. So if you're selling a $250,000 house, you'd expect to pay a professional about $2,500. But if you can't quite afford that, don't worry. Simply start with the consultation to figure out what you need to do to help buyers visualize the space as their future home.

You can pay a professional stager a one-time fee — usually around $300 — for them to tour the home and tell you what they think needs to be done. They'll leave you with a to-do list that can help you get the home set up and properly staged. And if you want to save some cash, you can do it all yourself.

4 simple upgrades that instantly boost the value of your home

You may not be DIY savvy like Tim "The Tool Man" Taylor on the show "Home Improvement." And you're likely not as rich as Amazon founder Jeff Bezos. So when it comes to making upgrades to increase the value of your home, skill and budget are big considerations.

Luckily, if you make these four simple changes, your house could be worth thousands of dollars more. And you don't have to be a handyman extraordinaire or a billionaire to get the job done.

Give the bathroom a makeover. Remodeling your bathroom can significantly boost the selling price of your home. However, completely updating the water closet isn't always cheap. If you don't want to dip into your savings for a completely new look, consider replacing the toilet seat, updating the faucets and cabinet handles, and getting a more modern-looking shower curtain.

Invest in a facelift for the kitchen. Hiring a contractor to redo your whole kitchen costs a pretty penny. But you may not need to pay through the nose for new counter-tops and top-of-the-line appliances.

A fresh coat of paint on your cabinets and new hardware can make the space look more contemporary. And if your appliances don't match or are worse for wear, you may be able to order new doors to make them look almost new.

Going green may help bump up the selling price. Energy-efficient upgrades are all the rage. Not only will they cut down your utility bills while you're searching for a buyer, but one study revealed that energy-efficient homes in Los Angeles sold for 6% more.

While new windows or solar panels may be out of your budget, simply adding new insulation, upgrading to energy-efficient appliances, and replacing old lightbulbs with LEDs could help you find a buyer.

Smart storage solutions wow potential buyers. Older homes often have smaller closets and limited storage space, which can turn away some buyers. But adding shelves or other storage areas could help you get more money for your home.

How (and when) to fire your real estate agent

Selling your home isn't a simple matter. That's why you often need to enlist the help of a real estate pro. And if you make the wrong choice when choosing a listing agent, you could wind up missing out on thousands of dollars. So how do you know if you need to fire your agent and switch to a new one?

- Your home isn't selling as quickly as it should. If your home is sitting unsold, you're still paying for utilities, property taxes, and other upkeep expenses. And if other homes in the area are getting snatched up while yours remains vacant, you might want to consider switching your agent to some-body who has more experience selling in your neighborhood.

- You don't see eye to eye with your agent. A good relation-ship is important. If you're having trouble communicating your needs or if they're not effectively marketing your home, look at other options.

Dropping your real estate agent isn't always straightforward. When you hire somebody to sell your house, you often have to sign a con-tract that guarantees them a commission. So even if you're the one who finds a buyer, your agent will still get a cut. And if you back out of the contract, you may have to pay a hefty cancellation fee.

First, have a conversation with your agent and try to work things out. If the situation can't be fixed, ask them to terminate the contract without penalty. If that doesn't fly, call the real estate brokerage and ask them if it's possible to work with a new agent. Most real estate firms will work with you to find you a new agent or resolve the problem. However, if they don't, you may need to consult a lawyer to see what legal options you have to get out of the contract.

Mortgage preapproval: Budget better and gain negotiating power

Shopping for a house? You'll need to know what you can afford before you can start narrowing down your search. And if you're not paying cash, that means you'll need to get a mortgage. The best way to know how much money you can borrow? Get preapproved.

Unlike mortgage pre-qualification — which just estimates how much house you can afford — the preapproval process involves a close look at your finances. That includes your income, assets, credit score, and debt. At the end, you'll have a better idea of how much you can borrow and what your interest rate and monthly payments might be.

And as an added bonus, having a preapproval on a mortgage can help you negotiate with the seller because you already have your finances in order.

So how do you start this process? Simply reach out to a bank or mortgage lender and let them know you want to get preapproved. But don't stop at one. To make sure you're getting the best rate, shop around and get quotes from a few lenders.

The hoax that could hijack your closing fund

When you're finally ready to close on a home, you'll need to transfer tens of thousands of dollars into an escrow account. And if you're not careful, scammers may pounce and steal your hard-earned savings.

Fraudsters send out emails with links to fake websites designed to look identical to the mortgage lending company you're working with. They have similar names, email addresses, and contact information, so some people don't think twice before transferring their funds to the scammers.

To avoid this scam, never wire money based on texts or email instructions alone. Make sure you've talked with a live person, and verify they actually work for your mortgage lender.

Found your dream home? Don't forget these hidden costs

Rosie thought she found the perfect deal on a new home when she was downsizing. She bought a little house in a quiet, suburban neighborhood with a much lower mortgage payment than her old home. But when it came time to pay her monthly bills, she discovered that she was actually spending even more on housing. Her mistake? She forgot to factor in the other costs — like utilities and home insurance.

Before you buy, ask if you can get utility bills from the current homeowner. You want a breakdown of the seller's electricity, water, and internet expenses so you can have a rough idea of what your monthly costs will be. If you can't get that info, ask your real estate agent if they can dig up an estimate based on similar-sized homes nearby.

Also get your homeowners insurance quote ahead of time. Depending on where you move or how big your home is, these costs vary. You might find that it's more expensive to get the same level of coverage on your new home.

Factor in maintenance fees, property taxes, and homeowner association dues, too. Eliminating these surprises will help save you from buyer's remorse down the road.

Sight unseen — tips for navigating the latest buying trend

Touring a home is an important step in deciding whether or not to make an offer. But in some cases, you may not be able to check out a house before pulling the trigger. If you're trying to secure a place out of state or want to buy in a competitive market, follow these suggestions to sidestep a dud.

Your real estate agent can tour the house for you. Ask them to take photos or use video chat to give you a virtual look at the place. As long as you trust their judgment, they could help you determine whether or not the home is worth it. If you need another set of eyes, consider asking a reliable friend or family member to walk through the house with your agent. Get them to report on lighting, smells, sounds, and size.

In addition, research the area as thoroughly as possible. Look up crime stats, contact the local city council to see if there are any major projects planned, and check out online forums and message boards to see what people are saying about the town.

Buy or rent: Easy rule of thumb gives guidance

Think paying rent is a waste of cash? After all, if you buy a home you may recoup your investment when you're ready to move. But believe it or not, you're not always better off as a homeowner.

Before you buy, consider how long you'll want to live in that house. If you're planning to settle down in a home for longer than five years, it often makes more sense to buy. But any shorter, and you may not make your investment back when you sell. You have to factor in closing costs, agent fees, and taxes when selling, and that can really eat into your profit.

31 | Relocating

> "Often when you think you're at the end of something, you're at the beginning of something else."
>
> Fred Rogers

What to keep in mind when trading towns

Every winter you head to warmer climates with your fellow snowbirds. So you may think your vacation spot is the perfect place to nest in your retirement. But before you take flight, consider these factors that could affect your retirement relocation plans.

Cost of living is an essential feature whether you're moving into a neighboring city or a whole new state. And that cost isn't limited to housing prices. Expenses from health care and travel to visit your family from a new home base could up your spending.

Look into the tax laws of the states you're considering. If you live in a high-tax state, you might benefit from moving into one with lower income tax. However, the details are key. In some states you're required to pay income tax, but you get a break on retirement income like Social Security and IRA distributions. Also evaluate property, sales, estate, and inheritance tax rates.

Don't let taxes be the sole thing guiding your decision, though. After all, you've spent years saving for a fulfilling retirement. Think about what kind of lifestyle you want and if the area you're interested in offers those perks at your price point.

For example, moving to an affordable college town may be the perfect fit for folks who want to stay active and engaged. Some large universities even specifically have retirement communities near their campuses that offer access to courses, social activities, and health care services. Plus college towns often have an abundance of culture, like theater performances and cafes, you can enjoy.

Senior living alternatives: Find a home that fits your lifestyle and budget

You've heard of independent living communities. This lifestyle is set up to keep you living in your own apartment or house while also having access to amenities like fitness centers, maintenance services, and extra security. But it can be costly, averaging $1,500 to $3,500 a month. Fortunately, this isn't the only way you can stay active in your golden years. Check out these cost-saving alternatives.

Sharing is caring — and cost-effective. Your kids are all moved out, and now their bedrooms sit empty. You can utilize this extra space to help pay your mortgage. House sharing is one option. You can rent out a room to a fellow senior if you're comfortable sharing community space. Besides a lower cost of living, you gain a built-in social group, and you and your roommates can share household chores.

Another option is called house hacking. In this scenario, you buy a multifamily property and rent out the units you aren't using. If you already own a fairly large house, you could also simply convert a space into a suite. For instance, a home with a finished basement or carriage house. Depending on how hot the market is in your area, you may even be able to turn a profit on top of covering your mortgage cost.

Join a retirement community without moving. Feel safe and comfortable in your current home? With virtual retirement villages, you don't have to leave your house behind to get community perks.

A local village can connect you to services like transportation, grocery delivery, and maintenance. These resources help you stay independent and less isolated. Your village may even host social activities you can join.

To find a village near you, visit the Village to Village Network at *vtvnetwork.clubexpress.com* and click on *Village Map* under the *About* tab. Use the search field or browse the map to find the phone number and website for the closest village. Keep in mind some of these communities require dues for access. Depending on where you live, this could be around $500 per year for a single person.

Honey, I shrunk the house. Average house size in the U.S. has increased by more than 1,000 square feet since the early '70s, but especially as you age, all that extra space may not be serving you well. Downsizing can lower your bills and reduce maintenance demands.

If you're ready for a dramatic change, tiny living could bring you huge savings. Tiny houses on average are a mere 225 square feet. That's eight times smaller than the typical home you'd find on the market. What you lose in square feet you gain in savings on your utilities, mortgage, and upkeep.

There's more than one way to go small. You can tow your tiny home with you, but if you want a more on-the-go option, an RV or a houseboat may be a better fit.

Clear clutter for a smooth path to a cost-saving move

Are you ever torn between keeping things or giving them away or selling them? Those feelings can slow you down when you're trying to declutter. Fortunately, there's a simple one-step process that will answer that question for you every time, with complete confidence and no regrets. Put the item in a box and store it for six months. If you don't need it in that period of time, you should donate or sell it. But if you want it before then, you can keep it.

Because this process hinges upon time passing, it's best to start going through your things long before you need to clear out for a move. Monica Friel, chief executive organizer at the professional organizing company Chaos to Order, advises going through your space on a regular basis to make sure you're not accumulating stuff you don't use.

"The home is the most expensive purchase that we make so we encourage people to really honor that space and don't just let junk pile up in it," says Friel. "Make use of that space, make it living space, and be intentional about what you're keeping and getting rid of."

Friel says moving is an excellent time to get organized since you have to go through all of your things anyway. But knowing what to keep or toss can be tough. Ask yourself these questions.

- When was the last time I used this?

- How frequently do I use it?

- Is there room for it in my new space?

- How hard would it be to replace if I got rid of it?

To save space, consider digitizing old papers or art and taking photos of objects with sentimental value that you don't need to hang on to. Enlisting a friend or professional to talk through your decisions to keep or discard an item may help, too.

Follow these rules and you'll soon have a clutter-free home. And you'll never miss what you got rid of. It may sound time-consuming, but this process could save you money. By purging before movers come, you'll have lower costs for packing and shipping.

Stay local to turn an easy profit on your unwanted possessions

Make clearing clutter before a move easier by starting in your community. Post items to local Facebook groups dedicated to buying and selling and you'll save yourself the trouble of shipping. Have a lot to get rid of? Host a garage sale. These five simple tricks could double your income.

- Spruce up your wares. Buyers want to purchase something usable, so clean up your items. And if it's an electronic device, stick in batteries to show all is in working order.

- Price compare. Check the retail value of your items online and then knock down the price by at least half. This will get you a reasonable price so your items sell, and make it worth your time and effort.

- Advertise well. Use bright signs to point cars around town toward your yard sale. And be sure to include the date and times. Post the details on sites like Craigslist or a local Facebook group to garner extra attention.

- Display intentionally. Create a flow between spaces so customers can easily move around. Group similar items together for a better shopping experience.

- Start on Friday. Increase your buyer turnout by hosting a two-day sale that starts on Friday. It's a great day to lure in serious shoppers, and because it's only the first day, you may have to negotiate less.

EBay for newbies — ways to win at selling

You want to get rid of the clutter, but maybe you think yard sales are too much work. Here's how to move the stuff out without the hassle, while still making money. Use eBay.

It's free to create an account at *ebay.com*, and you can set up your own online business or simply sell secondhand items from your home — just like an online yard sale.

Ready to clean out? Here's what you need to know if you want to sell your items on eBay.

- You'll pay a small fee to list items for sale — usually a flat, fixed fee.

- There is a 10% fee on the selling price of items, paid by the seller.

- You'll need to provide a comprehensive and honest description of the item, along with good quality photos.

- Set realistic delivery charges. In general, it is best to set the delivery charge at the correct amount for the item, or slightly higher, to cover your costs. Also include the cost of any packaging that you have to use. If in doubt about how much it will cost to post an item, have it weighed first.

- Never send the item until you have received payment from the buyer.

Buyers and sellers can communicate via messages on eBay. However, never give out any personal or financial details.

If there is any kind of problem with a transaction on eBay, report it in the eBay Resolution Center or, as a last resort, report it to the Federal Trade Commission at *ftc.gov*.

How to spot a bad moving company

You're handing nearly all your worldly possessions off to strangers when you book movers, so you need a trustworthy company. Start off by searching mover ratings on the Better Business Bureau site *bbb.org*, and ask your social circle for suggestions.

Contact your top three for a price quote. It's a big red flag if the company doesn't factor in your belongings or has a too-good-to-be-true offer. Always ask about extra costs that could be added to your bill.

If you're moving out of state, your mover must have a U.S. Department of Transportation number. Double-check their motor vehicle insurance and liability insurance, too. Missing these is a no-go.

Moving costs average $1,530 for short distances and can double if you move states, so price is a priority. But don't sacrifice security for a deal. Instead, lower your costs by moving in the offseason, October through March, or on a less popular weekday.

Prep your move early to stave off stress

Before you get to the nitty-gritty days of packing and relocating, creating a schedule is essential to stay on track for your ship-out date. And to ensure you don't make any money-wasting missteps.

"You want to have a good plan in place and a timeline for what needs to get done so that when the move date happens you're prepared," says Monica Friel of Chaos to Order. "Oftentimes the move comes and we're overwhelmed by not realizing how much there was to do."

Two months in advance. Start prepping now if possible. The first tasks on your list should include making a moving budget, researching moving companies, and purging your possessions.

In the next few weeks start gathering packing supplies, planning a garage sale if you're having one, and getting all your medical records from your doctor if you don't already have access. At the five weeks mark, book your movers and confirm the time and date of your move along with other details.

One month out. Time to begin boxing up nonessentials. This is also the time to notify membership programs, like the gym, and your utility services of your departure. Go ahead and set up utilities at your new home.

In the next two weeks plan how to use up your remaining food, arrange transportation for your pets and plants, and update your address with the USPS and your banks and credit cards. Of course, you also need to up the gear on your packing. Keep your valuables in a safe and separate place so you can move them yourself.

The final week. Double-check that your movers have the right time and place. Give your home a thorough final cleaning, too. The day before you leave, clear out your fridge and defrost the freezer. Then after everything has been cleared out on moving day, do a final sweep of the place to make sure you didn't leave anything behind.

Moving day survival kit: Must-haves for a comfortable transition

You've just arrived at your new home and are worn out from the excitement of the day. Now what? Well because you prepared a special survival kit of your essential items, you don't have to unpack yet.

Just open this one box and you're set until after you get a good night's sleep. Plus it is a safety net if your movers show up late and can tide you over until they do. Here's what you need in your bag.

- toiletries like soap, toothbrushes, and toothpaste along with toilet paper and a towel

- a comfortable change of clothing and pair of shoes

- water bottles and nonperishable snacks

- cleaning spray and a paper towel roll

- important papers like ID cards, tax and insurance documents, and moving information

- anything else you might need over the next few days such as medications and phone chargers

---

32 | Aging in place

> "Aging is not lost youth but a new stage of opportunity and strength."
>
> Betty Friedan

On the house: How to pay for safety upgrades

Big home renovations can be costly, and you may not have enough cash readily available. But if you're over 62, you may be eligible for a plan that could put thousands of dollars in your pocket now. With a reverse mortgage, the worth of your home can be reinvested into itself. And for as long as you live there, you'll never have to pay it back.

The first step is to shop around for a lender and compare terms and fees. Typically, you need to have 50% equity or more in your home to qualify for a reverse mortgage. That's because if you use this type of loan, you'll be borrowing against your equity. You keep the title to your house but don't pay your monthly mortgage.

Instead, your lender will send you money. This could be in the form of a lump sum, recurring payment, line of credit, or some combination of those options. Then you can use that money to pay for in-home care, home modifications, and other things you need in order to age in place.

Your loan accrues interest over time but only comes due when you and your spouse pass away, sell the house, or no longer meet qualifications. You'll never have to pay back more than your home's value, even if your loan exceeds it.

Reverse mortgages aren't your only option, though. There's more help than ever for seniors who want to live out their golden years — safely — in their own home.

Medicare and other private insurers typically won't cover home improvement costs. However, most states have home and community based services, which help pay for modifications and repairs so you can live independently and comfortably at your pad instead of a nursing home. The Veterans Administration, U.S. Department of Agriculture, and other government organizations also offer assistance to qualified individuals through grants.

In addition, local service providers may have programs and funding for home assessments, remodels, and more. To track them down, use the National Directory of Home Modification and Repair at *homemods.org/national-directory*.

Drastically improve 3 key spaces with inexpensive changes

You want to live independently for as long as possible. However, your current house might not be the home you should renovate.

"Aging in place doesn't mean you stay in the same home where you had your working career, raised a family, or something like that," says Louis Tenenbaum, founder and president of HomesRenewed, an organization whose goal is to increase the number of age-friendly homes. "It means a place you stick."

So your first step is to evaluate your house. Is it up a steep hill? Are there treacherously tall staircases? Properties with these features, as well as cramped first floors and tight maneuvering space in bathrooms and bedrooms, might not be good candidates for aging in place. But if the bones are good, start updating in these three spaces with inexpensive changes that have a big payoff.

Bring up your bathroom standards. "Falls cost a lot of money and falls change people's lives," says Tenenbaum. They're the most common cause of injury for older adults, and bathrooms are one of the biggest hazard zones. Making small changes can protect your future.

Start by installing grab bars in your shower and near the toilet. Three bars will usually cost around $140. Switch over to a taller, comfort-height toilet, or skip a new commode and secure a seat riser on your current one, instead. Add a nonslip bathmat and increase visibility by choosing towels that contrast with your walls and floors.

Craft your dream kitchen. Spills and flames pose major risks in the kitchen. So how do you keep the heart of your home safe? Creating designated work spaces is one strategy. Have places where you can work standing, but also add lower counters or a table where you can sit and rest your legs when you're tired. Each space should have task lighting to reduce risks like burning your hand or nicking yourself on a knife.

Your sink is a functional focal point, so consider buying a touchless faucet. They start as low as $100. If you need a new fridge, check out models with side-by-side doors, so you don't have to stoop to reach your freezer drawer. Replace cabinet knobs with bar or lever pulls for a quick and easy update.

Travel safely through your home. You shouldn't be afraid to walk around your own house. But staircases and long hallways may become daunting as you age, especially at night. Plug in a few motion-activated night lights around your house to illuminate your walkway on the cheap.

If you have a single rail on your staircase, add one to the other side, says Tenebaum. That way no matter which direction you're going, you can have your dominant hand rooting you to the steps. The railing should extend the entire length of your stairs.

The cheapest solution to reduce tripping, though, is to keep your floors clean and clear, and skip the area rugs.

Smart home devices make your life easier

Learning how to use new technology can feel painful. But a few choice selections for around your home can make your life easier in the long run. Google and Amazon are two big names in the home tech arena. Both offer devices you can control with your voice from across the room. Have a question? Ask Google or Alexa to look up a song title or a movie's leading actress.

These devices have more practical features, too. For instance, Google Home and Nest devices can create shopping lists, tell you the weather, or call a friend. Connect them to other smart devices like a thermostat or lights to control those by voice as well. Hands-free features are a huge help if you have mobility problems or arthritis.

Say, on the other hand, you have trouble remembering tasks. Your home assistant has your back. Smart speakers like Google Home let you automate a sequence of events with a simple command. For example, program your device to turn on the lights, alert you of scheduled activities for the day, and remind you to take your medication when you say, "Hey Google, good morning."

If you're concerned about privacy, you can delete old conversation transcripts and turn off its listening mode. So don't let technology intimidation keep you from trying devices that can help you stay connected and independent.

These caregiver resources can ease your load

The pandemic showed that traditional retirement homes may not be the safe haven people thought they were, says Louis Tenenbaum of HomesRenewed. If the spread of COVID-19 shifted your perspective on retirement facilities, you may be interested in aging in place. Which means you could require or become a caregiver later on.

Eligible caregivers to veterans can receive support from the Program of Comprehensive Assistance for Family Caregivers. You'll get training and financial assistance, which may include a monthly stipend. Another option is the Program of General Caregiver Support Services. It offers education, training, and other assistance like peer support mentoring.

Not a veteran? Check out the Paid Caregiver Program Locator at *payingforseniorcare.com/paid-caregiver/program-locator* to see if you qualify for a program that pays family members to care for aging loved ones. Or visit the Family Caregiver Alliance's Services by State tool at *caregiver.org/connecting-caregivers* to find local assistance, including caregiver compensation and government health disability programs.

33 | Home insurance

> "Doing something costs something. Doing nothing costs something. And, quite often, doing nothing costs a lot more!"
>
> Ben Feldman

Update your old house for a new and improved monthly premium

It's hard to beat the charm and character of an old home. But new houses have one major advantage — they're usually cheaper to insure. The reason? Older homes often have dated structural components, which will increase the risk of problems and drive up your premiums.

"Anything older than 10 years, you're going to pay more money," says Loretta Worters, vice president of media relations for the Insurance Information Institute.

But once you retire, you don't want your homeowners insurance rates to keep creeping up. So what's one of the best ways to bring those costs down? Make updates to your house bit by bit.

"You can then go to your insurance company and say, 'I've upgraded these things,'" says Worters. Follow her advice and consider these noteworthy changes.

- Roof. "When your roof is getting older and older, you're going to pay more money," she says. "A roof is like the foundation almost. If something happens to your roof, the whole house can collapse." Getting a new one is a big investment, but it can help secure your home and knock down your premiums by up to 20%.

- Plumbing. Water damage is a major problem for insurance companies. That means they'll slash your rates if you can show that you're taking steps to make your home leakproof. Address aging water heaters, faucets, supply pipes, and sewage lines.

- Wiring. Frayed wires in the wall could be a major fire hazard. Getting your electrical systems in tiptop shape will keep you safe and sound, plus it can lower your insurance rate. For example, switching riskier aluminum or knob-and-tube wiring to more durable copper could save you a pot of gold in the long run.

"If you make your home more resilient, you lower your insurance cost and you protect your home," says Worters.

Use these 7 secrets to slash hundreds off your insurance bill

The average American spends a whopping $1,300 each year on homeowners insurance. And if you live in certain states, you could be paying double that amount. But with a little know-how, you can get big savings on homeowners insurance.

Consider raising your deductible. This little-used option could bring your rates down by more than 35%. The reason? When you file a claim to fix damage to your house, you have to pay a certain amount out of pocket. But the more you're willing to front, the less your insurance company will charge you for coverage each year.

Buy all your insurance from one company. Own a home and a car? You need to get insurance for both, and companies will often offer discounts if you buy it from the same place.

Don't overdo your coverage. Many people think they need to get insurance coverage based on the real estate value of their house. But that's not the case. You need to get a policy that covers the cost to rebuild your home.

Disaster-proof your home. Live in an area with hurricanes or tornadoes? What about wildfires or earthquakes? Installing home upgrades to protect your property against natural disasters can slash your insurance bill.

Ask about a retiree discount. If you spend more time in the house, you can catch fires, leaks, and other problems early. And that means your insurance company won't have to worry as much about you filing big claims.

Let your insurer know you've paid off your home. If you don't have a mortgage anymore, you might get a discount on your yearly bills. The hope is that people who own their homes outright will be more likely to take better care of the property.

Adopt a healthy, responsible lifestyle. Surprise! By not smoking, you'll score a discount of as much as 15%. Work on your financial health by improving your credit score and you might save even more. Plus look out for the environment with paperless billing for another markdown.

Get smart — high-tech upgrades save you up to 20%

Considering upgrading to a Wi-Fi controlled thermostat? Want to invest in a burglar alarm or smoke detector that will send alerts to your phone when it goes off? These futuristic devices can add to the efficiency and safety of your home, but that's not all they can do.

"A lot of times people get discounts from their insurance company as a way of incentivizing them to invest in this technology," says insurance expert Loretta Worters. "You can get discounts from anywhere between 5% and 20% on your homeowners insurance premium."

How much you'll save depends on factors like your insurance company and the type of device. Security cameras and other safety gadgets are great options. And Worters says investing in things that can detect and stop flooding — like water shut-off sensors — are a huge plus for most insurance companies. "They spend millions of dollars every year on plumbing leaks. These are big problems," she says.

Interested in adding these upgrades to your home? Contact your homeowners insurance company before you pull out the checkbook. Some insurers offer discounts on devices, installation fees, and other costs.

 Damage control: Keep a weather eye out for this contractor con

After natural disaster strikes your town, you may be struggling to find a contractor to do the necessary repairs on your home. So when somebody turns up at the door claiming to be able to fix up your house, it sounds great. And even better? They'll submit the insurance claims for you.

But chances are these so-called helpers will scamper before they actually repair anything. So how can you make sure you're not falling victim to a scam?

"Oftentimes, if there's been a disaster in your state, the state insurance department may have a list of reputable contractors," says Loretta Worters, spokesperson for the Insurance Information Institute.

She also recommends avoiding people who ask for the bulk of the payment upfront. A reputable company will usually ask for about a third of the cost in order to get supplies, she says.

---

34 | Property taxes

> "In this world nothing can be said to be certain, except death and taxes."
>
> Benjamin Franklin

Expand your budget by deferring your taxes

Never pay property taxes again. It may sound too good to be true, but many seniors are eligible to defer their property taxes. Freeing up that money could make living on a fixed income more manageable.

Interested? Check if your state or local government has a property tax deferral program. Typically, these programs allow older homeowners to delay paying property taxes for as long as they live in their house. When they pass away or decide to sell their house, the taxes come due. The amount deferred has essentially been borrowed, so that balance plus interest are then paid back to the government.

Bill appeal — win your way to lower dues

Have your property taxes been hiked up an obscene amount this year? You'll be on the hook for that money if you don't file an appeal quickly. In some states, you have just 30 days.

That's why Hap Richardson, an attorney in Georgia who specializes in property tax appeals, says, "It's extremely important to look out for the notice of assessment." The first few months of the year is commonly when you'll receive this notice, which tells you how much your house has been valued. Here's what to do next.

Understand how property tax is calculated. The first step to knowing if you're paying too much property tax is to understand where these numbers are coming from. Your local government dictates the current tax rate. An assessor estimates the current market value of your estate, the land, and structures, using computer software or sometimes visiting your property.

Imagine they value your property at $400,000. The tax rate and your valuation are then multiplied together to get your annual tax bill. So a rate of 2% would mean an $8,000 tab.

Gather your evidence. Wow, $8,000 is a lot of money. But are you paying more than you should? First, make sure you're getting all the exemptions you're entitled to. Then get to work.

"When people appeal their property tax bill, they are arguing about the county's opinion of the fair market value," says Richardson. "So the biggest mistake people make is they argue about the wrong issue. They argue 'My bill increased $3,000.'"

But he says, "The way to win an appeal is 'You raised the valuation of my property 30%.' And if you can get them to lower the valuation then your bill is reduced proportionally."

Your job is to prove your property valuation is too high. So request a copy of your property tax card from your local assessor's office. Make sure information like number of bathrooms is accurate. You can also ask the tax assessor how they came up with their valuation number. Take a look at comparable homes in your area and see if there are any major differences between the assessments.

Most local governments have these public records accessible online.

Make your case. You've looked at a lot of information before you actually submit your appeal. But don't go overboard. Sending in a lengthy binder will put off the review board. The same is true for an in-person hearing.

"Prepare a succinct argument illustrating why your property tax bill is too high," advises Richardson, "for example, 10 to 15 minutes."

Remember, the tax change isn't personal, so don't get frustrated. "If you lose your temper, you lose," says Richardson. Hiring a lawyer can help you through this whole process.

Just for seniors: Special exemptions mean you owe less

"The homestead exemption is a discount on your property taxes for the house where you live," explains property tax attorney Hap Richardson. "The older you get, the bigger the discount. It's like a reward for getting old and staying alive," he jokes.

For instance, some states may have one exemption if you're 62 or older, then might eliminate your requirement to pay school taxes after you turn 70. Other states offer seniors a floating homestead exemption that increases with the value of the house to help combat inflation. The trick is that usually you're not automatically enrolled for these exemptions. You have to sign up yourself.

Want more property tax savings just for seniors? Certain states offer volunteer programs that allow you to work off a portion of your bill if you meet the requirements. For instance, in Boston a single senior over age 60 can have an income of no more than $40,000. Those who qualify can reduce their taxes by a maximum of $1,500 in exchange for 111 volunteer hours.

35 | Home maintenance & cleaning

> "The time to repair the roof is when the sun is shining."
>
> John F. Kennedy

Spruce up your house in half the time with these simple tips

Ever wondered how many hours you've spent tidying, scrubbing, dusting, and vacuuming your home? According to a recent survey, the average American parent spends about 282 hours a year cleaning their home. But if you want to keep your house spotless, you don't need to dedicate all that time to chores.

Start your morning by making your bed. It sounds strange, but if you do this as soon as you wake up, you'll get more done all day long. A small survey revealed that people who take a few minutes to tidy up their sheets feel like they're more productive than people who leave their beds unmade. The reason? Starting the day off this way may give you a sense of accomplishment that helps you get ready to tackle the day.

Keep your home clear of clutter. Clothes strewn across the floor and boxes crammed into every corner will slow you down while you're trying to clean. Before you even start with your vacuuming, mopping, and dusting, take a few minutes to put things away. You'll be surprised at how much faster you can clean when you don't need to pause to deal with clutter.

Work smarter, not harder. If you're running all over the house while you're cleaning, you're probably wasting a good bit of time. To cut down on your chore time, spend a few minutes devising a plan of attack.

Make a list of chores, and think about the order you're going to do them in so you don't have to backtrack. For example, if you need to let cleaning products soak for a few minutes before scrubbing, plan to use that time to tidy up another area so you're not waiting around.

Park your tools close by. A bucket or tool caddy stocked with cleaning supplies is a great way to keep the pace up. You won't have to keep doing laps around the house in order to get what you need to tackle every little mess. And if your vacuum can't reach from room to room, consider getting an extension cord so you don't waste time plugging it in over and over again.

Cheap household products clean from top to bottom

You don't need expensive cleaners to get your house squeaky clean. A pound of baking soda costs less than $1, and you can use it to tackle nearly any mess you can think of. In fact, a slurry from baking soda and water is perfect for degreasing kitchen cabinets and countertops. Discover the other cleaners already in your home.

- Vinegar. Stinky, smelly washing machines aren't just annoying. If the watertight seal isn't kept clean, it could fail and cause all sorts of other problems. Every so often, spray the gasket with white vinegar and wipe down. Then run 2 cups of vinegar through an empty cycle.

- Dishwashing liquid and rubbing alcohol. Mix 1/2 cup of water, 1/2 cup of rubbing alcohol, and a few drops of dishwashing soap to scrub shower walls and leave your mirror sparkling.

- Lemons and salt. Sprinkle a bit of salt on half of a lemon and use it to scrub your bathroom sink and bathtub. The acid can help blast away foul-smelling bacteria and leave your home smelling clean and fresh.

- Mustard. It may sound strange, but this pantry staple could actually be a powerful weapon in your arsenal of cleaning supplies. Mix a teaspoon of plain, yellow mustard with hot water and swirl it around in glass jars or other food containers to wipe out stubborn odors.

- Castile soap. You can use this all-purpose superstar for just about anything. Mix a few drops with water to make a cleaner that clears up messes on wood, stone, or tile. And if you have pets, you can combine it with lavender oil to create an all-natural shampoo to soften your pet's skin and fight fleas.

Annual checklist helps you head off pricey problems

You need to take your car in for regular oil changes and maintenance checks in order to keep it in tiptop shape. And the same idea holds true for your home, too. If you don't take care of it, problems can eventually turn into expensive fixes or major safety hazards. Do these simple tasks at least once a year to keep yourself safe and bypass costly complications.

Examine the weatherstripping and caulk around your doors and windows. Theresa Clement, a home improvement expert at MyFixitUpLife, recommends checking for damage, mold, or other signs that your seals are failing. The materials aren't designed to last forever, so you need to replace them before water or wind can cause major damage to your home.

Clean your dryer vents. The lint that builds up in your dryer is so flammable that outdoor enthusiasts often use it as a fire starter when they're out camping. And if you let it build up in your house, it's a disaster just waiting to happen.

Clean the lint filter after every load, but at least once a year you need to disconnect the outlet vent behind the dryer and clean out lint that's piled up. If your dryer is too heavy to move alone, or if it vents out to the roof, consider hiring a professional to help you out.

Don't forget to give your gutters a once-over. Leaves, sticks, and gunk in your gutter aren't just unsightly — they're bad for your house. Water can pool and infiltrate your roof or siding, leading to thousands of dollars in damage. Experts say you should clean them at least once in the fall and once in the spring. And if you're not comfortable climbing a ladder, hire a pro.

Inspect your crawl space, attic, and other infrequently visited areas. "Go into places you don't go to normally. Open up closets or go into nooks and crannies with a flashlight and look around to make sure that there isn't a problem lurking in a hidden spot," says Clement. "There are a lot of places that people don't notice or pay attention to in daily life." Look for signs of water intrusion, mold, or bugs.

Keep an eye on your chim-chimney. If your home has a fireplace, get it examined at least once a year. If it's clogged with soot and ash, it can cause dangerous gases to build up or fires to start.

Inspect all your safety systems. Smoke alarms and carbon monoxide detectors are useless if the batteries are dead or if the wiring is faulty. Take a few minutes to go around and test them every few months, and change the batteries every year.

4 fantastic ways to protect your deck

Who doesn't love to lounge on their deck or patio? But if you don't keep it cleaned and well maintained, your outdoor oasis can turn into an unsightly, expensive problem all too quickly. In fact, experts estimate that replacing your worn out deck could set you back more than $15,000.

The good news? You can make sure your deck lasts a long time by following these simple maintenance tips.

- Freshen it up with a spring cleaning. Nature can do a number on the wood or composite materials that make up your deck. If it stays too wet from puddled water and debris, it can mold, mildew, or rot. Routine cleanups as well as an annual deep cleaning will help you wipe out these problems. Just avoid using a high-powered pressure washer, as it can ruin the wood.

- Look for problem areas to catch them early. Every few months, inspect your deck for loose nails, rotting boards, or other signs of wear. Fixing one or two issues could prevent the entire deck from suffering further harm.

- Keep the area around your deck clear and tidy. Overgrown shrubs and trees are a breeding ground for rot and mold. If your deck is buried under a mountain of greenery, it could be causing major damage. Try to keep plants and limbs trimmed so they're at least a foot away from your deck.

- Don't let your decorations sabotage your deck. Outdoor rugs and furniture can transform the space into a cozy hangout, but they can also trap moisture and mildew. Clean under rugs regularly, and rearrange the furniture every few months to keep uneven sun exposure from wearing your deck down at different rates.

Is this perilous paint still lurking in your home?

Think twice before you start sanding off old paint in your home. If your house was built before the 1980s, lead may be hiding in unlikely places.

Paint companies used to add this heavy metal to their mixes because it helped the paint dry faster and keep moisture from seeping in. Even though it was banned in 1978, you can still find lead paint on the walls and window sills of older homes.

If you suspect you live in a home with lead paint, head down to the local hardware store and get a lead paint test kit certified by the Environmental Protection Agency (EPA). If you do find lead paint in your home, the EPA keeps a list of contractors who are certified to remove the hazard. Go online to *epa.gov/lead* and click on *Find a lead-safe certified firm* for more information.

Keep an ear out for these strange sounds you can't afford to ignore

Everybody's home has a few charming quirks. Maybe it's the whoosh of your furnace kicking on, or a creaky floorboard that you know to avoid. But in some cases, those odd noises you've learned to live with could be the warning signs of something much more serious.

"A house is made of organic materials, so it ages just like we age," says Theresa Clement, a certified aging-in-place specialist. "If we ignore the signs from our body, it could lead to a big problem. The same thing is true with your house."

Clanging and banging in your walls, for instance, could be a serious plumbing problem. Air in your pipes might cause a hammering sound and introduces the perfect conditions for rust and corrosion. And pressure surges can actually knock the pipes loose and cause your plumbing to spring a leak.

Don't take creaking floors for granted either, Clement adds. "Your floor could creak because of expansion and contraction," she says. "But it could also be something else like settling in your house." Settling can be so severe that the supporting joists aren't in place anymore. "You'll need to secure them and make sure that everything is structurally sound."

Also pay attention to strange noises from your appliances. Does your washing machine thud and knock around when you're doing a load of laundry? You may think it's just out of balance, but it could be the start of a more serious electrical problem.

"If you don't fix it, it could cause your washer or dryer to totally break down," says Clement. "And you don't want that."

Expert advice on choosing a contractor

Picking the wrong contractor can turn a simple project into a never-ending nightmare. You could wind up throwing away hundreds of dollars on a job that runs on too long and leaves your home a mess.

Fortunately, home designer Theresa Clement has some tips that can help you choose the perfect person for the job.

"Make sure they have a contractor's license, insurance, and an actual address and a phone number," Clement says.

She also recommends looking into their online presence so you can see examples of their work. Or better yet, visit a potential contractor's completed projects in person and talk with a few former clients.

And another thing to look out for? Verify that they're punctual and tidy. "If someone is late to meet you or if their truck is a mess, that's a red flag," Clement says. "How are they going to invoice you on time, show up on time, and make sure the parts they need to order are going to come on time?"

More resources

Aging and Health Technology Watch	*ageinplacetech.com*	N/A
American Cleaning Institute	*cleaninginstitute.org*	202-347-2900
Consumer Financial Protection Bureau	*consumerfinance.gov/ consumer-tools*	855-411-2372
Fall Prevention Center of Excellence	*homemods.org*	N/A
Federal Alliance for Safe Homes	*flash.org*	877-221-7233
Federal Housing Administration	*fha.gov*	202-708-1112
HSH	*hsh.com*	800-881-3660
Insurance Information Institute	*iii.org*	212-346-5500
National Aging in Place Council	*ageinplace.org*	202-939-1770
National Association of Exclusive Buyer Agents	*naeba.org*	800-986-2322
National Association of Insurance Commissioners	*naic.org/consumer.htm*	816-783-8500
National Association of Realtors	*nar.realtor*	800-874-6500
National Association of Senior and Specialty Move Managers	*nasmm.org*	877-606-2766
National Institute on Aging	*nia.nih.gov/health/topics/ aging-place*	800-222-2225
U.S. Department of Housing and Urban Development	*hud.gov*	202-708-1112
U.S. Department of Agriculture	*rd.usda.gov*	800-414-1226
U.S. Department of the Treasury	*makinghomeaffordable.gov*	888-995-4673
U.S. Department of Veterans Affairs	*va.gov/housing-assistance*	800-827-1000
USA.gov	*usa.gov/housing*	844-872-4681

UTILITIES & SERVICES

Stay up and running without breaking the bank

36 | Electricity

Apartment living: Small changes that yield big energy rewards

Saving electricity as a renter is hard. After all, any major modifications are subject to your landlord's approval. However, you can make changes around your apartment that save you cash without requiring a big investment.

Start with the lights throughout your abode. Brittney Gordon, media manager for the Energy Star Labeling Branch, recommends switching to LED bulbs.

"It is easy and it's becoming much more affordable than it ever was to have LED technology in your home," Gordon says. "An Energy Star LED bulb uses 90% less energy than a traditional incandescent bulb, and it will last you 15 times longer."

You can buy LED bulbs for less than $1 each, and they'll save you about $50 in energy over their lifetime, says Gordon. Multiply that number across all the lights in your house for some serious savings. And don't forget to turn off lights when you leave a room. Use task lighting instead of overhead lights to shave off more from your bill.

Another big energy sucker is power you're not actively using. Idle load includes devices in standby or sleeping mode that still draw power. Unplug these electronics as well as small appliances like toasters and hair dryers. According to the U.S. Department of Energy, you could save up to $100 to $200 a year.

Tier 2 power strips can help out, too. By plugging in one of these you can get an energy savings of up to 50% compared to pulling power directly from an outlet. That's because it uses advanced technology to cut power to your electronics when you're not using them.

Assistance programs help you buy energy-saving appliances

"A lot of people think that it's harder to save energy in their home than it is," says Brittney Gordon from the Energy Star Labeling Branch. But it's easier than ever to find efficient appliances. "As long as it has the Energy Star label, it means that it is certified to save you money, save energy, and help protect the environment."

Take an Energy Star heat pump water heater. It might cost more than a standard model, but the savings can add up to $3,500 over its lifetime. In the same way, you could save more than $700 by using an energy-efficient washing machine, refrigerator, and air purifier. Stack the savings even higher with Energy Star dryers, dehumidifiers, fans, and more.

The long-run gain sounds great, but buying new appliances can be pricey. Fortunately, you can track down programs that may help cover your costs.

Loop in local aid. Your power company may offer an assistance program that makes energy-efficient products affordable for you. Take Pacific Gas and Electric Company, which provides power to portions of California. Their assistance program provides free energy-saving upgrades to qualified customers. These changes may include a fridge replacement, water heater repairs, and LED lightbulb swaps. Georgia Power and Southern California Edison also have savings programs that offer similar home updates.

And the discounts don't end with appliances. Georgia Power, for instance, grants eligible seniors up to $24 off their monthly bill.

Round up big savings with rebates. Even if you don't qualify for free appliances from your power company, you still can avoid paying full price. Visit *energystar.gov/rebate-finder* to search for rebates in your area for Energy Star-certified products. Depending on what's available, you could chip off a big chunk of your cost, like $100 cashback on the purchase of a new clothes dryer.

You can also recoup some of the costs in the form of a tax credit from the federal government. For example, a qualified water heater in tax year 2021 might earn you a $300 credit.

Locate programs with one easy tool. The Database of State Incentives for Renewables & Efficiency (DSIRE) offers comprehensive information on programs for energy-saving appliances. To search for programs, go to *dsireusa.org*, choose your state, and click *energy-efficiency*.

You'll find info on rebates from local utility companies, tax credits, sales tax exemptions, and federal grants. For instance, just three clicks on this website leads Florida residents to a utility company rebate program. Those who qualify could get a $100 rebate for an energy-efficient cooking range or $500 on a water heater.

And savings aren't limited to appliances. Search the site for other energy incentives like solar technology. Heating and cooling rollbacks come in the form of programs for heat pumps, window replacements, fans, and more.

Hot tips to heat your water for less

Water heaters are an eyesore, so yours is probably hidden away in the basement or a closet. But out of sight, out of mind can be a problem. Water heaters are the second-highest energy user in your home.

Energy Star appliances can drop down that use 70% from a standard electric water heater. But switching yours out isn't the only change you should make.

Flushing your water heater can lead to lower electric bills all year long. That's because sediment builds up in your tank, which can lower its efficiency and can clog your water lines. So at least once a year, take just one hour for this maintenance. Experts recommend flushing once every six months or more depending on your water hardness.

Save even more by lowering the temperature of your water heater to 120 to 130 degrees. Also add an insulation jacket around your electric heater and insulation to the 6 feet of piping closest to the heater. When doing this, make sure to read your manufacturer's recommendations and avoid covering the top and bottom of the heater or its thermostat or burner.

You may also want to consider switching to a tankless water heater. They have to be serviced just once a year. And because tankless water heaters only produce hot water as needed, you don't lose energy, or money, from it waiting on standby.

4 major fridge mistakes that eat up expensive electricity

The convenience of home refrigerators swept the nation in the last century. But you better watch out. Your refrigerator uses more power than any other kitchen appliance. Avoid these four mistakes and you can keep it from consuming so much energy.

- Setting your fridge to the wrong temperature. You don't want it too cold, so adjust your fridge to 35 to 38 degrees and freezer to zero degrees.

- Not paying attention to the seals. Close the fridge door over a piece of paper so half is in and half sticks out. Give the paper a tug. If it comes out easily, you may need to replace the seals or adjust the latch.

- Letting your coils get covered in dust. Clean them off with a vacuum and coil cleaning brush for higher efficiency.

- Leaving liquids and foods uncovered in your fridge. Moisture released from them puts more work on your compressor.

Make a clean break from steep laundry costs

You have two hulking machines in your laundry room, a washer and dryer. They ease your workload but can make your energy costs soar. Energy Star machines are one of the best ways to save. For instance, their washers wring out water better than other machines, so your clothing needs less time in the dryer.

"Front-load clothes washers are the most efficient clothes washers to have in your home," says Brittney Gordon, from the Energy Star Labeling Branch. "They are 50% more water efficient than a top-load washer that has an agitator in it, and they use 45% less energy than a traditional top-load washer with an agitator."

If you're not in the market for new machinery yet, check out these small changes that can help lower your bill, too.

- Tossing in two felted wool dryer balls can reduce clothes drying time by one-third. This energy-saving gadget costs less than five bucks to make yourself with wool yarn. And unlike dryer sheets, they can be reused for years.

- Clean the lint trap of your dryer to keep it running at max efficiency.

- Save about $66 a year when you switch to washing your clothing in cold water.

- Only run full wash loads, but be sure not to over- or under-fill your dryer. Or avoid using your dryer altogether by air-drying.

How to gauge if solar panels are right for your home

Ready to step into the future? Solar power could be the renewable energy resource of your dreams. The upfront cost of solar panels runs from $15,000 to $20,000. That's pretty pricey, but over its lifetime this tech could save anywhere from $10,000 to $30,000 on your energy bills.

Plus you can knock down the expense with a tax credit. Systems installed in 2021 or 2022 may qualify for a 26% credit and those installed in 2023 may pick up a 22% credit.

But is it worth it? You can find tools online to help you decide if you're a good candidate for solar panels. Google's Project Sunroof at *sunroof.withgoogle.com* can assess how much sunlight hits your roof and provide estimated savings. EnergySage's solar calculator at *energysage.com/solar/calculator* can also estimate your savings when you go solar.

37 | Heating & cooling

"It doesn't matter what temperature the room is, it's always room temperature."

Steven Wright

Seal leaks to save more than $100 on your energy expenses

Want to detect air leaks in your house on the cheap? All you need is one buck. Shut a door or window over your dollar bill. If you can easily pull the dollar out, you're losing energy and need to seal it more tightly. Closing up your air leaks can knock 10% to 20% off your annual heating and cooling bills. That could equal savings of over $100.

Caulking around windows and doors is a good place to start, and it's an inexpensive update at about $30 or less. Also look for gaps around electrical outlets, baseboards, exterior corners, and dryer vents. And don't forget insulation.

"Nine out of 10 homes in the U.S. are under-insulated," says Brittney Gordon, media manager for the Energy Star Labeling Branch. "And by sealing air leaks and adding insulation to your attic, you can become more comfortable at home and save up to 10% on your annual energy bills."

One easy insulation project you can do yourself is using bubble packing sheets to seal up drafty, single or double glazed windows. The air pockets make it a good insulator. Plus it's inexpensive, especially if you're reusing some from a package.

Apply the wrap to the inside of your windows by spraying a light film of water on the windows and gently pressing the bubble side against it until it sticks. This trick will trap heat in your house, lowering your energy bills in the winter.

Slash utility bills with these household tips and government giveaways

Your walls, roof, and other barriers to the outside make up your home's envelope and shelter you from the elements. Maintaining the integrity of this envelope is essential because letting air leak in will raise your energy costs. The government can help.

The Weatherization Assistance Program (WAP) helps increase the energy efficiency of low-income homes. If you qualify, you could get over $4,500 worth of energy-saving improvements made to your house for free. Professionals will first perform an energy audit where they assess your house for the most cost-effective changes and any potential safety hazards. Then they'll take weatherization measures like maintaining or replacing your HVAC system, adding insulation, and repairing small leaks in your walls or attic.

> "The average American household spends almost half of its annual energy bill on heating and cooling their home. More than $900 a year on average," says Brittney Gordon from Energy Star. "By switching to an Energy Star-certified air source heat pump, you're going to save energy and money all year long."

These improvements decrease energy use and could save you more than $280 a year on your energy bill. Upgrades aren't reserved for single-family homes either. WAP may provide assistance regardless of whether you rent or own, or live in an apartment, house, or mobile home. Contact your state weatherization agency to apply.

If you're in need of emergency assistance, apply for the Low Income Home Energy Assistance Program (LIHEAP). This federally funded program offers cash grants to cover utility bills. Some states also offer energy-related home repairs through LIHEAP that can save you money in the long run.

Savings by design: Home decorating tips set the scene for lower dues

Who says making your house more resistant to the elements can't make it more beautiful, too? Use these tips to tap into home savings and superior style.

Finesse your fans. Ceiling fans add style to a space, but there's more. The direction your fan turns can impact your heating and cooling costs. A counterclockwise spin is great during the summer because it pushes cool air down toward you, lessening your need for AC.

Flip the switch in winter so the blades spin clockwise. That way your fan will pull cool air upward and drive warm air down to the floor. This could reduce your heating needs and cut your costs by 10%, says the Department of Energy's Building Technologies Office.

Cover your floors. An estimated 15% of your house's heat is lost through the flooring. By covering bare floors with carpet or throw rugs, you add a layer of insulation that traps in heat. Plus carpet feels warmer under your feet, so you won't need to crank the heat up as much to stay toasty.

Put your window hangings to work. Insulated cellular shades and window quilts provide the most protection from wind and cold. Exterior awnings, roller shades, and roller shutters, on the other hand, offer the best defense against the sun's heat. Visit *efficientwindowcoverings.org* for guidance on options that are best for your climate and window type.

Nurture your landscape. Interior changes can lower your heating and air costs, but shift your gaze outside for extra savings. Strategically planted trees can break the wind and offer shade. In fact, research by the U.S. Department of Energy suggests that three properly placed trees could save a household over $100 annually. Even just shading your outdoor air conditioner can improve its efficiency by as much as 10%.

The most effortless way to keep your home comfortable while saving cash

Turn back your thermostat by 7 to 10 degrees for eight hours each day, like when you're asleep or at work. This simple tip could save you $87 or more on utility bills and requires almost no work at all.

The smaller the difference in temperature between your indoor air and the outside, the lower your overall bill will be.

Although you can make these changes manually, a smart or programmable thermostat can start adjusting the temperature before you wake up or get back home. That way you won't be uncomfortable with the new settings.

The secret program that rewards you with money

With a one-and-done setup, load management programs make lowering your heating and cooling bills easy. Here's how it works.

A switch is installed to control major appliances, like your HVAC system and water heater. The power company then has the option to manage your energy use during peak power demand hours. Typically, these energy demand surges occur on hot summer afternoons and cold winter mornings.

In exchange for control, your power company pays you with a credit on your bill. For hot days, your AC compressor will cycle off for short periods of time while the fan continues to run. Depending on the program, this could give you savings of up to $25 a month in the summertime. When it's chilly out, your heat strips may be controlled for savings of around $15 for each winter month.

You may not even notice when the load management is active. But if you don't like it, you can have the switch removed.

Energy audit alert: Beware free inspections

Home energy audits are key to identifying where your home is wasting energy. A certified energy auditor can use tools like blower doors and infrared cameras to determine the best energy efficiency measures to take. But watch out for companies offering free audits.

Unlike specific diagnostic testing, these no-cost assessments often only give general recommendations about energy use from a quick walk-through. Even more concerning are salespeople presenting themselves as unbiased. A company that offers a free audit may suggest the product they sell regardless of your home's actual needs. Want a legitimate audit? Call up your utilities company to see if they offer them.

You can also do a basic assessment yourself using the EPA's Home Energy Yardstick. It will compare your energy use to similar houses and offer suggestions for improving your home's comfort while decreasing your bills. Try it at *energy star.gov/campaign/home-energy-yardstick*.

38 | Water

The easiest, cheapest way to detect and fix a toilet leak

It's hard to miss a dripping faucet or pipe. But you may be wasting money unknowingly if you have a leaking toilet. Over the years, the seal that keeps the water in the upper tank can start to degrade, which lets water drip into the bowl and down the drain even when you're not flushing.

"You could be leaking 50 gallons of water a day and not know it because you can't hear it or see it," says Ed Osann, director of national water use efficiency at Natural Resources Defense Council. "By the time you can actually hear a toilet running and see the ripple in the bowl, you could be leaking between 100 and 200 gallons a day."

So how can you tell if you have a leak? Drop 1/4 teaspoon of food coloring into the upper tank of your toilet and then wait

10 minutes. If the water in your toilet bowl changes colors, you've found a leak. "That's the easiest and cheapest thing you can do," says Osann.

And chances are, all you need to do to fix it is install a new flapper valve in the tank. "That might be a $10 item at Home Depot," Osann says. "If you have a handy house member or relative, it's not a major plumbing job."

But if you have an older toilet, you might be better off replacing it rather than fixing the leak. Toilets made before the mid-1990s didn't have the same efficiency standards, so they use a lot more water in each flush.

"If you have a toilet that is more than 25 years old, it will pay to have it replaced," says Osann.

How to quench your thirsty lawn without spending a fortune

A lush lawn could make your yard the pride of the neighborhood. But keeping your grass green might cause your water bills to skyrocket during those hot, summer months. Fortunately, with a little know-how you can keep your yard in tiptop shape and save money on your utilities.

Rethink your lawn mower setup. How you mow your lawn makes a big difference in how much water it will need. "A closely cut lawn will require more water than one that you let grow to a couple of inches," says water efficiency expert Ed Osann. So set your mower blade height a bit higher, to at least 2 inches.

Save time by leaving the grass clippings in the yard. The nutrients help your grass grow deeper roots so they absorb water better. Mulching mowers are great since they cut the blades into smaller pieces. You'll want to mow more often to avoid piles of dead grass that leave brown spots in your yard.

Ditch the timed irrigation system and opt for a hose instead. An automatic, timer-controlled sprinkler may seem like a great way to keep your lawn regularly watered, but it could be costing you a pretty penny.

"The data shows that people who have in-ground, automatic systems actually use more water than people who just have a hose and a sprinkler and turn it on when they think the lawn needs watering," says Osann.

Consider the layout of your yard. Big, grassy lawns may be nice if you have young kids who need a place to play. But if you're an empty nester, you might want a smaller patch of turf that requires less water and less maintenance. You can replace the grass with a different ground cover — like clover — that is more tolerant of dry spells.

You could also convert portions of your yard into a native garden that conserves H2O. If you're not sure what kind of plants work best for your area, reach out to your local water utility or park service. "They may have programs for learning about water-efficient gardening, or they may have demonstration gardens," Osann says.

Showerhead hunter: Expert tips improve your cash flow

You used to be able to find showerheads in the store that boasted an impressive flow rate of 5 or more gallons a minute. That meant you had a great shower, but it cost a king's ransom. If you still have an older showerhead, you could be using upwards of 1,200 gallons a month just to bathe.

Make the switch to a low-flow showerhead and cut your usage by more than half. Many people think changing out their showerhead means sacrificing the quality of their shower. "In reality, people are getting good showers from water-efficient showerheads," says Ed Osann from Natural Resources Defense Council. "At least they can."

The trick? You just need to know what to search for. "I recommend that people look for showerheads that have a variable orifice. Another way of describing them is 'pressure compensating,'" Osann says. And that's the phrase you're more likely to see on the label. "What that means is the user will get pretty much the same flow through the showerhead across a wide range of pressures."

He also recommends looking for showerheads labeled with the EPA's WaterSense approval. That means the flow rate will be capped at 2 gallons per minute. And you don't need to spend big bucks, either. You can find a high-quality, low-flow showerhead for less than $20.

Upgrade your faucet to save water in the kitchen

Are you turning all your attention to your shower, toilets, and clothes washer to save on water? Don't forget about your kitchen faucet. It accounts for the majority of your faucet water use, says Ed Osann, a leading authority on water efficiency.

From rinsing vegetables to washing dishes, flow rate makes a big difference. You can save water by switching to a more efficient faucet. The only problem? "WaterSense has not developed a label for water-efficient kitchen faucets," Osann says. So how do you know what to buy?

The maximum flow rate allowed by federal regulation is 2.2 gallons per minute, but check the rate on the package to find one that's lower. "Most major manufacturers are making a kitchen faucet that flows at 1.8 gallons per minute," says Osann, "and that can be a nice water saver."

39 | TV & movies

7 smart moves to keep cable — but cut your bill

Your cost for cable TV is probably higher than it's ever been. In fact, if you're like many viewers, you're paying $100 to $200 every month. And you can expect that bill to keep climbing.

While you could cut that cord completely, if you want to stick with cable, here are the top things you can do to whittle your bill down to size.

Compare bundling and unbundling. Sometimes it's a deal to get your TV, internet, and cellphone or landline contract through the same provider. But sometimes you'll save by using different companies for each service. Just asking about this may get you a better offer from your current provider.

Review your package. How many sports channels are in your lineup? And are you paying extra for shopping, children's, or foreign language channels you don't watch? That deluxe package you signed up for a few years ago may not truly reflect your viewing habits like it used to. So try dialing back to a more basic package and see if you notice the difference. Your wallet certainly will.

Jump on the latest promotion. Cable companies offer promotional prices at least once a year — oftentimes around the holidays. Call and ask about any specials they are running and get the details on when you might be eligible for the next one.

Say farewell to extra equipment. Are you still renting a modem? Do you have a DVR in every room? Each box or gadget that belongs to the cable company has a monthly fee attached. Pare these down and you'll pare your monthly bill down, too.

Question fees. Cable bills seem designed to confuse and bewilder. But you should know exactly what you are paying for. Grab your latest bill, your phone, and a pen. Call the customer service or billing department of your provider and have them explain each line item. Ask how you could eliminate some of the fees.

> Want a better rate on your cable, phone, and internet? Don't call the customer service department. Instead, try the cancellation department. Companies hate when customers leave and may be so eager for you to stay that they offer a better deal than your existing one. Hold your ground if the first offer is not to your liking. But don't push it too far and insist on something unrealistic, or they may just say "so long."

Bring the competition into play. Spend some time researching prices from other providers. Then, with the facts in hand, give your cable company a call and politely ask them to match a better deal.

Read your contract carefully. Understand what is and isn't allowed with your contract. Once you have a good understanding about this, you will be in a much stronger position to negotiate a better deal.

Flat and happy: A guide to keeping your TV up and running

Want to expand the life of your television? The following info will help keep it humming along for years to come.

- Switch your TV off now and again. Just like pretty much anything else, constant use will wear out your television. So turn it off if you're about to fall asleep or aren't watching.

- Use a surge protector to defend against voltage spikes.

- Avoid overheating. Most TVs have their ventilation system behind the screen, so keep at least 4 inches of distance between the back of your television and the wall.

- Never clean the screen with chemicals. Instead, wipe it down with a dry rag or duster after turning the TV off.

- Keep the contrast setting at a reasonable level. A higher contrast requires more energy, which cuts into the longevity of your television.

The world is yours with a streaming stick

You can watch just about any movie and TV show available — or listen to any kind of music — from the comfort of your living room. One little box, or stick, will open this world to you. All you have to do to get started is buy a device that provides the streaming service.

Take Roku, for instance. Traditionally, this has been a box which connects to your TV via an HDMI cable. But many people prefer a stick, which plugs into the HDMI slot in the back of your TV. You can purchase these from $29.99 upward, depending on the type of device.

Once you have bought your Roku device, link it to your Wi-Fi router by following the instructions on your TV. After that you can create a Roku account, and then you are all ready to start streaming movies and TV shows.

There is no charge for setting up a Roku account, which allows you to connect to the vast range of content it offers. And a lot of it is free, but you can also use your Roku streaming device to subscribe to services such as Netflix, or to rent or buy movies and TV shows.

Roku is just one of many hardware options you can choose for streaming. Others include the Amazon Fire TV, Apple TV, and Google Chromecast.

Suffering from buffering? Tips on avoiding streaming woes

Ever stream a favorite movie only to have it interrupted by a spinning circle or a "Loading, please wait" message? If so, a sluggish internet connection may be the culprit.

Fortunately, a few simple tricks may be all it takes to solve the problem. Here's what to do when your video download gets stuck on pause.

Make sure you get what you paid for. You can find the speed of your internet service by going to *speedtest.net* or *fast.com*. Then compare that number with the speed you signed on for with your internet service provider. Call the company if you find a dramatic difference between what you're getting and what you should be receiving.

Restart to improve your signal. Performing a reboot can do wonders when it comes to your internet connection. So turn off your TV and unplug your modem and wireless router for at least 30 seconds. Then plug in the devices and wait for the indicator lights to stop blinking. Turn on your TV, access your streaming service, and see if your video is no longer stalled.

Check the placement of your router. Did the preceding steps not work? It's possible that the location of your router is preventing it from working properly. Make sure it's in a central area of your home, and not in a closet or on the floor. Keep it elevated and away from other wireless devices, like laptops and cellphones.

No subscription required — 14 amazingly free streaming services

Is it time you gave up cable and started streaming instead? Go ahead and cancel. You can watch many of your favorite movies and shows for free.

Netflix, Amazon Prime, and Disney+ may steal the streaming spotlight, but you don't have to subscribe to major providers like these and pay an arm and a leg. There are plenty of free streaming services out there. Just be prepared to view a few commercials.

Crackle	crackle.com
Hoopla	hoopladigital.com
IMDb	imdb.com
Kanopy	kanopy.com
Peacock	peacocktv.com
Pluto TV	pluto.tv
Popcornflix	popcornflix.com
Redbox	redbox.com
Sling Free	sling.com/deals/sling-free
STIRR	stirr.com
the ROKU Channel	therokuchannel.roku.com
Tubi TV	tubitv.com
VUDU	vudu.com
XUMO	xumo.tv

Also check out free trials the major paid services offer. But don't forget to cancel at the end of the complimentary period if you don't want to continue, or you'll be charged.

40 | Phone & video calling

> "To effectively communicate, we must realize that we are all different in the way we perceive the world and use this understanding as a guide to our communication with others."
>
> Tony Robbins

Negotiate a better bill with your cell service

Phone companies don't want you to know how far they'll go to avoid losing a valuable customer. They may give you loyalty discounts or some other deal that lowers your monthly bill. But you have to ask.

Go into the conversation armed with details of offers at other companies, and know what you need out of your plan. Ramsey personality and personal finance expert George Kamel has a script to help you out.

Start by saying something like, "Hi I'm George, I've been with AT&T for 12 years now, and I'm happy with my service but my bill is just too high for my budget right now. Is there any way you can lower it?"

Your customer service agent may recommend switching to a lower plan, but be firm.

Follow up respectfully with something like, "I appreciate that. That's a good start but this isn't quite where I need to be. Is there someone I can speak to about possibly canceling my service? I hate to go, but if you can't help me I might need to switch providers."

This initial worker may not have the power to give you a special deal, but the supervisor or retention personnel you get transferred to might. Even $10 less monthly could be dramatic.

Take good notes and write down who you spoke to, when, and what they said. Make sure they add the new information to your account notes, and ask if you can get an email confirmation including the changes they agreed to. You may have to negotiate each year, but the savings are often worth it.

"If one hour can save you $300, that's a great hourly rate," says Kamel.

3 top-tier ways to save with your current carrier

Whether you're looking to save a buck on your phone bill for yourself or a loved one, the top tips are the same. Don't miss out on these key three from personal finance expert George Kamel.

Get automatic savings. "One of the best ways to lower your bill is to make sure you have signed up for automated payments or paperless billing," says Kamel. Because you're making your provider's job easier, they'll pass savings on to you.

You could get $5 to $10 dollars off your bill each month, for savings that add up to more than $100 annually. Promotion periods may offer discounts as high as $25 off per month.

Only pay for what you need. Using a limited data plan can feel like playing blackjack. If you go over your limit any given month, you lose in the form of fees.

It's easy to dodge overage charges, though, if you know how much data you're using. Go to your settings and turn on automated notifications to be alerted when you're close to your data limit. While you're in your settings, turn off background app refresh so you're not using data when you don't need to.

"Wi-Fi is going to be your best friend when it comes to limited data plans, so make sure you're using that whenever possible," says Kamel.

Cut out insurance costs. New phones can be pricey, so insurance may seem like a good investment. But Kamel says if you can't afford a replacement, that phone may not be in your budget anyway.

Instead, cut out the insurance to save $100 or more a year. Then set aside a few dollars each month to go toward a replacement if you need it. This way you guarantee you'll get a phone you want, versus the refurbished replacements offered by some plans.

Protect your phone from damage with a sturdy phone case and screen protector, and you may not need a replacement at all.

Switching plans makes saving money a cinch

Say you've tried to lower your bill with your current phone company, but it's not enough. It's time to follow through and switch providers. A recent survey by Consumer Reports shows more than half of their members who switched carriers said they saved money. The same could be true for you.

First, do some research to see if you're currently overpaying. Enlist a friend to help you compare the cost and fees from different providers, including various plans like unlimited data. Then check for new customer and senior discounts.

But don't just look at the numbers. Coverage is essential because your phone is worthless if you can't use it. Make sure key locations like your house and office are on the company's coverage map. Read through customer reviews to see if you'll have good access to assistance.

Secret shortcuts for speedier customer service

Ready to switch phone providers? It's frustrating trying to get through to most customer service departments — endless buttons to press and those tedious automated messages. How would you like to speak to a real person and bypass recorded menus?

Thankfully, it is still possible to get the human touch with almost every customer service call you make. Just check out the GetHuman website at *gethuman.com*.

Simply type a company name into the search box on the homepage to find the customer service details for that company. This includes the current wait time for a call, an option to skip waiting on hold, and an option to chat with an expert.

Stay connected: Unexpected apps help you keep up with family for free

Technology makes staying in touch with family easier than ever. Earn your no. 1 grandparent award this year by upping your game with these cheap ideas.

- Story time. Instead of paying for a special screen-sharing reading app that could cost you over $100 annually, use free video call platforms like Zoom, FaceTime, or Skype to share a good book.

- Movie night. Some streaming services like Hulu and apps like Kast let you watch a movie at the same time as a loved one. Many even allow audio, video, or text chats while you're watching.

- Walkie-talkie with a twist. Free apps like Marco Polo and Zello let you video or voice chat even when your schedules don't match up because you don't have to respond in real time. If you have an iPhone, audio messages work similarly.

More resources

Alliance for Water Efficiency	home-water-works.org	N/A
American Council for an Energy-Efficient Economy	smarterhouse.org	N/A
Benefits.gov	benefits.gov/categories/Housing%20and%20Public%20Utilities	N/A
Energy Saver	energy.gov/energysaver/energy-saver	N/A
Energy Star	energystar.gov	N/A
Environmental Protection Agency	epa.gov/watersense	N/A
Federal Communications Commission, Consumer Guides	fcc.gov/consumer-guides	888-225-5322
Federal Communications Commission, DTV Reception Maps	fcc.gov/media/engineering/dtvmaps	888-225-5322
Federal Communications Commission, Lifeline Program	fcc.gov/lifeline-consumers	888-225-5322
Federal Trade Commission	consumer.ftc.gov/topics/saving-energy-home	N/A
Low Income Home Energy Assistance Program	acf.hhs.gov/ocs/low-income-home-energy-assistance-program-liheap	202-401-9351
Low Income Household Water Assistance Program	acf.hhs.gov/ocs/programs/lihwap	N/A
National Council on Aging	benefitscheckup.org	N/A
Office of Policy Development and Research	archives.huduser.gov/portal/consumer/home.html	800-245-2691

EAT ON THE CHEAP

Bite-sized wisdom to pad your piggy bank

41 | Grocery shopping

> "We all eat, and it would be a sad waste of opportunity to eat badly."
>
> Anna Thomas

5 smart tips to live well on a tight budget

Living on a fixed income doesn't have to mean hard times when it comes to eating well. In fact, you can trim your grocery bill without cutting back on food. The following shopping secrets will have you spending less every time you're at the supermarket.

Fill up at home. How often have you made a last-minute dinner run at the store and ended up buying cookies and ice cream, too? Most likely you were shopping on an empty stomach. Better to nosh on a healthy snack like whole-grain crackers and hummus before heading out. You'll have more money — and a trimmer waistline — as a result.

Start with the cart. Shopping carts are getting larger and larger all the time. And with good reason. The bigger the cart, the more likely you are to fill it up with unnecessary items. So opt for a smaller cart or basket. And buy only the merchandise you need. It's one of the best things folks on a fixed income can do to bring down expenses, without living like a pauper.

Say yes to store brands. Did you know that the cost of store-brand food and drinks are, on average, 25% lower than name-brand products? They often taste alike — and are of the same quality — as their higher-priced peers. You can frequently find store-brand items to the right or left of their more expensive counterparts. No sales or coupons needed.

You'll want to stroll on past costly, pre-sliced fruits and veggies in the produce aisle. A store might, for example, charge a little over 60 cents for a whole, 10-ounce onion. Buy a similar onion already chopped up and you'll shell out $3.29. That's a whopping 430% more. Slice and dice your own onion once a week and save $139 a year.

Kiss temptation goodbye. Supermarkets sell billions of dollars worth of candy, soda, chips, and other products at checkout lanes annually. And oddly enough, the customers who buy these expensive treats are often the same ones who ignore them in the aisles.

Turns out, retailers strategically place these items by the register to lure you into an impulse buy when you're tired, distracted, and itching to leave the store. Don't fall for it.

Remember, cash is king. Bring a calculator to keep track of how much everything costs as you add merchandise to your basket. This will help prevent overspending. In addition, leave your debit or credit card at home and pay in cash. This way you won't become tempted to buy more than you can afford, allowing you to save money every month.

Eat well, spend less: Stocking the healthy, thrifty kitchen

Want to shop for healthy foods — which are often pricier than processed fare — without breaking the bank? It all comes down to laying the necessary groundwork, says Marcia Batista, a registered dietitian nutritionist in Apollo Beach, Florida.

"It's always helpful to have an idea of why you're going grocery shopping," she advises. To that end, Batista tells her clients to plan their meals for the week and to make a list of the necessary ingredients. She says it's also useful to look at the supermarket's circular of weekly sales. Doing so might even dictate the foods that go on your shopping list.

But don't stop there. Once you're at the grocery store, Batista says, don't automatically navigate to the fresh fruits and veggies. Huh? It makes sense when she explains that such produce, while nutritious, isn't always the most economical choice. After all, it spoils quickly.

"Buy fresh if you're going to use it right away," Batista suggests. Otherwise, opt for canned or frozen. Both have a long shelf life and generally contain the same amount of nutrients as fresh. Just be sure to select options without added sugar or sodium.

Batista further notes that many health professionals advise shoppers to stick to the perimeter of the store. Why? To avoid the high-calorie, nutrient-lacking processed foods — sugary drinks, massed-produced breads, and snack foods — in the middle aisles. But Batista says she hits the center of the store on occasion. That's where she finds healthy, go-to pantry staples like quinoa and canned and dried beans.

Both are excellent sources of plant protein. That makes these flavorful foods very nourishing — and much less expensive — alternatives to meat. Switching from animal to plant proteins is beneficial in so many ways, Batista adds. "It's going to be good for your wallet and also good for your health."

She has one more surprising piece of advice for people who think all organic foods are good for you. They're not.

Batista says people sometimes tell her that they buy organic gummy bears or organic toaster pastries. Her advice? Look at the ingredients in the product, not the label "organic" or "natural," to see how much nutrition you're really getting.

No scissors needed for big price cuts

Clipping, sorting, and carrying around paper coupons takes time and energy. But you can avoid the hassle — and still save a ton of money — by switching to digital.

So how do you start? Download your supermarket's app or go to the store's website. Log in or sign up for a new account by entering the appropriate information. This step links the electronic coupons you choose to your shopper loyalty card.

Next comes the fun part. Start saving by clicking or tapping on all the coupons you want — from batteries and shampoo to granola and seltzer. Fortunately, there's no need to run to the store right away. The coupons stay in your account until you purchase the corresponding item. Just remember that they carry an expiration date like their paper cousins.

Once you're at the supermarket, shop for your items and head to the checkout lane. But instead of sifting through piles of paper coupons at the register, scan your loyalty card or provide your alternate ID to receive your digital savings. Of course, you'll want to check your receipt to ensure that the store redeemed all your coupons. If not, see someone at customer service to get the problem fixed.

Prefer shopping online? Lots of grocery stores allow you to add electronic coupons to your virtual cart. Kroger, for example, accepts them if you pick up your groceries curbside but not if the store makes a delivery.

Cash in on a jackpot of coupons

Coupons and grocery shopping go together like Superman and Lois Lane. Because you'll certainly feel like a superhero when you score super savings at the checkout.

All you need to do is visit a website or download an app and you're ready to rake in the discounts. Check these out. Many even offer coupons on items beyond groceries — like travel, electronics, clothing, home goods, jewelry, toys, and more.

Coupons.com	coupons.com
CouponCabin	couponcabin.com
Coupon Craze	couponcraze.com
CouponAlbum	couponalbum.com
Coupon Sherpa	couponsherpa.com
RetailMeNot	retailmenot.com

And don't forget about cash-back websites and apps that offer money to shoppers after they purchase items. Options like *checkout51.com* and *ibotta.com* provide rebates when you submit your receipt.

Waste not, want not: Solutions for bloated food bills

Yikes! The average senior household spends more than $4,200 a year on groceries. That sure is a big chunk of change when you're living on a fixed income. But don't despair — these practical, money-saving tips will ensure you pay less every month.

It's shocking to hear, but U.S. households waste nearly a third of all the food they buy each year. One reason why? Perishable items pile up in the fridge, only to get thrown out after going bad. So limit your purchases of dairy, fresh fish, and salad fixings to those you'll eat between supermarket visits.

Still, you'll probably have leftovers. Eat them for lunch or dinner the next day. Or try repurposing parts of a meal. For example, you can puree last night's roasted veggies with some chicken broth. Voila! You've whipped up a nutritious and delicious soup in minutes.

Freezing leftovers for later use also prevents spoilage and saves money. How much? If you're part of a senior household, cutting your food waste could save around $1,000 a year.

Stack up your savings with this classic strategy

Want to get grocery items for pennies — or even for free? Then read on to discover a secret that stores hope you never learn.

Use two coupons — one issued by the manufacturer and the other by the store — on a single item. You'll go home with even fuller pockets if the item is on sale or, better yet, on a bargain rack.

Just be sure to check the retailer's policy. Some don't accept "stacked" coupons. And pay attention to the order in which you apply the coupons. Experts suggest you use those that require a minimum purchase amount first. That way other coupon discounts won't negate the deal by making the product fall below the required amount.

42 | Food storage

> "Throwing away food is like stealing from the table of those who are poor and hungry."
>
> Pope Francis

6 top tips for stay-at-home food safety

Food poisoning isn't only on the menu at your local restaurant. The home kitchen is the third most frequent location for the source of this illness — food contaminated with a nasty collection of bacteria or viruses. And that statistic just might be growing.

"With more people cooking their own meals at home, it's important to practice the highest standards of food safety, cleanliness, and hygiene," says Lisa Yakas, consumer product expert at NSF International, an organization that protects and improves global human health.

She advises you follow a few food safety tips to avoid risks like *E. coli*, *Salmonella*, yeast, and mold, which often cause foodborne illness.

- Once you've stocked up on groceries, don't stuff everything willy-nilly in your refrigerator. Air circulation is essential to keep food at the proper temperature. Organize items strategically so there's some space between.

- Place raw meat in a designated drawer or container to prevent juices from getting on other food.

- Allow leftovers to cool before storing them, but don't let them sit out at room temperature longer than two hours.

- Generally, eat refrigerated leftovers within three to four days. However, you can safely freeze most for two to three months. How to keep it all straight? Date every container before storing so you'll know when to discard.

- Ever watched someone toss a package of frozen chicken onto the counter to thaw? If so, that's one meal you'll want to pass on. This room-temperature danger zone is the perfect breeding ground for bacteria. Instead, defrost frozen food in the refrigerator, allowing four to five hours per pound. If you plan to cook an item immediately, it's safe to thaw it under running cold water or in the microwave.

- Don't panic if a packaged or canned food is slightly past its "Best used by" date. This is merely a guide as to flavor or quality — not safety. Likewise, the "Sell by" date tells the store how long to display an item for sale. But do pay attention to expiration dates. Toss anything that could be expired.

"Food safety, cleanliness, and hygiene within your home are all things you have 100% control over," Yakas points out, "and help ensure the health and safety of you and your loved ones."

Cool freezer hacks that stop food waste cold

"I love freezing food for so many reasons," says Andrew Zimmern, James Beard Award-winning chef and television personality. "In part because I can store fresh food and use it later." But he also relishes the challenge of coming up with new ways to make dinner from what he calls freezer finds.

It's a sentiment shared by lots of Americans who are reported to be putting food on ice at record rates — many purchasing extra freezers to keep all their stashed goodies preserved. But all is not cool in subzero land. A recent survey revealed people often feel stressed, not comforted, by the amount of unused food in their freezer.

When you end up having to toss out bricks of discolored meat, bags of shriveled produce, or mystery items rimed with freezer burn, you carry the guilt of having also just tossed a chunk of your hard-earned money right in the trash. Never waste your groceries or your greenbacks again with these nifty tips for organizing your freezer.

Label. Use masking tape and a permanent marker to ID and date any leftovers, homemade dishes, or bulk items you've repackaged. Feeling uber tidy? Color-code types of food with different colored markers or self-adhesive labels. For instance, green means veggies. Got it?

Align. Initially, freeze bagged liquids, such as soups or stews, flat. Once they're solid, store them vertically — just like files in your office. Super easy to flip, find, grab, and go.

Group. Stow like items in labeled bins. Pick some up cheaply at the dollar store or repurpose whatever you have lying around the house. Why not give new life to old magazine holders or even small plastic tubs missing their lids?

Rotate. Just like grocery stores shift their stock, swap your frozen goods around so nothing stays out of sight, out of mind. Place the newest foods in the bottom or near the back of your freezer. And move older items so they are next in line for use.

Classify. Allocate certain freezer shelves or areas for specific types of food. That way you'll know where to go looking for chicken. Or ice cream.

Itemize. Post a list of all your frozen food, with dates, on or near the freezer. Then check off whatever you use from this inventory. Nothing gets lost or forgotten. When it's time to cook or to shop, check the list. You'll know exactly what you have and what you need to buy. A dry-erase board or magnetic notepad is perfect for the job.

Storage wars: The best (and cheapest) containers for your fridge and pantry

Want to save money and the planet? Swap plastic for glass. Seems simple enough. Although plastic's long been the top pick for millions of products, health and environmental concerns have experts urging change.

If you need more convincing, when it comes to food storage, glass containers knock it out of the park.

Pinch those pennies with a dirt-cheap choice. A package of 12 mason jars suitable for storing, preserving, and even freezing, will set you back less than $9. Compare that to multiple boxes of zip-sealed bags or plastic containers, and you'll quickly learn the math speaks for itself.

Refill, reuse, and recycle. Glass washes and even sterilizes so well, you may not have to go out and buy all new containers. Run empty spaghetti sauce jars through a hot dishwashing cycle and, voila, instant storage.

Keep foods fresh and tasty. Choose a glass storage container and lid that seals with gaskets or by locking and you've got an airtight environment. No flavors, odors, or bacteria in or out.

To your health — avoid the perils of plastic. If you're in your kitchen zapping yesterday's pasta primavera in a plastic container, stop. Bisphenol A (BPA) is a chemical in many plastics that can break down and leach into your foods, especially when exposed to heat and harsh detergents. Glass, as any scientist will tell you, is chemically inert — which means it won't react to other elements and contains no compounds that can seep into your food.

 ### Spoiled rotten: Is your fridge killing your produce?

Lifeless lettuce. Slimy squash. Melting mushrooms. Ick. You just dropped over $11 down the garbage disposal.

Produce spoils faster than it should when your refrigerator's crisper drawer doesn't do its job properly — maybe because you're making these two very wasteful fridge fumbles.

- The humidity setting for your crisper drawer depends on the contents. Choose low humidity for foods that tend to rot due to escaping ethylene gas, such as pears, apples, peaches, melons, and avocados. Items that wilt, like leafy greens, need high humidity. Don't combine these different types in the same drawer or mix up the settings.

- Many fruits and vegetables emit water during storage. And perhaps you pre-wash items and put them away damp. Any excess moisture trapped in the crisper drawer with your produce will lead to rot and mold. The solution is to dry everything thoroughly before storing and line the drawer with clean paper or cloth towels to absorb any moisture. Just make sure to replace the towel whenever it becomes damp.

---

43 | Dining in

> "Cooking is at once child's play and adult joy. And cooking done with care is an act of love."
>
> Craig Claiborne

All in 1 — cook up savings with this convenient multipurpose gadget

So many appliances in kitchens these days — pressure cookers, slow cookers, yogurt makers, rice cookers, and more. Wouldn't it be nice if one gadget could do it all?

That's where multicookers come in. These appliances cover all of the above and then some — from sauteing and browning to roasting and steaming. Not only that, cooking time can be up to 70% faster than traditional methods.

Multicookers typically range anywhere from $50 to $200. Pricing often hinges on the model's size, cooking capabilities, and design features. Here are some things to know if you're in the market for one.

- Look for deals on Black Friday or Amazon Prime Day. These kitchen appliances — some of which even have the ability to air fry crispy sweet potato fries — also tend to go on sale in November and December.

- Multicookers come in lots of varieties — some have bells and whistles that you may not need. For example, you probably wouldn't want one with cake-making or bread-making features if you're not much of a baker to begin with.

- Be sure to pick the right size. A 3-quart cooker is best for making meals for one or two people, while the 6-quart size is suited for small households of up to four individuals. Have a large family that visits often? Consider an 8-quart version.

Pinch pennies with an order-in game plan

Uh-oh. You've settled in to binge watch your favorite TV series when your tummy starts to rumble. A thought crosses your mind. Why not order dinner through one of those food delivery apps? Just think — a tasty takeout meal dropped at your doorstep within the hour.

Not so fast. All that convenience can come with a hefty price. According to The New York Times, getting your food this way can cost up to 91% more than if you bought the same meal directly from the restaurant.

That's because most of the popular apps require a delivery fee, sales tax, and a service fee, too. If you want just a sandwich or two, you might even be hit with a "small order" charge. And don't forget that the delivery person should receive a tip equal to 20% of the entire bill, or $3 to $5, whichever is higher.

Of course, it would be less expensive to pick up your menu selections yourself. But if that's not an option, you can still cut the cost of staying home and satisfying your appetite for, say, chicken tikka masala. Here's how.

Go directly to the source. If you're hungry for a deal, shop around for restaurants in your area that offer free delivery. Many also sell gift cards that come with perks, which can offset taxes and service fees. Panera Bread, for example, has provided a free $10 bonus card with every $50 purchased in gift cards.

Split a dish and skip the extras. Are you a light eater? Consider ordering a less expensive appetizer as your main course. Or set aside half of your entree for lunch the next day. That way you'll get two meals for the price of one. And don't order drinks. Why spend $2 or $3 for a beverage that's probably already in your fridge? Same goes for dessert.

Watch for discounts. Be sure to check the websites of food delivery platforms like Uber Eats, DoorDash, and Grubhub for promotional codes and special offers. Some deals are available to new users, while others apply to everyone. Promos include free delivery and fixed discounts for certain purchase amounts.

Sign up for a subscription. You can subscribe to a food delivery service if you often find yourself ordering in. For $9.99 per month, for example, the Uber Eats Pass gives you access to free deliveries and a 5% discount on any order that costs more than $15. You may be able to try out the service for free.

Are meal kits worth it? A nutritionist weighs in on the trend

Mmmmm. Flaked salmon in citrus butter sauce with a tasty side of roasted green beans and Parmesan red potatoes. Sound like a treat you'd find only at a fancy restaurant? Not anymore.

Welcome to the world of meal kits — pre-measured, and often pre-prepped, boxed ingredients that come with cooking instructions. It's a fast-growing, multibillion-dollar industry that has taken online retailers and supermarkets by storm.

But are they a good idea? They can be, says Vandana Sheth, a California-based registered dietitian nutritionist. For starters, she says, prepared entrees are convenient alternatives for busy people who don't want to rely on fast food to fill their tummies. "A kit literally can transform a meal in 10 to 15 minutes," she says.

Though, she adds, it's important to make smart choices. Look at the label before buying a ready-to-make meal. Does it lack protein and fiber? If so, you could round it out by adding a big salad or some steamed veggies.

"All foods can fit into a healthy way of eating," she says. Just make sure you get enough produce on your plate.

And the price? Sheth says the cost depends on the retailer. And like anything else, you'll want to balance your wants with your needs. Tucking into a tasty plate of food without the stress of prepping certainly has its perks. But kits come with a price. You'll be paying for packaging, Sheth says, along with the convenience of someone else doing the leg work for you.

If you have time to shop for the ingredients yourself, she advises, you can customize your meals and might save a chunk of change.

Back from the brink: 4 tips for reviving food

Don't give up on that wobbly carrot just yet. Often all it takes is a little TLC to freshen up your slightly past-their-prime provisions. Follow these tips to keep edibles from ending up in the trash.

- Rehydrate wilted lettuce and cabbage by trimming a bit off the stem and immersing the entire vegetable in a bowl of ice water for 30 minutes or so. Hearty root veggies like yams, beets, and parsnips may need more time. Set the trimmed ends of stalk vegetables like celery and asparagus into a glass of cold water before placing it in the fridge. This works for carrots, too.

- Have unsliced bread that has dried out? Douse the crust with water before placing the loaf in a 350-degree oven for five to 10 minutes. You can bring chips and crackers back to life by microwaving them on full power for 10 seconds or so.

> Are you among the millions of Americans who drink 2 cups of coffee a day? If so, try this simple hack that can save you hundreds of dollars annually. Instead of buying pricey, single-use K-Cups that already contain ground coffee, purchase a reusable one and fill it yourself. You could save as much as 54 cents per cup of joe. That's $1.08 a day — or nearly $400 a year.

- If honey becomes thick with sugar crystals, place a pot of water on low heat. Once the water has warmed, take the pot off the burner and place the open jar of honey in it, making sure the water line stays below the lid. If your bottle is plastic, first spoon the honey into a sealable glass jar. Stir the contents with a teaspoon until the honey runs clear.

- Freshen up leftover popcorn by spreading the popped kernels evenly on a baking sheet. Then place the sheet in a 250-degree oven for roughly five minutes. Check every minute or so to prevent burning.

💬 More resources

Academy of Nutrition and Dietetics	eatright.org/food	N/A
Benefits.gov	benefits.gov/categories/Food%20and%20Nutrition	N/A
Environmental Protection Agency	epa.gov/recycle/reducing-wasted-food-home	N/A
Food and Drug Administration	fda.gov/food/resources-you-food/consumers	888-463-6332
Food and Nutrition Service	fns.usda.gov/program/assistance-seniors	N/A
FoodKeeper App	foodsafety.gov/keep-food-safe/foodkeeper-app	N/A
Iowa State University Extension and Outreach	spendsmart.extension.iastate.edu	N/A
Meals on Wheels America	mealsonwheelsamerica.org	888-998-6325
MyFridgeFood	myfridgefood.com	N/A
MyPlate	myplate.gov/eat-healthy/healthy-eating-budget	202-720-2791
National Agricultural Library	nal.usda.gov/fnic	301-504-5755
National Center for Home Food Preservation	nchfp.uga.edu	N/A
Natural Resources Defense Council	savethefood.com	N/A
Nutrition.gov	www.nutrition.gov/topics	N/A
SNAP Education (SNAP-Ed)	snaped.fns.usda.gov/nutrition-education/nutrition-education-materials	N/A
Supplemental Nutrition Assistance Program	fns.usda.gov/snap/supplemental-nutrition-assistance-program	800-221-5689
U.S. Department of Health and Human Services	foodsafety.gov	N/A

WHEEL & DEAL

Drive down the price of getting there

44 | Fuel costs

> "A dream without ambition is like a car without gas
> — you're not going anywhere."
>
> Sean Hampton

Fill up on fuel savings with these maintenance moves

Keeping your car in good shape takes a little bit of elbow grease.
But these three straightforward maintenance strategies can help
you get more bang for your buck at the gas pump.

Regularly replace your spark plugs. Your spark plugs may be
the culprit if your fuel economy suddenly drops. All it takes to
increase your gas mileage up to 30% is changing them out.

Keep your tires properly inflated. Tire pressure slowly drops
each month. "Having tires with lower pressure than what is recommended on your doorjamb sticker can affect performance,
tire longevity, and fuel economy," explains deputy auto editor at
Consumer Reports, Jeff Bartlett.

Underinflated tires waste approximately 1% of all gasoline
consumption annually, according to the U.S. Department of
Energy. For you, that means proper tire pressure can save a couple
of cents per gallon. That's on par with what you might save with

a loyalty program. Properly inflated tires typically last longer and are safer, too.

Don't let your gas level veer toward empty. "Keep at least a half-tank of fuel at all times," says Bartlett, "especially when there is a risk of shortages, say, due to a lack of gasoline delivery drivers to meet travel demands, or when a major storm or hurricane is imminent."

But there's more. Getting too low on fuel can affect the fuel pump, causing overheating and expensive repairs. Plus condensation that forms in the empty part of your tank in cold weather could lead to engine or tank corrosion and frozen fuel lines.

The driving habits that keep your tank fuller longer

Enhancing fuel efficiency on the road isn't just up to your car, it's your job, too. "Your driving habits can play a significant role in fuel economy," says Jeff Bartlett of Consumer Reports. "When you drive, follow the speed limits and drive smoothly." Use these tips to adjust your driving patterns and get the most out of your money.

Curb jolty driving. Bartlett recommends avoiding hard acceleration and braking whenever possible. Zooming forward uses more fuel, and stopping hard wastes the fuel you just used to reach that speed. On the highway, this aggressive driving style could lower your mileage 15% to 30%.

"Smooth acceleration, cornering, and braking also extend the life of the engine, transmission, brakes, and tires," says Bartlett.

Click on cruise control. This feature can help you maintain a steady, money-saving pace. Just don't use it when the roads are wet and slippery, you're in heavy traffic, or you're going down winding roads. And when setting your speed, keep in mind that driving above 60 mph will reduce how many miles you can travel on your tank.

"Higher speeds exact a toll in fuel consumption," says Bartlett. "Speeding up from 55 to 75 mph is like moving from a compact car to a large SUV."

Chart the best driving route. Choosing the most efficient course to the grocery store doesn't just save you time running errands, it can save you money, too. Traffic leaves you sitting on the road as you burn through your gas and money, so avoid rush hour if possible.

Order your stops so you're not backtracking and using unnecessary gas. If possible, pick roads with higher-quality surfaces as bumpy streets take away your forward momentum.

Don't be lured in by unnecessary gas upgrades

Trying to keep your car in tiptop shape? You may think the more expensive fuel is worth your dollar. But unless you have a high-performance vehicle, hold off.

"Save your money and skip premium gas unless it is 'required.' This is indicated on the fuel filler door," says auto expert Jeff Bartlett. "Many cars list it as 'recommended,' which means it is optional. If there is only midgrade or premium fuel available, this will work fine in a car that is rated for regular gasoline."

It's an entirely different story when it comes to Top Tier gas, although the names may seem similar. Where premium fuel is meant for specific types of vehicles, Top Tier just means the gas has more engine-cleaning additives than other fuel. It may be worth the extra investment because it prevents carbon buildup in your engine, which can reduce your mileage on a tank of gas.

However, you don't have to go hunting for it. When prices of gas skyrocket, choose what's convenient and competitively priced. When fuel costs drop back down, pump Top Tier gas to clear out the crud that may have built up. Certain gas stations, like BP, Exxon, and Shell, offer Top Tier gas.

45 | Car insurance

> "As for the future, your task is not to foresee it, but to enable it."
>
> Antoine de Saint-Exupéry

Save more when you drive less

You retired a few years ago and are driving less than ever before. But have you told your car insurance provider?

"Seniors are often overpaying on premiums because insurers are still charging them based on previous information, like they were going to work and commuting," says Michael DeLong, a research and advocacy associate with Consumer Federation of America.

If you know to ask, insurers will reward you for racking up fewer miles. One option is a pay-per-mile program. Unlike a low-mileage discount, which simply offers money off for driving less, pay-per-mile is a separate plan calculated based on exact mileage.

"For people who don't drive often or people who only drive short distances, this tends to be very affordable and can actually save you a significant amount of money," says DeLong.

Some companies, like Metromile, are entirely based around this model. Other big names like Nationwide and Allstate offer it as well. With these programs you pay a small flat rate each month, say $45, plus a per-mile fee.

Imagine you drove 24 miles every day in June for a total of 720 miles. If your per-mile rate is 6 cents, your mileage cost for the month would be $43. Now add the $45 flat fee for a total of $88. Compare that to the national average of $124 a month, and you're talking serious savings.

The fewer miles you drive, the more you'll save. You could even cut your car insurance costs by as much as 50%.

Going on a road trip? No worries. Oftentimes the company will cap your daily mileage cost. For instance, with Metromile and Nationwide's SmartMiles, any distance you drive over 250 miles in one day is free.

Vehicle monitoring: Weigh discounts against privacy concerns

Want a pay-per-mile insurance plan or a safe driver discount? Plug in one device and soon your car will be sending detailed driving reports to your auto insurance company. Depending on the program, it may collect data on mileage, speed, braking patterns, and more. Your insurer can then use this information to adjust your premiums.

The benefits? "It could encourage safer driving behavior and ensure that your insurance premiums are based on your driving record as opposed to unfair factors like your credit score, gender, or job," says consumer advocate Michael DeLong.

But risky habits behind the wheel could actually increase your premium. Plus privacy concerns are a key drawback, so ask what safeguards the company has. You should know what information they're collecting and make sure they won't sell that data. Most states don't regulate these devices, so you need to do your homework.

Most important steps to get the best monthly rate

"I can't wait to shop for car insurance," said no one ever. But do these two steps and you could shave hundreds off your premiums. Now that's something to look forward to.

Gauge your needs. Start by evaluating the value of your car. The general rule of thumb says it's time to drop comprehensive and collision insurance when annual costs add up to more than 10% of your car's value. These policies cover damage to your vehicle and aren't usually a good investment if your car is worth less than a few thousand dollars.

Your state's required minimum liability coverage likely won't be enough if you cause an accident that results in injuries and damages for the other person. That's why many experts recommend you supplement that amount to match your net worth.

Compare plans. Online price quote tools are a convenient way to compare your options. Be sure to use exactly the same information with each company, though. Making a chart can help you visualize the differences, says insurance expert Michael DeLong.

"Even relatively small differences could save you a significant amount of money," says DeLong. "Don't let yourself be rushed."

Pay less on your premium with these discounts

The average American pays $1,483 a year for car insurance. Yikes. That's enough money to fund a three-day vacation for two at Disney World, including park tickets, food, and a stay at a four-star hotel. So how can you cut your costs? Check out these discounts.

Sign up for defensive driving. "You can refresh your driving skills with a defensive driving course," says Michael DeLong of the Consumer Federation of America. "It provides evidence that you're a safe driver, and it could also qualify you for a discount."

Deductions from completing a state-approved safety course are often only available for those age 55 and up. Just one perk of being a senior.

Earn accident avoidance accolades. Get rewarded for your safety behind the wheel when you keep your driving record accident-free. If you're in an accident, you'll lose this bonus.

To avoid losing out on your claim, too, DeLong recommends getting a second opinion and not just trusting your insurer. If they undervalue your claim, they won't have to pay you the full value.

Boost your credit score. "It's not widely known but auto insurers do use your credit score to influence your rates," says DeLong. "People with fair or poor credit get charged a lot more, sometimes hundreds of dollars more, even if they have perfect driving records."

So improving your credit score by keeping your credit card spending low and paying your bill on time can actually help lower your auto insurance.

Update your vehicle to be tech savvy. Your insurer may knock down your bill if your car has modern safety features. Savings might accompany anti-lock brakes or an anti-theft device.

But pay attention. Anti-theft discounts, for example, generally only apply to comprehensive insurance, which covers vehicle theft. This will do you no good if you only have liability.

Make paying simple. Get a thank you from your insurance company in the form of a discount when you go paperless. Setting up autopay could also keep a few extra bucks in the bank. Check whether these are one-time or recurring offers.

46 | Car maintenance

"Take care of your car in the garage, and the car will take care of you on the road."

Amit Kalantri

Swerving big-ticket breakdowns: ID these sounds and smells early

It's hard to tell if that clanking and thumping you're hearing while driving is just typical road noise or if there's something more serious going on with your car. And are you sure that funky smell is drifting in through the open window, or is your engine trying to warn you that something is going wrong?

Pay attention to these odd sights and smells. If you notice them lingering for more than a few minutes during your drive, it may be a sign that you need to get the car fixed before a more expensive problem breaks your wallet.

- Screeching and scraping when you hit the brakes could mean your brake pads are wearing thin. And if you hear a grinding, too, it may be time to get the calipers and rotors replaced.

- High-pitched squeaks and squeals suggest you have a problem with an engine belt slipping. Fixing this could be as easy as cleaning dirt and grime off the belts in your engine. If that doesn't erase the problem, replacing the belt might do the trick.

- Notice a sweet, almost syrupy smell? Your engine is probably leaking coolant. You need to get this fixed as soon as possible. If the coolant runs out, your engine could overheat and fail.

- Persistent smoke and burning smells could be a few different problems. Acrid, burning odors could point to an oil leak in your engine. Or if you notice strong exhaust smells in your car, you might have a dangerous carbon monoxide leak.

Stick to this schedule to keep your car running for years

A car that lasts 200,000 miles may have seemed like a pipe dream years ago, but modern vehicles are more reliable than ever. As long as you keep up with regular maintenance and look after your ride, you could make it last practically a lifetime.

"Anticipating your vehicle's needs before problems strike is important," says John Nielsen, AAA's managing director of automotive engineering and repair. "While it may seem that skipping maintenance and repairs can save money in the short term, staying on top of car care can save drivers hundreds of dollars in the long run."

Follow this mile-by-mile maintenance schedule to keep your wheels on the road.

Every 5,000 miles. Oil lubricates all the intricate, moving parts in your car's engine to make sure they don't overheat and cause your car to break down. But over time it gets dirty and less effective, so it needs to be regularly changed out. If you use synthetic oil in your car's engine, you may be able to go up to 10,000 miles between oil changes. And if your car is older, it may need more frequent attention. Put a fresh oil filter in every time you change the oil, too.

Every 10,000 miles. Your tires don't wear out evenly when you drive your car. Mechanics recommend getting them rotated and rebalanced at regular intervals so that your tires wear down slower and more evenly.

Every 15,000 miles. Dusty, dirty air can clog up your car and cause major problems, so the engine has an air filter that protects it from tiny particles. But if you let too much dirt build up, the filter won't work properly. Depending on your car's engine, you may only need to replace the air filter every 30,000 or 35,000 miles. Check your owner's manual for more info.

Every 30,000 miles. Brake pads wear down a tiny bit every single time you stop the car. And over time, they become less and less effective. Their life span may depend on the material used in the pads and what kind of driving you do. For example, if most of your miles are on the highway, your brakes could last as many as 80,000 miles. Ask a reputable mechanic to inspect your brakes if you're not sure they need to be replaced.

Every 50,000 miles. Your car needs some major TLC when it hits this milestone. Get a mechanic to flush the transmission fluid. You should also inspect your battery, spark plugs, and ignition wires to see if any of them need to be replaced.

"Consumers who forget or ignore recommended maintenance ultimately pay higher repair costs," warns Nielsen. Adopt this agenda and it's a win-win.

Get your check engine light diagnosed without spending a dime

Every car that's hit the market since 1996 is equipped with a tiny computer. And when things go wrong, the computer can recognize there's a problem and turn on your check engine light to warn you.

The only issue? You need a special tool to access that computer and see what the problem is. That's where on-board diagnostic (OBD) scanners come in. They link up to your car and give you a diagnostic code that describes the problem.

You might think these tools are only for professional mechanics, but you couldn't be more wrong. You can buy one for around $30. Or take your car to an auto parts store, where they may scan it free of charge. Once you have an idea of what needs to be fixed, evaluate if you can do the repair yourself or research how much the job will cost so you're not scammed by a shady mechanic.

Replace this overlooked — and cheap — item once a year

Few things are worse than getting caught on the road in a sudden downpour only to discover your windshield wipers don't work anymore. Instead of smoothly clearing the sheets of water off of the glass, the brittle rubber leaves a wet smear across your windshield. It's annoying, ugly, and downright dangerous. The fix is surprisingly cheap and easy. Make replacing your windshield wipers a regular part of your car's maintenance schedule.

Because wiper blades are made of rubber, they won't last forever. They could crack and dry out within six months to a year depending on your climate. Fortunately, a new set of blades can cost as little as $20. And installing them is incredibly simple. Even if you're not an experienced DIYer, you should be able to follow the instructions on the box and change the blades out in a matter of minutes.

However, if you're not up to the task, you don't need to pay a mechanic to get the job done. Many auto parts stores will install new windshield wiper blades for free when you purchase a set from the store.

4 essential items to keep in your car at all times

Stranded in a parking lot by a dead battery or a flat tire? You may have to pay a hefty fee to get your car towed to the nearest mechanic's shop. In fact, the average cost of a tow clocks in at $75 to $125. That's not including what you'll have to spend to get your car running again.

But you can easily prevent some roadside emergencies. All you need to do is keep these essential maintenance items in your car.

- The owner's manual. This important document will tell you all sorts of info about your car, such as what kind of oil your car needs and your recommended tire pressure. If you have it in hand, you'll be well-equipped to handle quick roadside maintenance. And if you lost your manual, or you bought a used car that didn't come with one, don't worry. Search for it online or contact your car's manufacturer or a dealership to order one.

- Jumper cables. If your battery dies, your car isn't going anywhere. However, with an inexpensive pair of jumper cables and help from another motorist, you may get your engine firing.

- Duct tape. Sideswiped in the parking lot? Your sideview mirror may be left dangling from your car. And driving without being able to check your blind spots is a recipe for disaster. But with a bit of all-weather duct tape, you may be able to temporarily reattach loose items or broken parts of your car.

- A spare tire and all the tools you need to use it. A flat tire won't leave you stranded if you have all the proper tools. Check if your car came with a spare. Many manufacturers leave it out in order to reduce the car's weight and improve the fuel economy.

Failed an emissions test? You may save hundreds with these simple tips

Most states require you to get an annual smog test in order to keep your car on the road. While they're usually cheap, quick, and easy, a failed test could mean you're staring down an expensive repair bill. But if you don't pass the first time around, don't panic. These three tips could help you save hundreds.

> Do you actually need to get an emissions test every year? You might be surprised to find that you're eligible for an exemption that lets you opt out of these annual inspections. Some states allow older vehicles, brand-new rides, and hybrids to skip out on smog tests. Others may let seniors who drive less than 5,000 miles a year get a pass. Check your local regulations to see where you stand.

See if your state will foot the repair bill. Before you go into your own pocket for emissions-related repairs, check with your local government. The assistance program in California, for example, pays up to $1,200 in repairs, while the one in Arizona offers up to $900.

These programs aren't available everywhere, though. Ask the emissions testing station manager for more information if you fail a smog test.

Newer car? Take it to the dealership. It can take a bit of time before you notice something is defective with the emissions system after you buy a new car.

That's why the government requires dealerships to cover the cost of emissions-related repairs if the car has less than 24,000 miles on it or is less than two years old — whichever comes first.

Save the receipts for a repair waiver. You have to take your car to be retested after failing an emissions test. And if you fail the second time around, you may not be eligible to renew your vehicle registration.

But some states offer repair waivers that will let you ignore the results of a smog test if you've already spent the required minimum on repairs. The rules vary from state to state, so check with your local tag office to find out more info.

47 | Car buying & selling

> "Everything in life is somewhere else, and you get there in a car."
>
> E. B. White

This 1 purchasing habit could save an amazing $250,000 over a lifetime

Trading in your car every few years to buy a shiny, new one is as good as throwing your hard-earned cash down the drain. According to Liz Weston, a personal finance columnist with NerdWallet, simply holding off buying a new car for about 10 years or so can save you a quarter of a million dollars over the years.

In her book, *Deal with Your Debt: Free Yourself from What You Owe*, she crunched the numbers and found that an average person who buys a car every five years will wind up spending a lot more money on their car payments than someone who waits 10 years before getting a new one.

"Just on the payments alone, you're saving $250,000 by owning it longer," Weston says. Plus older cars are often cheaper to insure, so the hidden savings can be even higher. And it's never too late to start using this strategy.

Worried that holding on to your car for too long could leave you with expensive repair bills? "J.D. Power says 200,000 miles is essentially the average before the typical car starts needing major repairs," Weston says. "So if you drive about 15,000 miles a year, that's 13 years of driving."

And to get even more savings? Buy a car that's a few years old. Cars lose value fast in the first few years, so shopping for a used auto can get you a great bargain without compromising on reliability.

"If you buy a two- or three-year-old car, you've let the first owner take that big depreciation hit and you can still drive it 10 years easily," says Weston.

Car shopping? The most important things to do before you head to the dealership

"People walk into a dealership with a target on their back," says certified financial planner Liz Weston. That's why, when you're shopping for a car, going in unprepared is the worst thing you can do. To make sure you're not taken advantage of, follow her advice.

- Research the market value of the car you want ahead of time. Weston recommends bringing the paperwork in to show that you know what you're talking about. It will put you in a firm position to bargain.

- Reach out to a bank or credit union to get approved for a loan before you even step foot in a dealership. If you have your financing lined up, you don't have to settle for the high rates that dealerships often offer.

"If only you do those two things, you'll be head and shoulders above other folks walking in," Weston says.

3 key steps to car selling success

Selling your car is no easy undertaking. If you're not careful, you could price the car too low and get fleeced. Or you may ask for too much and spend months and months trying to offload your old auto. To get the most money out of your car, try these tips and tricks.

Price your car right the first time around. Can't decide how much you should sell your car for? Use appraisal tools — like Kelley Blue Book or Edmunds — to get a rough estimate for how much the car is worth. It's also a good idea to check out local forums, such as Craigslist or Facebook Marketplace, to see how much cars like yours are selling for in your area.

If you need a bit of extra advice, consider getting a mechanic to appraise your car. Not only can you sniff out potential issues that would ruin a sale, but you can highlight features of your car that are in good shape.

Boost the curb appeal. If you're trying to sell your house, you'd give it a thorough cleaning and make sure the landscaping is in tiptop shape. So why wouldn't you give your car the same treatment? Get it detailed and washed to help draw in prospective buyers.

If you're making an online listing, you'll need good pictures of the car. Find a well-lit area and take photos from a variety of angles. Include pictures of the interior, trunk, engine, tire tread, and odometer — to show the current mileage.

Don't be afraid to negotiate. Trading your car in at the dealership or selling it to a used car retailer is easy, but it'll leave you with less money in your pocket.

However, if you want to get every last cent out of your ride on the open market, you'll need to be able to negotiate with a buyer.

Set a price that you're not willing to go below and stick with it. Don't let a sob story or strong-arm tactics force you into a bad deal. If you're not happy with the offer — or if you feel like a buyer is wasting your time — be ready to walk away.

Use these smart shopping tips to buy online

Considering a new car? Online government surplus auctions may catch your eye. These websites sell everything from furniture and electronics to vehicles and building supplies. And if you're a savvy shopper, you may be able to score a killer deal using websites like *govdeals.com* and *gsaauctions.gov*.

But whether you're using a government auction or simply shopping for used cars online, you need to be careful when buying a car — sight unseen or otherwise. If you're thoughtless, you could end up with a lemon. Fortunately, a little bit of research could help you avoid an expensive mistake.

Stick with a car that has a good reputation. Some makes and models have common problems that could leave you with costly repair bills. Before bidding on a vehicle, do some research about the car to see if there are any well-documented issues.

Look for red flags in the vehicle history. If you can, get a history report from *carfax.com*. Scan it over to learn how many owners the vehicle has had, check whether or not it's been in any major accidents, and see if the previous owners kept up with the regularly scheduled maintenance.

Verify that the vehicle doesn't have a salvage title. This means it had some kind of significant damage in the past.

See if you can get an independent inspection. While you may not be able to check out the car in person before you pull the trigger, that doesn't mean you can't get it looked at. Research well-reviewed, reputable mechanics near the seller, and ask if you can get them to take it for an inspection.

This will help you catch any major mechanical issues that may cause a headache down the line. Just make sure you're the one who picks the mechanic, though, so you know you can trust the report.

Sellers beware: Hit the brakes on this common escrow scam

You're a sales superstar. You prepped your car, advertised it with finesse, and negotiated like a champ. Now it's time to close the deal. But if you fall for this growing scam, you'll forfeit your ride.

Scammers will often offer to use an escrow service to safely transfer the money to you. The only problem is that they'll enlist the help of shady — or even nonexistent — companies. And you'll only find out that the money isn't actually there after you've signed over the title to your car.

To avoid this scam, research the escrow service before finalizing the sale. Or find a reputable company and ask the buyer to use it instead. Don't sign over the title before the money is in your hand. Other con artists use fake money orders, wire transfers, or checks to scam you out of your car.

Buying isn't always better: Future-proof your drive by leasing an electric car

"Fuel economy is one of the most important factors to consider when buying a new car," says Jeff Bartlett, deputy auto editor for Consumer Reports. "Even when gas prices are down, they won't stay that way forever."

And when it comes time to shop for a new car, you may decide you want to leave the gas pump in the past and go for an electric car. But instead of buying, it may be smarter to opt for a lease instead.

"Generally leasing is a not a great idea because you're owning the car through its biggest depreciation period," says personal finance expert Liz Weston. But that isn't necessarily the case for electric cars. "Because technology is changing so fast, everybody who knows cars says to lease an electric car."

And that's not the only reason to choose a lease. Some states offer tax rebates or other incentives for people who lease alternative fuel vehicles, so you may find you can get a great deal on the car.

Considering a used electric car? If you're interested in a used vehicle, you'll need to make sure the battery is in good shape. They have a limited life span and can be quite costly to replace, so ask if the battery is still in warranty or if it has failed in the past.

💬 More resources

AAA Fuel Price Finder	member.acg.aaa.com/ga/driving-safety/fuel-prices.html	N/A
Alternative Fuels Data Center	afdc.energy.gov	N/A
AutoMD	automd.com	N/A
Car Care Council	carcare.org/car-care-resources	N/A
CARFAX	carfax.com	N/A
Consumer Financial Protection Bureau	consumerfinance.gov/consumer-tools/auto-loans	855-411-2372
Edmunds.com	edmunds.com	N/A
Federal Trade Commission	consumer.ftc.gov/topics/buying-owning-car	N/A
GasBuddy	gasbuddy.com	N/A
Insurance Information Institute	iii.org/insurance-basics/auto-insurance	N/A
Kelley Blue Book	kbb.com	N/A
National Association of Insurance Commissioners	content.naic.org/consumer/auto-insurance.htm	816-783-8500
National Automobile Dealers Association	nadaguides.com	N/A
U.S. Department of Energy	fueleconomy.gov	N/A
USA.gov	usa.gov/cars	844-872-4681

AT YOUR LEISURE

Cut-rate ways to live it up

48 | Computers & cellphones

No. 1 way to penny-pinch on your next computer

Who doesn't love a bargain? If only you had a crystal ball to predict the next price cut on your must-have electronic device. Then you could turn your bargain hunt into a reality.

Well, no need for fortunetellers. Simply wait until the latest model of a device is released. Manufacturers and retailers want to clear their inventory of older products to make room for the newest desktop computers, laptops, tablets, and smartphones. And that's when you can snap up last year's version for a steal.

If you time it right, you can get a relatively new device for a bargain and never have to pay full price. As soon as new models hit the market, check out the manufacturer's website to see if they have special offers on the older products.

Even if a device is from the previous year, it will still have good specifications and should be able to do everything that you need it to do.

The secret word that can save you big bucks

If you're looking to buy an electronic device — or even an appliance — one word can help you find a bargain. That word is "refurbished."

A lot of companies offer desktop computers, laptops, tablets, cellphones, and printers that are returned and then rebuilt or restored to their original, or better, working order. To find these, look at the websites for the following companies, and type into the search box "Refurbished," "Trade in," or "Trade up." Some offer trade-in programs only periodically, so check back with the website if you don't see one currently available.

Apple	apple.com
Best Buy Outlet	bestbuy.com
Dell	dell.com
Hewlett Packard	hp.com
Newegg	newegg.com
Overstock	overstock.com
TigerDirect	tigerdirect.com
Walmart	walmart.com

Remember to be a little extra careful when buying refurbished computer equipment. Check that it has been wiped clean of any previous content, make sure the specifications meet your needs, look for a warranty, and verify the return policy.

Avoid warranty woes and protect your purchase for free

It's Murphy's law that something will go wrong on your cellphone or tablet right after the manufacturer's warranty runs out. But did you know you can extend that warranty for free? It's a secret, money-saving tip most people aren't aware of.

Many credit card companies offer up to an additional year of protection beyond the manufacturer's warranty on certain products.

If this benefit is available through your credit card — check your cardholder agreement to find out — all you have to do is use your card for the purchase. Then save all your paperwork so you can submit a claim if necessary.

The Federal Trade Commission suggests you take these steps to avoid any problems or misunderstandings regarding a manufacturer's warranty.

- Read the warranty before you buy. Make sure you understand exactly what protection you're getting.

- Print out a copy of the warranty and keep it with your records.

- Save your receipt and file it with the warranty. You may need it to document the date of your purchase or prove that you're the original owner.

- Look for an address to write to or a phone number to call if you have questions or problems.

- Perform required maintenance and inspections on the product.

- Don't abuse or misuse the product. That may void your warranty coverage.

> Smartphone running a bit slow? Instead of buying a new one, speed it up by clearing the phone's cached data, getting rid of apps you never use, and deleting old messages. You can also store your videos and photos on a cloud-based service to free up room on the phone.

Dare to compare and spend less

You remember the good old days when you would run from one store to the next, checking to see who had the lowest price on an item. All that running around — maybe not the good old days, after all.

Well, today is truly the better day because you can comparison shop online and let your fingers do the running. Just log in to a website that performs the comparisons for you.

You can review the prices on a wide range of products, and then go straight to the site with the best offer and buy the item. No easier way to save. Have some frugal fun on these price comparison websites.

Bizrate	bizrate.com
Google Shopping	shopping.google.com
Pricegrabber	pricegrabber.com
Shopping.com	shopping.com
Shopzilla	shopzilla.com
Yahoo Shopping	shopping.yahoo.com

Delete doesn't always do it — wipe private info off your computer for good

Before you discard, sell, donate, or recycle your old computer, make sure no one else can access any of its contents. Follow smart security protocol and know that when a file is gone, it's really gone.

Take out the trash. When you delete something from a desktop computer or laptop, this only places a file into the Recycle Bin on a Windows machine, or the Trash on a Mac. Take the next important step and right-click on the Recycle Bin or Trash icon, and click on the option to empty it.

Use an app. Third-party programs can guarantee deleted items stay deleted. These are known as file shredders, and they permanently delete any files and folders you select.

File shredder apps are designed for desktop computers and laptops, and they are generally downloaded from their own websites. Take a look at these.

Alternate File Shredder	alternate-tools.com
File Shredder	fileshredder.org
Ccleaner	ccleaner.com
TuneUpMyMac	tuneupmymac.com

Reset your device. Even when something has been deleted permanently from a hard drive, specialist software recovery companies can still sometimes retrieve it. This is why you should wipe your hard drive clean before you dispose of it. Resetting the device is a way to wipe the hard drive and return it to its original factory settings.

These are the steps for a Windows desktop computer or laptop.

1. Navigate to *Settings* then *Update & Security* and then *Recovery*.

2. Click on the *Get started* button under the *Reset this PC* heading.

3. Click on the *Remove everything* button to get rid of all of your personal files, apps, and settings.

For a Mac using macOS, the process is different.

1. Shut down your computer and then turn it on again.

2. As it starts up, hold down the *Command + R* keys until the Apple logo appears on the screen.

3. When the macOS *Utilities* window is displayed, click on the *Disk Utility* option, and then on the *Continue* button.

4. Click on the Mac hard drive, usually named Macintosh HD, and click on the *Erase* button.

5. Keep the default options in the next window, and click on the *Erase* button to remove all of the files, photos, passwords, and anything else you have created on your Mac.

Tablets and smartphones can also be reset to their factory condition from within the device's settings app.

High-tech trash: Smart uses for your old gear

It's time to upgrade. But, oh, what to do with the computer or laptop you don't need anymore? Before anything, make sure you've wiped your private information off the device and you have reset it to its original factory condition. Then consider one of these ideas.

Sell it. Computing equipment can find a good home on a shopping website such as eBay. Even if you don't receive a huge amount of money for it, at least it will be taken off your hands. There are also a number of websites where you can trade in computing equipment. Two to look at are Wirefly at *wireflytradeins.cexchange.com* and Nextworth at *nextworth.com*.

Give it to family and friends. Grandma won't mind that your iPad is a few years old. She'll still be able to locate her friends on Facebook and send emails to her grandkids.

Recycle it. Want to help conserve resources and natural materials while ditching your old tech? The Environmental Protection Agency recommends you recycle your electronics at a certified facility. Use your ZIP code to search at *e-stewards.org/find-a-recycler* or *sustainableelectronics.org/find-an-r2-certified-facility*.

Donate it to charity. Old electronics are gratefully received by some charity organizations, particularly those that use it for training adults and young people in need. One to try is the National Cristina Foundation at *cristina.org*.

Bagging bargains: How to save money every time you shop

The online world is a great place to find a range of money-off deals and bargains — if you know where to look.

One super site for checking out all of the discounts available to you in your area is Flipp at *flipp.com* — or download the Flipp app to your phone or tablet. Use Flipp to find all the local offers and circulars for stores near you by simply entering your ZIP code.

Check out these other money-smart apps and websites for saving on just about anything you can imagine. You'll never again pay full price.

DealNews	*dealnews.com*
Hip2Save	*hip2save.com*
RetailMeNot	*retailmenot.com*
Slickdeals	*slickdeals.net*

49 | Travel

> "The most beautiful thing in the world is, of course, the world itself."
>
> Wallace Stevens

Fly past airport checkpoints for free

Airport security — a test of patience, grit, and moral strength. What would you pay to bypass this torment? How about next to nothing?

That's right, enrollment in two programs that allow you to breeze through airport security can be yours for the asking.

TSA PreCheck. Five years of PreCheck, run by the U.S. Transportation Security Administration, costs $85. But over 30 credit cards or loyalty programs cover the application fee or let members use rewards points to pay for it. Go online to *tsa.gov/precheck* and click on *Loyalty Programs* for a full list.

CLEAR. Membership in this privately operated program fast-tracks you through security at more than 50 airports for $179 a year. However, several Delta- and United-branded credit cards offer discounted CLEAR membership. And some frequent flyer programs will knock almost half off the enrollment fee, or grant you complimentary CLEAR membership. Visit *clearme.com* for details.

Don't fall for phony reviews

Because online ratings influence travelers so much, a whole industry of scammers has sprung up, offering fake positive reviews for restaurants, hotels, and other businesses to buy and post. Be wary of evaluations that are all completely positive, are all short, contain lots of exclamation points, or don't have many details. Follow these tips for more genuine information.

- Look at only the most recent reviews, since past issues may have been addressed.

- Pay special attention to those written by travelers like yourself — whether a senior couple, a solo tourist, or an extended family group.

- Check multiple sites for reviews on the travel business or activity. You should get a fair consensus across the board.

10 costly rental car mistakes (and 1 thing you should always do)

You know it's crazy to pay for insurance through a rental agency rather than getting coverage for free through your own carrier or a credit card. But are these 10 other rental missteps on your radar?

- Forgetting to price compare smaller companies against the biggies.

- Ignoring mileage, whether it's overbuying unlimited miles for a short trip or thinking you have unlimited miles when you don't.

- Allowing the rental agency to include tolls in your contract. Many add hefty surcharges.

- Not watching the clock. Return your rental even a couple of hours late and you may get charged for an entire additional day.

- Paying for GPS or other extras you don't need.

- Overlooking rewards and loyalty programs.

- Prepaying for gas. You'll spend more per gallon and shell out for gas you probably didn't use.

- Failing to use membership and group discounts, such as those through big-box stores, clubs including AAA or AARP, and affiliations like the military.

> It may seem convenient and cutting edge to pair your phone with the Bluetooth in a rental car, but it also allows the car's computer to upload your personal information. This info is then available to anyone driving that car. Hello ID theft.

- Renting at the airport. Rates are usually higher here than at other locations.

- Paying upfront for a rental car. If plans change, you'll likely have to ante up a cancellation penalty or even the full amount. Since many companies allow free cancellations, you should never have to prepay.

And always, always ask for a free upgrade. What have you got to lose?

Live the high life in the low season

Lull. Shoulder. Off-peak. It has many names but senior travelers call it brilliant. And unexpected. And affordable. Of course it's traveling when the majority of vacationers are staying home.

Why offseason is the best season for your wallet. Most destinations are particularly attractive to travelers at certain times. Skiers want to hit the Rockies when the snow is plentiful. Beach bums herd the kiddies to the coast when school is out and the ocean is warm. But savvy seniors have the luxury of going whenever they want. The perks are plentiful.

- You'll pay less for almost everything — airfare, car rental, lodging, and sometimes entrance fees to attractions like theme parks.

- You can take advantage of special low-rate package deals designed to entice visitors during a slow time of year. You may even snag an upgrade.

- Smaller crowds? Yes, please. That means less waiting, more options for seats at restaurants, and maybe even your pick of hotel rooms or rental cars. You'll have space to spread out, which might make you feel safer from all the risky bits that go hand in hand with crowds — like thieves and germs.

Do your homework to avoid nasty surprises. There could be a reason no one visits Thailand in September. Can you say monsoon? Weigh your tolerance for heat, snow, and rain when thinking about an offseason jaunt. Weather will usually be your biggest consideration. In addition, find out what attractions, restaurants, and accommodations will be closed.

So what are some top spots for offseason travel — still with lots to do and good food, too?

- beach destinations in the fall
- ski resorts in the summer
- national parks in winter
- big cities in the fall
- Europe between November and March

Seniors travel cheap with a little online help

Make your escape a little more budget-friendly by using the internet to find the very lowest rates on airfares, car rentals, accommodation, and entertainment.

Cheap Caribbean	cheapcaribbean.com
Expedia	expedia.com
Goibibo	goibibo.com
Kayak	kayak.com
Orbitz	orbitz.com
Priceline	priceline.com
Skyscanner	skyscanner.com
Travelocity	travelocity.com
TravelZoo	travelzoo.com

50 | Active living

Backhand health care costs with pickleball

What would you do with an extra $1,000 this year? Take a trip? Pay a bill? Buy that something-something you've had your eye on? You can fund that shopping splurge, make new friends, and get physically fit. All by playing pickleball.

A study published in the medical journal *BMJ Open Sport & Exercise Medicine* found that adults who stayed physically active as they got older had lower health care costs — saving $800 to over $1,000 a year, depending on their level of hustle and the age they began exercising.

Of course, pickleball isn't the only way to gain these benefits. Any aerobic workout will do. But it's a surefire way to strengthen your heart, lower your blood pressure, and raise your metabolism. Plus, it's fun.

Don't be intimidated, thinking you must be the next Chris Evert or Jimmy Connors. Pickleball is ideally suited to seniors who may be slowing down.

- The court is smaller than a tennis court, which means you don't have to move much — especially if you play doubles — or hit the ball too hard.

- You use a sidearm motion to volley rather than overhand. Much easier on shoulder joints. Plus the paddles are large and light, meaning less muscle and grip strain.

- The plastic pickleball travels more slowly than a tennis ball. Easy-peasy to see and hit.

- You can play indoors or out, making this a year-round sport suited for every climate.

> Gardening is great fun and even greater exercise. Connect with others while enjoying this healthy hobby through online gardening groups. Search social media platforms — like Meetup and Facebook — as well as organizations like The Garden Club of America at *gcamerica.org* for local clubs offering plant and seed swaps, free expertise and advice, and, of course, inspiration. Priceless.

Look for pickleball courts at your local gym, fitness center, recreation park, YMCA, or community center. Then go online to the USA Pickleball Association at *usapa.org* for rules, tips, tournaments, leagues, and more places to play.

Surprise! The most astonishing place for free stuff

When is a library not a library? When it is a gateway to a world of fabulous and free activities. Maybe you've never thought to look past the books, magazines, and media offerings. If so, you've neglected the loads of benefits this public resource has on call. Items available at your library will vary, so have a chat with the helpful folks at the circulation desk to see what's on their shelves.

Outdoor play. If nature beckons, then you could — literally — check out a state park pass, a backpack brimming with hiking gear, or other equipment to make your next excursion more thrilling. Save anywhere from a few bucks to hundreds of dollars by borrowing instead of buying.

- air mattresses
- bicycles
- camping tents

- croquet sets
- fishing poles
- kayaks

- lawn games
- snowshoes
- tennis rackets

Indoor fun. Support your current hobby or try out a new one, all free with a library card. Your taxes paid for it — use it.

- 3D printers
- board games
- butter churns
- cake pans
- iPads
- jigsaw puzzles
- karaoke machines

- knitting needles
- microscopes
- musical instruments
- party supplies
- popcorn machines
- sewing machines
- woodworking tools

Take the bite out of skyrocketing pet costs

Almost 1 out of every 5 American households adopted a cat or dog during the COVID pandemic. "This incredibly stressful period motivated many people to foster and adopt animals," says Matt Bershadker, president and CEO of the ASPCA. More households now face the fact that owning a pet can cost — well — four legs and a tail.

Basic annual expenses for a cat will set you back about $900. And for a dog almost $1,500. This includes everything from surgical vet visits to toys.

Bring that fur baby home for less. You'll pay big bucks for a purebred from a breeder. A more frugal option is to look into rescue organizations or shelters and follow these tips.

- Negotiate if the fee doesn't already include spaying or neutering, microchipping, or vaccinations.

- Wait for special events when adoptions are free.

- Choose an adult or older dog or cat rather than a puppy. These are traditionally harder to place in homes and may be cheaper to adopt.

Dish it up with fewer dollars. Pet owners spent an estimated $44 billion in 2021 on food and treats for their best friends. That's a lot of kibble. Why not use these money-saving tricks and avoid paying top dollar?

> You might be eligible to get your money back if your recently bought pet becomes sick or dies within a certain time period. Find out if your state has a pet purchase protection law by going to the Humane Society's website at *humanesociety.org* and searching "puppy lemon laws." Their FAQ page links to a state list.

- Sign up for a food subscription service.

- Join pet food rewards and loyalty programs.

- Buy in bulk.

- Replace or supplement commercial food with homemade. Just check with your vet first for guidance.

Pet Rx — keep them paws-itively healthy. Your pet is family. But you'd prefer they stayed bright-eyed and bushy-tailed without your finances going belly up.

- The average yearly premium for an accident-and-illness pet insurance policy in 2020 was $342 for cats and $594 for dogs. Consider it if your pet has a medical condition or if you don't have the reserves to cover the cost of an injury. Otherwise set up an emergency pet fund for the unexpected.

- When you find yourself facing a hefty medical bill, ask your vet to work with you. Often they have payment plans that will fit more easily into your budget. And have a conversation before services are rendered. Perhaps you can forego optional tests or treatments.

- Don't pay full price for pet meds. Just like human drugs, many have generic options. Then comparison shop at warehouse clubs, big-box stores, online pharmacies, and online pet supply stores.

51 | Clothing

> "Care for your clothes, like the good friends they are."
>
> Joan Crawford

The hottest shopping spots for savings

Updating your wardrobe doesn't have to blow your budget. You can save as much as 90%, when you know where to shop. At the top of the list are online resale sites like thredUP and United Apparel Liquidators. They make brand-name clothes available at bargain-basement prices, all without you having to leave the comfort of your home.

If you like the in-store experience or want to try things on, your local thrift stores and consignment shops are hot spots. There you can find great quality, as well as low, low prices. As an added bonus, shopping secondhand reduces the need for new clothing production and saves items that still have life in them from the landfill. This helps reduce fashion waste and protects the environment.

Bear in mind that store layout shouldn't define your trip. Clothing doesn't have a gender, so when browsing keep your eyes open to all available items. If you see a cool sweater in a section you don't usually shop in, don't be afraid to snap it up. What you shouldn't ignore is the clothing label. This will help you determine the quality of the fabric and whether it needs any special care when laundering.

Don't let yourself get carried away by the sweet deals, though. You can rack up a big bill even shopping discounted clothing. So before you start looking, make a list of what you want or need. Then set a spending limit and stick to it. This will help you save money and keep your house clutter-free.

Cha-ching: Reward yourself every time you shop

Rumpelstiltskin may have been able to spin straw into gold, but you can do him one better — and turn your paper receipts into cash.

Simply download an app onto your phone and scan receipts from restaurants, grocery stores, or retailers. That's it. Depending on which app you use, your receipts are converted into cash or points that you can redeem at stores or via gift cards.

Maybe you're a fan of store loyalty cards, but not so much of the clutter they make in your wallet. Enter the oh-so-simple, high-tech solution. Keep all your loyalty cards on an app on your smartphone. Then simply bring up the card on your phone when you're in the store, and never miss a bargain again. Three to have a look at are Reward Cards, Stocard, and VirtualCards.

Go to the app store for your Android or Apple device and check out shopping rewards apps like these.

- CoinOut
- Fetch Rewards
- Ibotta

- Receipt Hog
- ReceiptPal
- Shopkick

Always read the fine print before you download an app so you're aware if they collect personal information or require a link to your credit or debit card. Some receipt apps ask you to take part in market research in order to get the full range of rewards.

Extend your clothing's life span with these top care tips

When it comes to filling your closet, always choose quality over quantity. Invest in well-made staples that you can wear year after year. For the sake of your clothing's longevity, you should also be aware of their special care instructions. And use these additional tips to make your favorite pieces last.

Watch your machine usage. Having a washer and dryer in your home and at the ready makes doing your laundry easier, but some articles of clothing, like jeans and sweaters, don't need to be washed after just one wear. Donning them a few times before washing them again will help extend their life.

When it's time to wash, use cold water if possible. This will help protect your clothing from shrinking and fading. Afterward, a drying rack or clothesline will be gentle on your clothes and won't damage elastic. Plus you'll save on your electricity bill with these two changes.

Skip over-sudsing your duds. Are you using too much laundry soap? You'd be surprised by how much is enough. You need just 1 to 2 tablespoons of liquid detergent in a standard washer or 2 teaspoons in a high-efficiency machine. Too much soap can leave a residue which is why more detergent will make your clothes attract more dirt.

Store your wardrobe the right way. Plastic and wire hangers can stretch your clothing out of shape. Invest in wooden hangers that will last longer and keep your clothing in better condition. Skip hangers entirely for heavy sweaters, and fold them instead. Keep your clothing out of damp, hot, or sunlit spaces, which can all cause damage.

Invest in your delicates. Protect your undergarments and other pieces that need a gentle touch by sticking them in a delicates bag before washing. If you have the time, take the extra care to hand-wash them.

Ditch your iron. Choose the wrong temperature and you could do serious damage to your favorite button-up. Fortunately, all you need in order to get wrinkle-free clothing without the iron is a simple DIY recipe. Mix 1 cup of distilled water with 1 teaspoon of fabric softener. Then just spritz on a mist of this homemade formula to your hanging garment, smooth over the creases with your hands, and watch the wrinkles disappear.

Visible mending — creative way to make your wardrobe last longer

You may have learned how to repair your clothing growing up, but with online shopping and long store hours it's easy to have fallen out of the habit. However, in the last few years DIY repairs have seen a resurgence with visible mending.

This technique embraces the flaws of a worn piece of clothing. Imagine patching a torn-through knee with a colorful fabric or embroidering over grass stains. You can extend an item's life, save money, and add your own personal touch to your clothing.

Not a master mender yet? Now is a great time to learn with tutorials on YouTube and sewing blogs. And since you're accenting the imperfections of a piece anyway, you don't have to fret about getting everything just right all the time.

Books & music

> "A day out-of-doors, someone I loved to talk with, a good book and some simple food and music — that would be rest."
>
> Eleanor Roosevelt

Download digital books in a snap

You never have to be without a good book again. Thanks to online bookstores, a treasure-trove of publications are available for you to download onto your reading device, wherever and whenever you have internet service.

You may have to pay for most of your e-books, but you'll find a considerable number of free titles, too. Some online stores offer free samples, usually consisting of one or two chapters, that you can download to see if you like a particular book. Here are your main options for acquiring e-books.

Amazon Kindle. Since Amazon began as an online bookseller, no surprise it also has a major presence in the e-book market. Through the use of its own Kindle e-reader, Amazon has built up a large library of e-books, accessed through the Kindle Store on the Amazon website.

There is also a Kindle Unlimited option, which is a monthly subscription service providing access to over a million e-books as well as magazines and audiobooks.

Apple Books. On your macOS, iPadOS, or iOS devices, go to the Books app (formerly called iBooks) and tap on the *Book Store*. From here you can search by category, title, author, or keyword. Then filter for free items, and start downloading.

eBooks.com. This is an independent e-book store and has over a million unique titles. You can read their e-books online or download to a variety of devices.

Google Play Books. It started as Google eBooks in 2010, was renamed in 2012, and began supporting audiobooks in 2018. For Android users, the Google Play Books app operates in a similar way to the Books app on an Apple device. You will access, purchase, download, and read content using the app.

Kobo. The Kobo catalogue contains over 5 million titles you can download and read using their app or one of their e-readers.

Special website provides free e-books galore

Looking for more free books? You can't do any better than Project Gutenberg, found at the website *gutenberg.org*.

Named after one of the first pioneers of printed books, it has over 60,000 free titles. You'll find numerous classics, such as *The Adventures of Tom Sawyer* by Mark Twain and *Oliver Twist* by Charles Dickens.

You can download and read these books on any e-reader and also online on the Project Gutenberg website. And you don't even need to register.

Project Gutenberg titles are free because their copyright has expired. That means every year more works are eligible to be included in this tremendous free catalog.

The sound of music: 5 free services hit a streaming high note

Real music lovers are mad about streaming services with their vast libraries of songs, albums, artists, and more. If you're unfamiliar with this concept, listen up — you're in for a real treat.

They operate in a similar way to streaming services for movies and TV shows. You sign up and then access the musical content you want. The good news is you can stream music on your desktop computer, laptop, tablet, or smartphone. Link your device to some Bluetooth enabled speakers, and let the two-stepping begin.

Some streaming services are free, but you will probably have to put up with occasional ads. Most paid-for options offer a free trial, with the ability to create a family account so that several people can have access to the same service.

Here are some of the top music streaming services.

Amazon Music. This e-commerce giant offers four music streaming options.

- Amazon Music Free gives access to top playlists and thousands of stations, but you will hear ads.

- Amazon Music Prime, included with your Amazon Prime membership, offers 2 million songs, thousands of playlists, personalized streaming stations, and no ads.

- Amazon Music Unlimited is a fee-based subscription that does not require a Prime membership, but you'll get a reduced rate with one. You have access to more songs and more features with Unlimited.

- Amazon Music HD is for the true audiophile. For a monthly fee you can listen to millions of songs in High Definition (HD) and Ultra High Definition (UHD).

Apple Music. Access Apple's streaming service from the Music app on devices using macOS, iPadOS, and iOS.

There is a three-month free trial, and then you can choose a subscription option from Individual, Family, or Student.

Pandora. Another independent streaming service, Pandora's specialty is giving users the means to create playlists based on a range of criteria and types of music. Pandora also offers a huge selection of podcasts.

Spotify. Independent of the major technology companies, this is one of the most popular music streaming services. You can sign up for a free trial, but then will have to pay a monthly fee. For this you get unlimited commercial-free music from the huge Spotify catalog. There are also Family, Student, and free ad-supported plans.

YouTube Music. In 2020 the Google Play Music service moved to YouTube Music. You now have the option of a free version with ads or the ad-free, paid-for subscription version, YouTube Music Premium.

Want to play an instrument? Tap into these websites

Maybe you want to teach yourself the guitar. Or perhaps you fancy a songwriting career. Either way, you've lucked out. Modern technology makes achieving both goals easier than ever. And the best part? It's free.

All you have to do is boot up your laptop. Coursera, an online learning platform, offers a wide range of music classes. Go to *coursera.org* and click *Explore Free Courses*. You can type in the kind of lesson you're looking for at the top of the page.

Another option? The Berklee College of Music provides a variety of courses and downloadable handbooks at *online.berklee.edu*. To see what's available, click *All Free Music Resources* under the *Resources* tab.

And let's not forget YouTube. The website's videos run the gamut — from directions on how to play "Take Me Home, Country Roads" on the ukulele to setting up a drum kit. Find what you're looking for at *youtube.com*.

More resources

Academy of Nutrition and Dietetics	eatright.org/fitness	N/A
American Wool Council	americanwool.org/wool-101/care-tips	N/A
Coats Group	coats.com/en/Information-Hub/Care-Labels	N/A
Coin Laundry Association	findalaundry.org/stain-removal	N/A
Cotton Incorporated	thefabricofourlives.com/care-tips	N/A
Environmental Protection Agency	epa.gov/recycle/electronics-donation-and-recycling	N/A
Federal Trade Commission	consumer.ftc.gov/articles/avoid-scams-when-you-travel	N/A
Libraries.org	librarytechnology.org/libraries/uspublic	N/A
National Institute on Aging	nia.nih.gov/health/exercise-physical-activity	800-222-2225
National Library Service for Blind and Print Disabled	loc.gov/nls	888-657-7323
National Thrift Store Directory	thethriftshopper.com	N/A
Nutrition.gov	www.nutrition.gov/topics/exercise-and-fitness	N/A
WorldCat	worldcat.org/libraries	N/A
U.S. Department of State	travel.state.gov	N/A
USA.gov	usa.gov/travel-and-immigration	844-872-4681

GLOSSARY

401(k). An employer-sponsored retirement savings account funded by pretax employee contributions that may or may not be matched by the employer. Withdrawals from a traditional 401(k) plan are treated as taxable income, typically after retirement.

Ad valorem. A tax that is based on the assessed value of an item or service. Prime examples include property tax and sales tax. *Ad valorem* is Latin for "according to value."

Adjustable-rate mortgage. A home loan with an interest rate that adjusts over time based on market conditions. Such loans are usually named according to the length of time the interest rate remains fixed, followed by the length of time the interest rate can go up or down.

Adjusted gross income. Gross income — including wages, dividends, capital gains, and retirement distributions — minus adjustments to that income. Adjustments include such items as education expenses and contributions to retirement accounts.

Advance directive. A legal document that specifies the medical treatment a person wants if he becomes too ill or injured to make decisions. An advance directive may also give someone else the power to make those decisions.

Aging in place. Circumstances in which older adults remain in their homes and communities as they age instead of moving to an outside facility.

Amortization. The process of reducing or paying off debt with a series of fixed payments spread out over time. More interest and less principal is paid in the early years of the loan. The debt is paid off at the end of the payment schedule.

Annual percentage rate. The yearly interest rate charged on a credit card balance or loan. The term also represents the annual rate of return on an investment, such as a certificate of deposit.

Annuity. An insurance contract that pays out a fixed amount of money to the policyholder over a specific period of time.

Anti-Kickback Statute. A federal law that makes it illegal for someone to use Medicare coverage and a manufacturer coupon or other drug discount at the same time.

Applicant tracking system. A software used by employers to collect, store, and screen the resumes of job candidates. In many cases, the software filters applications based on keywords, education, former employers, and skills.

Area agencies on aging. Public or nonprofit agencies designated by a state to address the needs and concerns of older adults. These agencies coordinate closely with other organizations to provide information, programs, and services at the state and local level.

Asset allocation. The diversification of retirement accounts across stocks, bonds, and cash. The objective is to align the allocations with goals, risk tolerance, and time horizon.

Average daily balance. A key number used to compute how much interest is owed on a credit card balance. To figure out the average daily balance, credit card issuers multiply the daily interest rate by each day's balance.

Backup withholding. A tool used by the IRS to ensure it receives the taxes it is owed. When applied, it requires that taxes are withheld on payments that normally aren't subject to withholding, such as interest payments and dividends.

Balance transfer credit card. A credit card used to transfer balances from high-interest credit card accounts. Balance transfer cards usually offer a low or even 0% interest rate for a limited time. However, users of these cards often have to pay a fee based on the total amount of debt they are transferring.

Balloon mortgage. A type of home loan that features an initial period of low monthly payments, at the end of which the borrower is required to make a lump-sum payment to cover the balance of the mortgage.

Balloon payment. The larger-than-usual final payment that comes due at the end of the loan term on a balloon mortgage.

Beneficiary. A person or organization designated to receive proceeds from a deceased person's estate, including money from life insurance policies, retirement accounts, and trusts.

Capital gain. The profit that is realized after selling an asset — stocks, bonds, and real estate, for example — that has grown in value. Capital gains on such investments owned for more than a year are taxed more favorably than those held for less than a year.

Capital loss. The financial loss that occurs when a security or an investment such as real estate is sold for less than the original purchase price. Taxpayers can use capital losses to offset capital gains.

Certificate of deposit. A type of savings account that generally pays a higher interest rate in return for keeping the funds deposited for a fixed amount of time.

COBRA insurance. COBRA stands for the Consolidated Omnibus Budget Reconciliation Act. This federal law allows former employees to continue with their workplace health insurance plan for a limited period of time.

Collateral. An asset that lenders accept as security against a loan in case a borrower cannot repay the loan. For example, most mortgages are collateralized by the homes that the mortgages helped buy.

Community spouse resource allowance. The amount of assets a "healthy" spouse is allowed to retain before the spouse needing long-term care is eligible for Medicaid. Such amounts vary by state.

Consumer price index. Used to gauge inflation, the consumer price index is a measure of the change in cost of commonly purchased goods and services.

Conventional loan. A type of mortgage that is not secured by a government agency. Borrowers typically have to meet stricter requirements, such as a high credit score and more money for a down payment, to qualify for a conventional mortgage.

Copay. A fixed amount paid by an insured individual for covered services. It is usually paid at the time a service is received, such as when visiting a doctor's office.

Cost-of-living adjustment. An increase in Social Security benefits to counteract the effects of inflation. Cost-of-living adjustments for the Supplemental Security Income program are generally the same as those for Social Security.

Credit bureau. A credit bureau tracks the credit history of borrowers in order to generate credit reports. Financial companies buy this information to help determine the risk of extending credit to a potential customer.

Credit freeze. A tool used by consumers to avert financial fraud. It prevents the release of details on an individual's credit report, which keeps lenders from extending new lines of credit in that person's name.

Credit lock. A consumer product offered by credit bureaus that limits access to an individual's credit report. Unlike a credit freeze, which is free, a credit lock may require monthly fees.

Credit report. A summary of a borrower's past and present credit accounts and payment history. It is used by potential lenders to decide whether or not to offer credit and on what terms.

Credit score. A number from 300 to 850 that represents the likelihood that a person will repay debt on time. The score is based on an individual's credit report. In general, high scoring individuals are more likely to get a loan with favorable terms.

Data breach. A security incident that affects the confidentiality, integrity, or availability of data. A breach may involve the theft of Social Security numbers, personal health information, passwords, or credit card numbers.

Debt-to-income ratio. This ratio is equal to a person's combined monthly debt payments divided by gross monthly income. Lenders use this number, which is expressed as a percentage, to determine borrowing risk.

Deed of trust. An agreement between a home buyer and a lender at the closing of a property. Used in place of a mortgage in some states, this document affirms that a designated third party holds legal title to a financed property until it is paid off according to the terms of the loan.

Delinquent debt. A type of debt in which the borrower fails to make agreed-upon payments to the lender in a timely fashion.

Direct burial. The burial of a body shortly after death without a viewing or funeral services. This type of burial is generally less costly, and funeral homes must offer it on their price list.

Direct Express debit card. A prepaid debit card option that allows recipients of federal benefits to receive funds electronically. Users don't need to have a bank account because the funds are deposited into the card account on a designated payment date. The card can be used to make purchases, pay bills, or get cash.

Discount point. A fee paid upfront to a mortgage lender in exchange for a reduced interest rate over the life of the loan. One discount point costs 1% of the mortgage amount.

Dividend. A portion of a company's profit paid to shareholders. Paid on a regular basis, dividends are one way investors earn a return on their stock purchases.

Diversification. The process of owning different investments in order to reduce the effects of volatility in the markets and raise the potential for increasing returns.

Do not resuscitate order. A legally binding physician's order made at a patient's request. It states that if the patient's heart or breathing stops, cardiopulmonary resuscitation (CPR) should not be administered. A do not resuscitate order doesn't mean "do not treat" — only that CPR should not be attempted.

Dollar-cost averaging. A strategy in which investors use a fixed amount of money to buy shares of stock over regular intervals. The main benefit of this approach is to reduce investment risk.

Dual eligible beneficiaries. Individuals who qualify for both Medicare and Medicaid health insurance benefits.

Durable power of attorney for finances. A legal document in which one person gives another the right to make financial decisions on his behalf. It can become effective immediately or during a medical crisis, such as when the principal becomes physically or mentally incapacitated.

Durable medical equipment. Certain health care products, including walkers, wheelchairs, and oxygen tanks, that help an individual complete daily activities in and around the home. Many insurance plans provide coverage for these items.

Durable power of attorney for health care. A legal document in which one person gives another power to make health care decisions on his behalf. It becomes effective when the principal is unable to make those medical wishes known.

Earnest money. A deposit that signals a buyer is committed to purchasing a home. Sometimes called a "good faith" deposit, this money is held by a third party while the seller takes the home off the market and the buyer completes an appraisal and home inspection.

Emergency fund. Money set aside for large unexpected expenses, including medical bills and home repairs.

Equity. A home's current fair market value minus the outstanding balance of all mortgages or liens on the property.

Escrow. A legal agreement in which a third party holds money or assets until the two parties involved in a transaction meet certain conditions. It is usually associated with real estate transactions, but can apply to any scenario in which funds will pass from one party to another.

Executor. The person responsible for carrying out the terms of a deceased individual's will. Executors work for the estate from the time of passing until probate is complete.

Expenditure. The total amount of money that is spent on a good or service.

Explanation of benefits. A statement from an insurance company explaining the payments it will cover for medical services provided to an insured party.

Firewall. A computer network security system that monitors incoming and outgoing traffic. Firewalls are used to protect computers and networks from malicious software and traffic.

Fixed expenses. Ongoing costs, including rent, mortgage, and insurance payments, that don't regularly change in amount or frequency.

Fixed interest rate. An interest rate on a loan or mortgage that doesn't change for a set period of time. This results in payments remaining the same over that term.

Fixed-income assets. Investments that generate a regular stream of cash flow. The amount and timing of these payments are known in advance. Bonds are the most common type of fixed-income asset.

Full retirement age. The age at which a person is eligible to claim the full amount of Social Security retirement benefits earned throughout a career. Full retirement age is determined by the year in which a beneficiary is born.

Funeral rule. A ruling enforced by the Federal Trade Commission that requires funeral homes to disclose the cost of their items and services. It protects the consumer from mandatory packaged funerals and encourages price comparisons among funeral homes.

Geriatric care manager. A trained and licensed professional who can identify a senior's needs and find resources to ensure those needs are met.

Government impersonation. A scam in which callers claiming to be government representatives use fear and intimidation to trick victims into turning over personal information or money. Legitimate government agencies never call, email, or text to request money or personal data.

Government pension offset. A federal provision that reduces the amount of Social Security benefits a spouse or survivor can claim if that individual is also receiving a government pension in which no Social Security taxes were deducted.

Grandparent scam. A swindle in which a caller pretends to be a grandchild in need of immediate funds to deal with an emergency. The con artist's insistence on not sharing information about the request is a hallmark of this scam.

Green burial. An environmentally sustainable practice in which the deceased is not embalmed. The body is placed in a biodegradable coffin or shroud before being buried in the ground.

Gross income. Refers to all income received by an individual before taxes and other deductions. Sources include wages, rent, interest income, and dividends. Gross income is sometimes referred to as pretax income.

Hard inquiry. A request by a lender or credit card issuer to check a person's credit report before deciding to extend a loan or line of credit. A hard inquiry may temporarily shave a few points off a person's credit score.

Health care proxy. An individual who is legally appointed in an advance directive or medical durable power of attorney to make health care decisions on behalf of another person if illness or injury prevents that person from making medical decisions.

Health savings account. A type of savings account used by people with high deductible health insurance plans to pay for out-of-pocket medical costs. The account is funded with pretax dollars.

Home and community based services. A Medicaid waiver program that allows beneficiaries to receive services in their home or community instead of in an institutional setting.

Homestead exemption. A legal provision that reduces the taxable value of a home. This helps to lower the amount of property taxes a homeowner is required to pay.

House hacking. A strategy that involves renting portions of a primary residence to generate income that is used to offset the costs of owning the home.

Identity theft. A term used to refer to all types of crime in which someone illegally obtains and uses another's personal information to commit fraud or gain other financial benefits.

Immediate annuity. A type of annuity designed to provide guaranteed payments — whether for a lifetime or a set number of years — in exchange for a lump sum of cash. The payments start within a year.

Individual retirement account. A retirement savings account that allows a person to contribute pretax dollars that grow tax deferred until withdrawals occur at age 59 1/2 or later. Contributions to an IRA are typically tax deductible.

Inflation. A general rise in prices over a period of time. It reflects the decline of a currency's purchasing power.

Initial enrollment period. The seven-month period when someone is first eligible for Medicare. This timeframe includes the month of the person's 65th birthday, and the three months immediately before and after.

Intangible asset. A nonphysical asset that holds long-term value. Examples include stocks, bonds, patents, trademarks, and copyrights.

Interest rate. The amount a lender charges a borrower for the use of money. It is expressed as a percentage of the amount loaned. An interest rate can also apply to the amount earned on a savings account or certificate of deposit.

Intestate. When a person dies without a valid will, he is said to have died intestate. In such cases, state laws decide how to distribute the deceased individual's assets.

Irrevocable living trust. A legal document detailing how an individual's assets should be distributed among heirs. As it is irrevocable, the terms can't be changed or terminated, except under limited circumstances. Such trusts are usually made to transfer wealth or reduce taxes.

Joint life insurance. A life insurance policy that covers two people. Such policies can pay benefits after one policyholder dies or after both of them die. The policyholders don't have to be married.

Joint will. A will signed by two people in which the surviving party inherits the estate. The document often also sets the terms for distributing the estate after both individuals have died. A joint will is irrevocable after the first party dies, meaning the surviving party cannot change its terms.

Jumbo loan. A mortgage used to finance high-priced properties that exceed the loan sizes set by Fannie Mae and Freddie Mac. Also called a "nonconforming" loan.

Lady bird deed. An estate planning tool that allows individuals in certain states to protect their homes as an inheritance without jeopardizing Medicaid eligibility.

Lease purchase agreement. A contract in which the buyer and seller of a home agree to a lease period followed by the sale of the property. Typically, a portion of the rent is used for a down payment, but the renter is still responsible for securing financing for the purchase of the property.

Liquid asset. An asset that can quickly and easily be converted into cash. Examples include money withdrawn from a bank account, stocks, bonds, and money market funds.

Living will. A type of advance directive that specifies the medical treatment a person wants if he is too ill or injured to make decisions. Some states combine a living will and health care power of attorney and call it an advance directive.

Long-term care insurance. Private insurance coverage that helps pay for home health care, nursing home care, and adult day care in the event the insured has a chronic health condition or becomes incapacitated. Several types of long-term care policies exist.

Look-back period. States require a person applying for Medicaid coverage for long-term care to disclose all financial transactions he or she was involved in during the five years before applying. This look-back period is designed to identify people who transferred assets to qualify for Medicaid.

Lump-sum distribution. A distribution or payment within a single tax year of a retirement plan participant's entire balance. The money is given all at once, as opposed to being paid out in installments.

Malware. An umbrella term that describes any malicious software designed to invade, damage, or disable computers, computer systems, networks, and mobile devices. Examples of common malware include viruses, worms, spyware, and ransomware.

Medicaid. Funded by the federal government and the states, this insurance program provides health care coverage to low-income families and individuals. Eligibility and benefits can vary widely from state to state.

Medically needy program. States with this program can offer Medicaid benefits to individuals whose health care expenses significantly reduce their income.

Medicare. A federal health insurance program for individuals age 65 and older as well as people with long-term disabilities.

Medicare Advantage. A type of health plan offered by private companies that contract with Medicare to provide Medicare Part A (hospital insurance) and Part B (medical insurance) benefits. Some Medicare Advantage plans cover costs not covered by Medicare, including vision and dental expenses. Most include prescription drug coverage.

Medigap. Health insurance coverage provided by private companies that is designed to pay for costs not covered by parts A and B of Medicare. These costs may include copayments and deductibles.

Mirror will. Wills that are nearly identical, typically with one spouse leaving all or most of their estate to the other and then to their children. Either party is free to change the terms of the will at any time.

Money market account. An interest-bearing account at a bank or credit union that may include check writing and debit card privileges. Money market accounts may pay a higher interest rate and require a larger minimum deposit than traditional savings accounts.

Mortgage pre-qualification. An estimate of how much a potential borrower is likely to be approved for, based on information about the individual's basic finances, including debt, income, and assets.

Mortgage preapproval. This involves a thorough analysis of the potential borrower's finances, including credit history, debt-to-income ratio, and employment history. The lender uses those details to determine the type and amount of loan the individual can qualify for.

Multiple listing service. An online database for real estate professionals to share information on properties that are listed for sale.

Mutual fund. A professionally managed fund that pools investors' money to purchase a wide range of securities. Each fund investor owns shares that represent a part of the portfolio's holdings.

Net income. For a wage earner, net income is the money an individual gets in a paycheck after accounting for deductions like retirement plan contributions, taxes, and health insurance.

Net worth. A measure of wealth found by calculating the value of things owned by a company or individual and then subtracting all debts.

Nonemergency medical transportation. A government program that provides transportation to and from medical appointments. It is available to eligible Medicaid and Medicare beneficiaries.

Older Americans Act. A federal law that promotes the well-being of seniors through volunteer opportunities, health services, caregiver support, transportation, and home-delivered meals. The Older Americans Act created the Administration on Aging, the main federal agency tasked with carrying out the objectives of the law.

Original Medicare. A fee-for-service health plan managed by the federal government that has two parts. Part A covers hospital insurance, and Part B covers medical insurance.

Overdraft fee. The amount a bank charges for making a transaction that exceeds the amount of money in an account.

Palliative care. Medical care focused on relieving the pain and stress that comes with a serious or advanced illness. Patients under palliative care can continue to receive curative treatment.

Patient assistance programs. Programs sponsored by pharmaceutical companies to provide free or discounted medications to people who can't afford them.

Payday loan. A short-term loan with a high interest rate. Payday loans are meant to be repaid with the borrower's next paycheck.

Pension. A retirement fund for an employee that was paid into by the employer, worker, or both. Payouts typically hinge on how long an individual worked for an employer and salary amount.

Permanent life insurance. Unlike term life insurance that covers an individual for a fixed period of time, permanent life insurance provides coverage that lasts a lifetime. This type of insurance also has a cash value component that the policy owner may borrow against.

Personal asset. Cash and other things — including real estate, cars, and savings and retirement accounts — owned by an individual that have monetary value.

Personal liability. A type of debt that includes current bills, future payments owed on assets like cars and houses, credit card balances, and loans that an individual has.

Phishing. A type of cybercrime in which scammers attempt to obtain personal information. While most attacks come via email, con artists may also use social media channels and mobile phone text messaging.

Portfolio. The combined holdings of investment assets, including stocks, bonds, commodities, and real estate.

Prepayment penalty. A fee that some lenders charge if all or part of a mortgage is paid off early. Typically, a prepayment penalty only applies if the homeowner pays off the entire mortgage balance within a specific number of years (usually three or five years).

Prescription discount card. A free, downloadable card that acts like a coupon. When presented at participating pharmacies, it provides discounts on prescription drugs.

Private mortgage insurance. Insurance needed for a mortgage that carries a low down payment — usually less than 20% of the purchase price of the home.

Probate. Legal process of administering and distributing the estate of someone who has died.

Property tax deferral. A program that allows eligible seniors to postpone payment of all or part of their property taxes until a later date.

Property valuation. An assessment of the value of a piece of real estate. It is based on several factors, including the location and condition of the property.

Pyramid scheme. A fraudulent system of making money that relies solely on new investor recruitment fees instead of sales of a particular product or service. Promoters typically promise investors a high rate of return in a short period of time. At some point the venture collapses, and the majority of recruits who invested late in the scheme lose their money.

Qualified retirement plan. A retirement plan that meets IRS rules and offers tax advantages. Such plans encourage workers to save for retirement by deferring income taxes on contributions and earnings. Most employer-sponsored retirement plans are qualified plans.

Ransomware. A type of malicious software that blocks access to a computer system or data until the victim pays a ransom. In many cases, the ransom demand comes with a deadline.

Required minimum distribution. The minimum amount that must be withdrawn annually from a traditional IRA, 401(k), or other retirement savings plan once the account owner has reached the age of 72.

Reverse mortgage. A loan available to homeowners 62 years or older that enables them to convert part of the equity in their home into cash. The loan doesn't become due until the borrower sells the home or vacates the property.

Revocable living trust. A legal document that spells out how the grantor of a trust wants his or her assets to be distributed after death. Such trusts are flexible in that the grantor has the option of amending the terms at any time. Revocable trusts do not have to go through probate.

Revolving debt. A type of debt that doesn't require fixed monthly payments. This type of debt most often comes from credit cards.

Rider. An amendment to an insurance policy that changes its coverage or terms. Riders generally offer extra benefits in exchange for higher premiums.

Risk tolerance. A measure of an investor's ability to withstand losses on an investment. Someone with a high risk tolerance, for example, is more likely to risk losing money in exchange for higher potential returns.

Rollover. The movement of funds from one retirement plan to another. If done properly, rollovers are usually nontaxable.

Romance scam. A type of fraud that occurs when a con artist adopts a fake online identity to gain a victim's trust. The scammer then uses the illusion of a romantic relationship to get money from the victim, often by claiming that the funds are needed to help resolve a crisis.

Roth 401(k). An employer-sponsored Roth 401(k) plan is similar to a traditional plan. However, employee contributions are made with after-tax dollars and won't be taxed upon distribution. Income earned on the account, from interest, dividends, or capital gains, is tax-free.

Roth IRA. A retirement savings account funded with after-tax dollars. This allows for tax-free growth and tax-free withdrawals to individuals who are at least age 59 1/2, as long as they have owned the account for five years or more.

Second mortgage. A loan taken out on a property that is already mortgaged. The lender uses the borrower's equity in the property as collateral.

Secured debt. A debt tied to a piece of property that the lender can seize in the event of payment default. Common types of secured debt are car loans and mortgages, in which the creditor can seize the auto or home to satisfy the debt.

Soft inquiry. Sometimes called a soft pull or soft credit check, a soft inquiry allows credit card companies and other businesses to review credit data not associated with lending decisions. Soft inquiries don't impact credit scores because they aren't attached to an application for credit.

Spam. Unsolicited digital junk mail that is sent out in bulk. It is often sent via email.

Spending down. A financial strategy in which applicants for Medicaid can receive benefits even though their income exceeds Medicaid limits. By spending that excess money on medical bills, the applicant's income can become low enough to qualify for Medicaid in a given month.

Spendthrift trust. A type of trust that limits the beneficiary's access to funds held in the trust.

Spoofing. A type of scam in which con artists attempt to garner personal information by impersonating a legitimate government agency or business. Spoofing is done via email, text messages, and caller ID.

Staging. The act of improving a home's appearance so that it sells quickly and at top price. Examples include removing clutter, adding fresh towels in the bathrooms, and arranging furniture so that a room feels spacious.

State Health Insurance Assistance Program. A federally funded program that offers free counseling services to seniors and their families so that they can better understand Medicare. Through grants directed to the states, these services are provided over the phone and face to face.

Supplemental Security Income. A federal income supplement program funded by general tax revenue. It is designed to help aged, blind, and disabled people who have little or no income. The program provides money to meet basic needs for food, clothing, and shelter.

Surprise billing. This happens when a person with health insurance gets an unexpected bill after unknowingly receiving medical treatment from a health care provider or facility that is out of their plan's network.

Tangible asset. An asset with a physical presence. Examples include homes, cars, art, boats, jewelry, and business property. Tangible assets are frequently used as collateral for loans.

Tax credit. A dollar-for-dollar amount of money that can be subtracted from the amount of income tax an individual owes. For example, if someone owes $1,000 in income taxes but has a $400 credit, he would have to pay only $600.

Tax deduction. A provision — often a personal or business expense — that reduces the amount of income subject to tax. By lowering an individual's taxable income, a deduction reduces the amount of tax that person has to pay.

Telehealth. The use of telecommunications to deliver health care services and patient education from a distance. Telehealth can include live video conferences, the electronic delivery of medical records, and remote patient monitoring.

Term life insurance. A type of insurance purchased for a specific term, say 10 or 20 years, that pays a death benefit to beneficiaries if the policy owner dies within that time frame. The policy expires when the term ends, but may be renewed or converted to another type of insurance contract.

Title insurance. A policy that protects home buyers and mortgage lenders from third-party claims on a property. Such claims generally don't show up in the initial title search and arise after the real estate closing.

Treasury bill. Short-term government securities that mature within one year. Treasury bills are issued at a discount to their full value. Buyers get the full value when the bills reach maturity.

TRICARE for Life. A health insurance program provided by the federal government to Medicare-eligible military retirees and their dependents. TRICARE for Life acts as a supplement to Medicare.

Two-factor authentication. A security process in which users must provide two authentication factors to verify their identity before accessing data. It is used to protect online accounts from unlawful access.

Umbrella insurance. A type of insurance that provides additional coverage beyond the liability insurance in regular homeowners or auto policies.

Universal life insurance. This type of insurance is similar to whole life insurance in that both provide lifelong coverage, pay a death benefit, and build up cash value. However, a universal life policy offers the flexibility of adjustable premiums and death benefits.

Unsecured debt. A common form of debt that has no collateral backing it. If the borrower defaults, the lender cannot seize property to pay the balance but must resort to debt collectors or legal action. Examples of unsecured debt include student loans, credit card charges, and utility and medical bills.

Variable annuity. A tax-deferred retirement product whose payments are determined by the value of the annuity's underlying investment portfolio. Fixed annuities, on the other hand, provide a guaranteed payout.

Variable expense. Costs that change from month to month, such as how much someone pays for groceries or gasoline. These expenses are influenced by day-to-day choices and can rise and fall depending on one's use of products and services.

Variable interest rate. An interest rate on a loan, credit card, or mortgage that goes up and down over time.

Veterans benefits. A variety of benefits and services offered by the U.S. Department of Veterans Affairs for eligible veterans, dependents, and survivors. They include pensions, health care benefits, educational assistance, and burial and memorial services.

Virtual currency. A type of unregulated electronic currency that functions as a medium of exchange. It is issued and controlled by its developers and used and accepted among the members of a virtual community.

Volatility. The amount and frequency in which an investment fluctuates in value.

Whole life insurance. A type of life insurance that provides a set amount of coverage for an individual's entire life. Whole life policies pay a death benefit, but also build up cash value. Policy holders can access that cash as the funds grow. Premiums on such policies never increase as a condition of coverage.

Will. A legal document detailing how an individual wishes his assets to be distributed after death. A will can also appoint guardians for minor children.

Windfall elimination provision. A requirement that reduces the size of an individual's Social Security retirement and disability benefits if that person receives pension benefits based on work-related earnings that weren't subject to Social Security payroll tax.

Withholding. Money withheld from an employee paycheck based on the number of allowances that the worker claims. Employers withhold money for federal income, Social Security, state, and sometimes local income taxes.

INDEX